Religion,

Federalism,

and the Struggle

for Public Life

Religion,

Federalism,

and the Struggle

for Public Life

Cases from Germany, India, and America

WILLIAM JOHNSON EVERETT

New York   Oxford • Oxford University Press 1997

Oxford University Press

Oxford   New York

Athens   Auckland   Bangkok   Bogota   Bombay   Buenos Aires
Calcutta   Cape Town   Dar es Salaam   Delhi   Florence   Hong Kong
Istanbul   Karachi   Kuala Lumpur   Madras   Madrid   Melbourne
Mexico City   Nairobi   Paris   Singapore   Taipei   Tokyo   Toronto   Warsaw

and associated companies in
Berlin   Ibadan

Published by Oxford University Press, Inc.
198 Madison Avenue, New York, New York 10016

Oxford is a registered trademark of Oxford University Press

Library of Congress Cataloging-in-Publication Data
Everett, William Johnson
Religion, federalism, and the struggle for public life / William
Johnson Everett.
   p.   cm.
Includes bibliographical references and index.
ISBN 0-19-510374-2
1. Federal government—Religious aspects—Case studies.
2. Religion and state—Germany—History—20th century.   3. Religion
and state—India—History—20th century.   4. Religion and state—
United States.   5. Germany—Politics and government—1945–
6. India—Politics and government—1947–   7. United States—Politics
and government.   8. Germany—Religion—20th century.   I. Title.
BL65.S8E84   1997
322'.1'09—dc20   96-21159

9 8 7 6 5 4 3 2 1

Printed in the United States of America
on acid-free paper

For

James M. Gustafson,

Teacher, mentor, friend,

Who first introduced me to the ethical significance of ecclesiology

Preface

This book is a comparative study of the engagement between religion and constitutionalism in three diverse federal republics—Germany, India, and the United States of America. It explores the deep but often subtle ways that religion, especially patterns of religious organization, can either foster or undermine the search for public life within a federal structure that both protects pluralism and also seeks to enhance greater unity among peoples under common law. I have grounded this exploration in the particulars of historical contexts, first in the role of the churches in Germany's "peaceful revolution" of 1989–90. Then, against this more developed case study, I turn to specific court cases in India and the United States to examine further the intricate contest and collaboration between various forms of religious organization and federal-republican orders in these two very different countries.

The impetus for this study began with my effort to set forth a way Christianity might reconstruct its fundamental symbol of Kingdom of God so as to engage more fully and critically the dominant political forms of our own time. This constructive theological task demanded a rigorous engagement with both political theory and law. Moreover, the global struggle for more adequate public life and federal order demanded that this inquiry be extended to other cultures and religious traditions. This book can offer only a first report on such an ambitious undertaking. Rather than yielding a comprehensive theory about this complex relationship, it seeks to deepen our understanding of the complexity and importance of this question.

To order this inquiry I have focused on two central connections in Western tradition between religion and federal republicanism—that of covenant and that of assembly. These two hinge concepts point us to the political ideas of federalism and publics, on the one hand, and to religious ideas of covenantal fidelity and religious association, on the other. This focus yields both some normative ethical commitments and a path of analysis. Normatively, I am seeking ways to advance the struggle for public life within a federal order, both by searching out possible religious resources for it and by providing some critical basis in religious traditions for guiding it. Analytically, I want to find out how in fact religious traditions may or may not provide such resources, especially if they possess covenantlike conceptions and practices that might enhance federalism or if they display patterns of free religious association that might augment the struggle for public life. Conversely, I want to examine ways that religious beliefs and organization might resist, subvert, or transform the federal-republican project.

These studies would not have been possible without the support of numerous people and institutions over the past seven years. A Lilly Endowment grant to the Candler School of Theology at Emory University enabled me to work with Prof. Wolfgang Huber, then of Heidelberg University, on the intersection of law, ethics, and ecclesiology in the fall of 1989. Emory University provided a research grant to assist my further research in Germany and India in 1991–92. The Protestant Institute for Interdisciplinary Research in Heidelberg provided both funding and facilities, not to mention a very helpful staff, to assist my research in Germany. Prof. Huber, now Bishop of Berlin-Brandenburg, continued his collaboration with me in Heidelberg, both at the institute and in joint teaching at the university, providing a constant flow of insight, information, and conversation to sharpen my analysis. The South Asia Theological Research Institute at the United Theological College, Bangalore, India, hosted my research in India in the summer and fall of 1991. Finally, through the Project on United Methodism and American Culture, funded by the Lilly Endowment through Duke University, I was able to collaborate with Prof. Thomas E. Frank, of Emory University, on the portion of this book devoted to United Methodism and the Pacific Homes case.

Numerous others were indispensable to this study. Pastor Gerd Decke, long active in ecumenical work as a study director in the Lutheran World Federation in Geneva, as a pastor in the Hessen-Nassau Evangelical Church, and now as Theological Secretary for the Horn of Africa and South Africa with the Berliner Mission, provided crucial guidance in my German research, including long hours of editorial assistance as well as establishing contacts with key participants in the events of 1989–90. Dr. Hans-Richard Reuter, of the Protestant Institute for Interdisciplinary Research, frequently clarified the mysteries of German ecclesiology as well as provided gracious hospitality during my stay in Heidelberg.

Prof. K. C. Abraham, Director of the South Asia Theological Research Institute, not only hosted my stay in Bangalore but provided constant guidance for my research. Profs. Frederick Downs and Hunter Mabry, of the United Theological College in Bangalore, contributed further to my understanding of historical and sociological dimensions of my research, along with many others inside and outside the UTC community. I am also indebted to Prof. T. K. Oommen of Jawaharlal Nehru University, whose many conversations with me provided invaluable sociological perspectives on the relation of religion and government in India. Finally, Prof. M. Thomas Thangaraj, at Emory University, has over the years been a constant sounding board for my explorations of religion and culture in India.

I also want to express my indebtedness to Prof. Max L. Stackhouse, of Princeton Theological Seminary, who for many years has encouraged and stimulated this comparative inquiry into the relation of covenantal religion and public life, both through his writing and many conversations with me as well as by instigating my first trip to India in 1988.

I also want to thank Scott Paeth, my research assistant, for his help in the final stages of this book, which he proofread with great patience and care.

In all of these travels and long hours of research and writing, I have been supported daily by my wife, Sylvia, whose rich artistry has lifted my spirits and whose constant care has made it possible for me to sustain this lengthy project. My greatest hope is that these reflections might enable all of us to participate more fully in the Wisdom she has so stunningly rehearsed in her art.

W. J. E.

Boston, Massachusetts
and Waynesville, North Carolina

Acknowledgments

Chapter 2, "The Churches and Germany's 'Peaceful Revolution' of 1989–90," is a revision and translation of my work *Neue Öffentlichkeit in neuem Bund: Theologische Reflexionen zur Kirche in der Wende,* which was published in 1992 by the Forschungsstätte der Evangelischen Studiengemeinschaft (Protestant Institute for Interdisciplinary Research) in Heidelberg, Germany. My translation and publication in this volume is by kind permission of the institute.

Chapter 3, "Religious Organization and Constitutional Justice in India," is a revised version of my article "Religion and Federal Republicanism: Cases from India's Struggle," which originally appeared in *Journal of Church and State,* volume 37, Winter 1995, pp. 61–85, and is published here with permission of the *Journal of Church and State.*

The section in chapter 4 subtitled "Methodism and the Quandaries of Republican Federation: The Pacific Homes Case" (pp. 269–305) is being published as part of the chapter "Constitutionalism in United Methodism and American Culture," coauthored with Thomas E. Frank, in a volume edited by Russell E. Richey, Dennis M. Campbell, and William B. Lawrence entitled *Connectionalism: Ecclesiology, Mission, and Identity* (Abingdon Press, 1997). This portion is published here with the permission of Abingdon Press.

Contents

Religion,

Federalism,

and the Struggle

for Public Life

Introduction

The end of the Cold War has released tribal, ethnic, religious, and regional conflicts that had been repressed by the East-West struggle for most of the century. A world supposedly divided between communism and capitalism has revealed itself once again to be rent by conflicts between groups that appeal to their biological roots and those that appeal to reason and consensus for legitimation. The terms of basic conflict on the globe have been radically altered within a few short years, whether we are speaking of eastern Europe, Russia, India, or Africa. In all these cases religion and religious organizations have played key roles on both sides of this conflict.

To grasp this intricate interplay we must go beyond the ways we have understood the relation of religion to communism and capitalism. We also have to think anew about the deep connections of religion to corporate economies and constitutional democracies, as well as to the traditional bonds of kinship, ethnicity, and race. In short, we need to rethink not only how we approach the central issues of human governance but also how they are related to religion. Cold War perspectives rooted in liberation theology as well as in Protestant, Evangelical, and Catholic responses to totalitarianism must enter the new fires of human struggle to be melted down into more suitable images for our thought and action.

In the dramatic upheavals in various countries over the last few years we encounter not only desires for better economic circumstances but also deep longings for an authentic and fully participatory public life. With these struggles comes also the effort to construct new constitutional forms by which to develop and preserve this new public life. These new constitutional orders invariably require more complex and resilient federal structures. We see these struggles for renewed federal republics not only in the newly unified Germany but in eastern Europe, the former Soviet Union, the Middle East, and South Africa, not to mention India and Canada. The bloody and tragic experiences in the former Yugoslavia, as well as the breakup of the Czechoslovakian Federation, have vividly dramatized the failure of such efforts to fashion a new federal and constitutional structure that can preserve a newly won public life.

Some aspects of these struggles are as old as John Locke's attack on patriarchy and Roger Williams's defense of religious liberty. The defense of gender equality in public life, earlier adumbrated by John Stuart Mill and Mary Wollstonecraft, has gained new and deeper meaning. Henry Maine, after serving many years in India, called this fundamental difference in social orders the clash between "status" and "contract"—between a social order based on position within a clearly graded community and one based on the conjunction of individual wills entering into agreements.[1] This conflict between democratic and traditional society was temporarily suppressed by the Cold War, only to resurface with its demise in the early 1990s. The Cold War's ideological framework assumed the victory of "modern" forms of government over traditional society. What we face in this post–Cold War period is not so much the end of the "modern" era as it is a return to the effort to construct democratic and federal republics not only in the midst of large-scale economic corporations but in the face of traditional cultures that appeal to biological bases for social order. Ancestry, gender, race, kinship, and with them the deep structures of language and religion challenge the effort to build political life on voluntarism, universal human rights, constitutional law, and democratic participation, just as the large corporate forms of capitalism have also threatened the popular participation necessary to democracy. The resurgence of ethnic nationalisms reminds us that in constituting a complex political order we are not dealing with a simple progression from one social form to another but with an intricate dialectic among these forms. How then might we best approach this complex dialectic?

At the core of our inquiry is the observation that whether in the South Africa of resurgent kingship and civic multiracialism or in the Russia of bureaucratic socialism and revitalized populism, people are trying to establish and maintain a legitimate constitutionalism that enables them to carry on a public life of self-governance. This constitutionalism cannot be a paper veil for a dictator or a small elite but a fundamental structure of governance rooted in a people's deepest values and institutions. Otherwise, a constitution is simply a facade for coercion rather than a product of persuasion and agreement. Legitimation of constitutional order is a process embedded in the depths of a people's culture. The task of legitimating and structuring this constitutionalism draws finally on profound religious dynamics. This book is an effort to understand the roles played by religious values and organizations in contemporary constitutionalism so that we can develop a political and theological theory to guide our thought and action.

Such an inquiry generates numerous questions. What are the peculiarly religious issues that are at stake in the establishment and maintenance of these federal-republican orders? What are the ways religious traditions, organizations, and perspectives can and do engage other institutions vital to democratic participation in a federal political order? Finally, what role can religious faith and organization play in the struggle for federal-republican government in the diverse cultures of our world? To begin this inquiry we need to remember the intense and peculiar relationship between religion and the rise of federal republicanism in Europe and America.

The Religious Cradle of Federal Republicanism

Western constitutionalism has been deeply shaped by the traditions of republicanism and federalism. Most modern constitutions have tried to establish a system of publics within a federalist order. Over the past 200 years these republics have steadily expanded their scope of democratic participation. Christianity, with its 1,500 years of imperial and monarchical accommodation, has often resisted modern constitutionalism, but it has also borne concepts and practices that have reinforced federalism, free public assembly, and conciliar decision making.[2] Both of these traditions are fundamental to the development of modern polities. I will argue that the intertwined traditions behind these two concepts have a peculiar power and validity for shaping our understanding and response to the struggles we see in our new political and economic era.

In the past 300 years European and American political thinkers generated the belief that public life requires a basic constitution that articulates the relationships between independently legitimate polities. This federalist conception is rooted in the biblical tradition of covenantal thought and practice. Covenantal orders are based in promises and agreements rather than status and command. The idea of *covenant* points to the struggle for bonds of trust that are flexible enough to create and accommodate change but also durable enough to bind generations together in obligation to the Creator and the creation.

The idea of a *public* directs our attention to the need for patterns of expression and negotiation that burst the limits of appeals to biology and kinship for ordering human relationships. Within a public, strangers as well as friends are treated as equal citizens engaged in argument about their common good. The notion that the church, like the synagogue that spawned it, is fundamentally an assembly—an *ecclesia* or *congregatio*—called out from the households of the people has always given rise to the principle that decisions are to be made in councils under the guidance of the Holy Spirit.

This conciliar ecclesial ideal has contributed strongly to the development of the idea of public life, especially in the congregationalism of Protestant countries but also in the recent rise of "base communities" in the Catholicism of Latin America after Vatican Council II.

When taken together with the idea of federalism, especially as it appears in the covenantal tradition, the idea of the public generates the approach to government we call federal republicanism. The more familiar term "constitutional democracy" usually denotes the effort to establish a federal-republican order in which all adults have equal admission to the public life of self-governance. However, these publics are varied in size, scope, and authority. They are linked in a complex "covenant" of constitutional law that seeks to balance power with power and authority with authority. The power arising in public association is thus channeled and constrained within the bonds of an overarching constitution.

Thus, in the federal-republican perspective people do not participate in self-governance as an undifferentiated mass of equal individuals. They participate through smaller publics where they share interests, memories, loyalties, and ways of speaking and acting that enable them to negotiate agreements for their common life. These agreements can then be set forth in larger publics through some system of representation. Federal republicanism always seeks to take into account the specific historical context within which these publics emerge and pursue relationships with wider publics without losing their own integrity. While it has some general characteristics, which I will present shortly, it also takes a multitude of forms in various historical and cultural contexts. While this variety may blur federalism's intellectual profile, it nevertheless offers people a general framework for seeking local participation within the larger vision of a global federal-republican order. The inquiry advanced in this book rests on the assumption that this is the central struggle of our time and that it can secure lasting success only if it deals with the ways religious traditions can shape and legitimate as well as undermine it.

At this point those of us fed by these traditions need to rethink and recast them in the light of a richer sense of global plurality as well as interconnection. Are these religious and political traditions peculiarly "western" and "biblical" patterns or can they be fostered in analogous ways in other cultural and religious milieus? The present struggle for new constitutional orders will ultimately fail unless it can be grounded in people's deepest affections and habits. This is the dimension of religion that must undergird any structure of authority. This book is an effort to discern how the essential elements in this European-American experience might engage not only the new challenges of the post–Cold War era but also some of the deep cultural and religious values and dynamics of other societies. How can these covenantal and ecclesial traditions, along with their political partners—federalism and republicanism—be reclaimed and recast in our own time?

The Frame of Inquiry

It should already be evident that this inquiry will focus on constitutions—their basic structure and dynamics in their social setting. More acutely I want to examine their relationship to their religious milieus and the religious institutions of the people. This relationship is manifested in the way the constitution depends on deep commonly held beliefs and values for its legitimation. It also emerges in the actual relationships between government and religious institutions. Thus, just as I focus on constitutionalism on the political side I will focus on "ecclesiology" on the religious side.

The term *ecclesiology* means first of all "the study of the church." I use the term in this Christian sense but also expand it to mean the study of any form of religious assembly—whether it be in synagogue, mosque, or temple. The ecclesiological question is: How do people who share a common faith organize themselves? How does their faith and practice achieve enduring institutional and organizational form? In these ecclesiologies we see the practical expression of religious beliefs, values, and orientations. It is primarily through these ecclesiologies—these enduring collective religious behaviors—that religion interacts with and shapes other institutions. Some religions have a highly developed institutional ecclesiology, as in the Roman Catholic Church. Others have a diffuse or almost nonexistent ecclesiology, as with Hindu devotionalism. These differences are crucial in understanding the significance of religion for public life. A study of ecclesiologies in this sense thus lies at the center of the exploration of the relation of religion to federal republicanism.

This study has both a descriptive and normative dimension. Descriptively, it seeks to understand the actual relationships that exist between particular forms of religious organization and the constitutional orders of federal republics. In examining these relations between religion and government I will also have to take into account the way other institutions, especially family and economy, deeply affect this relationship. In light of the tension between the values of democratic republics and those of kinship, monarchy, and patriarchy, I will pay close attention to the way values and patterns of race, ethnicity, patriarchy, and extended kinship condition both ecclesiology and constitutional order.

Normatively, this study assumes the positive value of federal-republican orders, distorted as they may often be, but it also seeks to search out ways both political theory and theology should be transformed in light of the general values of this religio-political tradition and the basic conflicts of our time. This purpose leads us to look for the possible religious resources in these differing contexts that might shape and support the federal-republican venture as well as those that might oppose it most strongly. I am similarly concerned with ways these religious resources might also stand in critical judgment over against certain developments in these federal republics. In short, I want to enhance the critical dialectic between these two protagonists in our historical drama by clarifying it and suggesting ways it might be deepened.

I have chosen to look at these religious and political dynamics through specific case studies involving religion and constitutional order. Case studies enable us to focus on specific issues in actual historical and cultural contexts. They force us to attend to the ways people actually think about the wider assumptions underlying the institutions shaping their lives. Each case, anchored in particular conflicts, interests, and aspirations, opens us up to the wider structural contexts of kinship, ethnicity, and economic organization shaping the interaction of law and religion.

The Plan of the Book

To begin, I shall first present a basic theoretical framework within which these descriptive and normative dimensions might be understood. The covenantal-federalist and the conciliar-republican traditions provide us with theories for understanding as well as evaluating the relation of religion and political order in these three cultures. I shall propose the idea of "covenantal publicity" as a bridge term that picks up both the religious content of the covenantal and ecclesial traditions and the political content of federalism and republicanism. This theoretical lens will focus the inquiry throughout the book.

I will then use this lens to explore the dynamics between religious organization and federal-republicanism in three different contexts—Germany, India, and America. Within these specific contexts we can begin to forge tools to help us understand the dynamics they have in common as well as the distinctive ways they shape the federal-republican struggle. Such a comparative case study approach is faithful to the federal-republican sense of historical embeddedness as well as to the contemporary challenge of knitting together local, regional, and global public orders.

Each of these countries has been informed by contrasting religious traditions, even within Christianity. Each country has had quite different political histories. But they also share some important commonalities. India and the Federal Republic of Germany developed their modern federal-republican constitutions in 1949–50. At the same time, both countries witnessed the birth of new efforts at church federation or union—in Germany the formation of the Evangelische Kirche in Deutschland (1948) and in India the establishment of the Church of South India (1947). Their political constitutions, though different in some very important ways, were deeply shaped by the federal constitutions of the United States and similar countries. Their new ecclesial constitutions, though shaped profoundly by indigenous historic circumstances, sought to enhance member participation and accountability of the church for the society around it.

The United States, though not reformed politically after World War II, saw the formation of the National Council of Churches (1950), successor to the Federal Council of Churches, and along with Germany and India the formation of the World Council of Churches and the United Nations, both in 1948. All of these political and ecclesial formations sought to enhance participation of groups through some sort of federal system of representation. All of them were committed to expanding the sphere of individual responsibility and participation in wider publics. All of them arose against the backdrop of racist horrors and holocausts of that terrible war.

In a sense these case studies could be taken up in any order. I have chosen to explore Germany's revolution of 1989–90 first. For English-speaking readers it has the veneer of familiarity yet also takes us beyond the usual categories of Anglo-American ecclesiology and constitutional history. Moreover, it lifts up in a dramatic way essential religious and political components of the struggle for public life in a federal order. I then consider India, whose dominant Hindu heritage, colonial experience, and sheer diversity challenge Euro-American values and organizational patterns at a fundamental level. At the same time, its close connection to English culture and government gives us a few familiar signposts to guide us into this complexity. Issues of women's rights, religious freedom, and compensation to former untouchables are shaped both by India's new constitutional order and by ancient ethnic and religious traditions. Finally, the study considers America, hopefully informed by a new perspective, to pick up some seemingly marginal cases that illuminate crucial issues in the relation of religion to federalism and public life in the United States. American Indian claims to sacred land sites and the entanglement of the United Methodist Church in a multimillion-dollar lawsuit reveal peculiar problems in the meaning of religion, of church, and of the foundations of federal-republican constitutions.

In light of these case studies we can then turn to the task of identifying some common threads and themes pervading these struggles. This comparative awareness can help us refine our understanding of federal-republicanism and its relation to religious values and organization. We can clarify the central challenges confronting the struggle for covenantal publicity and begin to identify ways that both religious and political orders might change in order to advance people's struggles for more adequate federal republics.

One

Envisioning the Engagement

Behind the contemporary struggle for more adequate federal re-publics lie two themes that are deeply rooted in biblical religion and classical political philosophy. They are the themes of *covenant* and *publicity*. The concept of covenant arose from ancient treaty relationships and came to have a religious meaning through its use in Jewish and Christian theology. In general, by "covenant" I mean a set of mutual obligations forming people's common life and established through solemn agreement. By "publicity" I mean people's effort to establish public spheres and participate in them. These two concepts are rich with further meanings derived from their biblical and classical roots that can orient us to the dynamic of federal-republicanism shaping our era.

The concepts of covenant and of publicity have both normative and descriptive import. They are both theologically constructive and sociologically analytical. As normative concepts they evoke in a deep symbolic way values, commitments, and ultimate orientations embedded in the traditions of Judaism and Christianity. The inquiry of this book arose within the widely shared commitment to a common life informed by the values they bear. The effort to pursue these values leads us immediately to the analytical question of how patterns of covenant and publicity actually exist or are absent in specific cultural contexts. At this point we draw on these concepts not merely to guide our conduct but to improve our vision of what is around us.

Covenant and publicity thus serve also as analytical devices for describing our world. They are heuristics that press us to certain kinds of questions about social and political life. They provide us with lenses for interpreting the political facts of our time. With their help we see some things that other concepts might let us overlook, much like infrared glasses enable us to see in the dark. They are bridges between analysis and ethical construction. Awareness of this dual role should accompany our use of these concepts. Even the most scientific looking of concepts, like "system," "function," or "pluralism," also bear this duality, usually without our realizing it. Description and prescription in the social sciences have a closer relationship than is often acknowledged. While the burden of this study is more analytical, there are also times when the analysis begins to point to normative possibilities. Sometimes this shift will be obvious; other times it will be buried in the narrative in a more subtle manner. Awareness of the dual functions of these key concepts can be heightened if we first turn to the meaning they have had in our religious and political development. We can then place these concepts within a sociological framework that will guide our inquiry into the relation of religion to federal-republican life in contemporary societies.

Religion and Federal-Republicanism

Our modern concept of a public sphere and of the meaning of life in a republic is intertwined with the concept of the church as it emerges in the New Testament and its first centuries in the Roman world. Moreover, our modern conception of federalism—that is, a constitutional order uniting relatively autonomous publics—is grounded in ancient Hebrew notions of covenant.

In both respects the biblical traditions have a valuable heritage that can orient us to our political life as well as critique it. Moreover, we have a rich though often forgotten history of religious and political reflection on these themes to awaken us to the many combinations they might form. While concepts of covenant and publicity do not yield specific prescriptions for our political problems, they provide some tools for approaching them and seeing how religious traditions and forms of organization might engage the political sphere in critical ways. First I will examine the family of terms surrounding the idea of the public. Next I will turn to the tradition of covenant and federalism.

Ecclesia and Publicity

In public relationships people emerge out of the private spaces of their lives into arguments about their common existence. We emerge out of the privacy of our homes into a public sphere, where we meet strangers and speak with them, not because we know them personally but because we have a common concern about living together on this planet. This is the dynamic of councils as they were known in the *kahal* or *edah* of ancient Israel, the *ekklesia* of the Greek *polis*, or the senate of the Roman republic.

In the kahal elders came together to deliberate about laws and policies for the common good of Israel. It was a kahal that decided to elect Saul king even though Samuel told them life with a king would be difficult (1 Samuel 8). But the elders were concerned about defense, security, and stability. They wanted to be like other nations who had kings to lead them to war. So they secured a king, and it was that monarchy that finally destroyed the power of the kahal, though it reemerged under foreign occupation as the council of the synagogue.

When Greek-speaking Jews translated their Hebrew texts into Greek they drew on the Greek word ekklesia as the word for kahal—the assembly. The ekklesia was simply the public assembly that deliberated upon and decided the affairs of the polis, the ancient Greek city state. The ekklesia was the assembly of those "called out" from their households and from ordinary economic life in order to appear as equals engaged in argument rather than as kinfolk obeying the elders. In the household people related to each other in a hierarchical pattern of subordination—elder over younger, men over women, parents over children and slaves. But in the polis people were equal, not because they were equal in physical ways but because they were equals before the law. The ekklesia therefore created a historic departure from family relations as the means to order the way we govern ourselves.

The early Christians, while they had many metaphors to describe themselves—Followers of the Way, Body of Christ, sheepfold, house, etc.—chose as their distinctive term the one that was used for the ancient Hebrew council—ekklesia. This group would be known as the ekklesia of Christ. The word was so important to their identity it was taken directly into Latin and remains as the root word for church in the Romance languages.

The other word closely tied to *ekklesia* was the Latin word *res publica*, "public affairs." From this root comes our modern conception of a republic, which is governance conducted in an open assembly by citizens who agree to be ruled by laws rather than by the often arbitrary decrees of a ruler.

Thus, the history of the church as ecclesia was inextricably tied up with the origins of our modern concept of a public. The early church put proclamation—public speech—at the heart of its life. With it came appeal to individual conviction as crucial to conversion and faith. It was this activity of publicity that upset the imperial order and brought persecution upon the church. Though suppressed by the adoption of imperial, patriarchal, and monarchical order after Constantine's adoption of Christian faith in the fourth century, this spark of conciliar publicity has continually reemerged and in our own time gained new prominence in a world of church councils, federations, and all manner of associations of Christians and interfaith assemblies.

Characteristics of Publicity

"Publicity" embraces all the activities that go into the creation of public life, whether in the ecclesia or in the republic. It is an activity in which people profess their convictions and search for agreement about their common life. Indeed, they have to express their convictions honestly in order to search for agreements that will rest on genuine commitment and mutual trust.

This public sphere can only arise where the bonds that tie family, work, land, and religion together as a fused ensemble have loosened. There is less of an automatic connection between people's family position and the kind of work they do. Land is not under the control of ancestral obligations but can be used or transferred in a variety of ways. Religion becomes a matter of choice more than filial duty. In these and other ways people are practically forced to come together in some sort of public space to decide how to construct their relationships in the common sphere they share. Four characteristics are central to publicity: *participation, plurality, persuasion,* and *commonality.* [1]

PARTICIPATION—FROM EQUALITY TO ACTION. Participation is the capacity of individuals to express their opinions and beliefs before others in a search for their common good. It therefore implies a rough equality among participants, lest some coerce others in the process of argument. Participation is sometimes limited to a few, as in an oligarchical council, or opened up to the many, as in democratic societies. The procedures by which people participate and how they reach decisions are then peculiar to each ongoing assembly. These are matters of its "polity," which rest not only on wider cultural and institutional structures, such as the structure of the family and of work, but also on deep values. How a society balances change and stability, for instance, will affect whether decisions are made by unanimous consent or by majority vote.

Hardly any polity is able to allow all citizens to participate in every decision. Even in villages, it has usually been the elders, the men, or others who have gained certain distinctions who represent the whole. The theory of representation is thus crucial to any theory of participation and legitimate decision making. Representation, we must add, is not merely the way one person might serve the wishes of her or his electors but also how the smaller council represents the founding principles and the future hopes of the people. What, in fact, is being represented in the debates of the council? Is the spirit of the founders there? Is the spirit of the revolution or acts that established the council being represented in its decisions? These too are questions of representation and participation that make a strictly democratic notion of a public inadequate even if normatively crucial as a starting point.

PLURALITY—FROM AGGREGATION TO ARGUMENT. Plurality means not only that there will be a variety of personal standpoints but that a variety of groups will emerge in the public sphere. This is part of the associational dynamic of any public. Because people can voluntarily associate around common interests or beliefs, enduring polarizations are difficult to maintain within the public. Plurality is not merely an unfortunate occurrence but enables human beings to find wisdom and truth. Alone we are "idiots," but with others we can come closer to truth. Plurality of association is necessary not only to pursue greater truth but to foster freedom as well. Freedom is the capacity to choose among alternative associations. It is a way of being in relationship, not a way of escaping relationships. Both truth and freedom are relational.

Plurality, however, is not always a matter of voluntary association. Many of the groups that participate in the public are constituted by the relatively involuntary bonds of family, kinship, origin, birth status, race, and gender. These too are part of the plurality of a public, even if their own constituting principles diverge from the free association of the public's own constitution. The racial politics of South Africa and the United States and the caste politics of India show us how categories of race and birth have been used both to subvert public life through apartheid and segregation and to strengthen public participation through policies of affirmative action and redress. How voluntary and involuntary groups are related in a public constitutes a critical question in my study here. It shapes each of the cases I will examine, though in quite different ways.

PERSUASION—FROM ARGUMENT TO PROMISE.   Persuasion is the process by which participants are brought to common action on the basis of shared beliefs, interests, or conclusions about the case at hand. It requires a capacity for clearly expressing our intentions, seeking to appeal to the present convictions of the listener. It then requires that we hear others in order to ascertain the common ground by which we might come to agreement. It requires the imagination and courage to propose new ways of piecing together the fabrics of our separate lives into a common garment.

Persuasion is thus quite different from command as a principle of common life. Persuasion is to the public what command is to the army. Persuasion is the operation of reason, command the operation of the will. This means that underlying persuasion is the faith that there is a shared rationality to which both speaker and hearer subject themselves in an argument. Common action is not simply dependent on the capacity of one person or group to overwhelm another by force. For persuasion to occur, then, all participants must have access to the same facts as well as share in the same notions of rationality and logical argument. Thus, the conditions of persuasion are similar to those of ordinary contracts, a connection that was transparent to modern advocates of republican governance.

COMMONALITY—FROM NECESSITY TO AGREEMENT. Persuasion requires not only a rough equality of power but also a common language and frame of reference for carrying on argument. Thus, it demands some minimum commonality of culture. Commonality rests in a shared world of meaning that makes possible the voluntary argument of the public. A public exists because people have something in common to argue about. Commonalities reside in the patient work of culture as well as in natural circumstance, climate, and geography. Without them there is no basis for authoritative decisions.

Provision for this commonality is often seen as one of the vital contributions of ethnicity, religion, kinship, and race. Because human bonds are so fragile, people must inevitably fall back on the necessary givens of their biological and cultural past in order to sustain their mutual promises and expectations. These "biologistic" appeals are somehow natural and necessary, and appeal to them is socially inevitable, the necessary preconditions for public civility.

A public grounded in covenants offers a different way of approaching the commonality needed for civil governance. It seeks to go beyond the bonds of biology broadly conceived without totally rejecting them. In doing this, it also has to find ways that they can be transmuted into patterns of promise and publicity rather than coercion and exclusion. One example for thinking of this relationship is to look at the way the natural bonds of parenthood have to be transformed into covenants of an increasingly public character in order to articulate, maintain, and enliven the relation of parent and child over the years.

Not only do publics need the four qualities I have just spelled out, they also have to be small enough to enable people to carry on common argument about matters that concern them. The Christian ecclesia emerges in particular congregations. The universal church can only be present in local assemblies because the dynamic of publicity requires a scale larger than the clan and smaller than the anonymous mass. The same holds for republics as well. A republic inevitably has to be a public of publics in order to maximize participation, plurality, and distribution of power. How this republic of publics is constituted raises the question of federalism.

Covenant and Federalism

To attain a more comprehensive scale of unity, a group of publics must turn to some system of alliances, compacts, and confederations in order to defend themselves externally and meet some of their internal needs as well. Moreover, their internal life must rest on an elaborate set of agreements of the people that hold them together in a more or less voluntary but highly committed way. Both of these needs—for internal cohesion and external defense—have historically led republics to a federal form of association.

Since the early Hebrews and Greeks, publics have turned to federal forms such as leagues, confederations, and alliances to maintain themselves internally and externally. Federalism itself reaches back to the ancient Hebrew concept of covenant. Covenantalism was derived from ancient treaty formulas and then given its theological meanings in Hebrew culture. From Hebrew covenant and Greek and Roman leagues came the evolving modern forms of federalism. The Latin word for covenant is *foedus*, from which we have the English word "federal." Federalism is thus not only a system for sustaining and interrelating publics but a framework for religious thought and practice as well. It is one in which the very understanding of God in Israel was shaped by the federal orders of the ancient world. It is therefore a key metaphor for bridging faith and politics.

A covenant is a set of promises among relatively independent parties to secure a common future. Like publics, covenants were historically the first step beyond kinship for establishing durable and trustworthy human relationships. In their ancient biblical form covenants were ways of relating people to the center of their deepest commitments and of relating themselves to each other, to their governors, and to the land on which they live. Covenantal thinking is thus a complex way of approaching a variety of relationships in terms of mutual promises.[2]

The Biblical Model of Covenant

Covenantal relationships assume that there are at least two relatively independent parties to the set of promises. In Israel we find that this mysterious God YHWH is one who seeks to enter into covenant. This is not merely a mode of God's activity. It is essential to who God is. God is a covenanting God. Human beings do not merely flow from the divine essence but exist with freedom before the Divine. The relationship of divinity and humanity comes to focus in the ever-surprising story of their promises. This means that the eyes of faith focus on the expectations they have of each other, the hopes that sustain them, and the way promises are broken and taken up again.

As the prime actor in covenant making, God is also the ground for upholding the covenant. God is not only the object of our solemn oaths but also the source of those ultimate allegiances, values, and assumptions about reality that enable us to trust the promises of the other covenanters. Every covenant, then, must have a sense of ultimate common allegiance in order to sustain it. In the biblical understanding God is not merely a metaphysical ground but an active party shaping and sustaining the covenant.

The second party, the people, is more than a solitary individual. God's covenant is with a whole "house" (the Hebrew *bayith* or the Greek *oikos*) comprising buildings, land, family, and intertwined generations. The people of this "house" are not an automatic unity. They gain a unity as a result of a covenantal process that is known to them through their story—not the timeless round of seasonal necessities but the unique and surprising ways they have been sustained over time. Their history is the outcome of promises made and kept, broken and renewed. Thus, the people are also intrinsically covenantal inasmuch as they take their historical existence seriously. Thus, covenant making in the Bible usually begins with a recitation of the story of grace, sin, and liberation that brought Israel to that point. That is how they know who they are as a party to covenant.

Finally, there is another party, often overlooked—the land. In one sense it is the "property" of the trust between God and Israel. It is the gift or trust that goes with the promises and their honoring. But in another sense it too is a kind of party to the covenant. It cries out, it dies, it flourishes. It participates in the covenant according to its own dynamics and integrity, sometimes as witness, sometimes as partner. It is not simply at human disposal but precedes humanity as God's first covenantal partner in creation. From the covenantal perspective, it has legitimate claims and standing in the web of covenant upholding life.

God, people, land—these are the parties constituting a "full covenant" in Israel. It is among these three parties that the web of covenantal promises is spun out. It is this intricate set of obligations that supports the system of law obligating all the parties to common action. to be faithful to each other through this law, this Torah. In the biblical concept of covenant we find the peculiar sense of law as binding, voluntary agreement. It is law as "constitutional," which means that the people are bound together not simply by family, tribe, race, inheritance, or nature but by a legal framework that "constitutes" them as a people.

In the interaction of these three parties, we recognize that at some points God's claims and initiatives are stressed and at other times the human parties emerge with greater equality. Sometimes even the land's claims are central, as in the prophecies of Isaiah (Isaiah 49, 55). The welfare of each of the parties depends on the faithfulness of the other two. Covenant always implies some kind of interdependency maintained through faithfulness to promises that secure the future. This is the heart of covenantal, or federal, theology.

Two Patterns of Covenant

Covenant can take two structural forms. The first, highlighted by George Mendenhall over 40 years ago, is a hierarchical or "suzereignty" form drawn from ancient treaties between stronger and weaker parties.[3] The strong party proposes the treaty, and the weaker party acquiesces in it because of its need. This, argued Mendenhall, is the form of God's covenants with Noah, Abraham, and Moses (Genesis 9:8 and 15:18; Exodus 24:3-8). It is the covenantal form for the giving of the Commandments. Of course, as Israel's history develops, we find other passages in which God honors Israel's freedom even as God seeks to maintain the bond of mutual faithfulness to this covenant. This covenant becomes the model for God's relation to David and his kingdom, where it functions to guarantee God's everlasting commitment to the

Israelite monarchy. It can be everlasting because it depends basically on God's initiative and faithfulness.

The second form, as in the covenants between Abimilech and Abraham, Jacob and Laban, and Jonathan and David, is an egalitarian one, joining two equals in a solemn bond (Genesis 21:27, 31:44; 1 Samuel 18:3). This is a covenant of alliance and friendship more than of dependence. We find it also in the sense of covenant among the tribes of Israel and then among the disciples and Jesus, who seeks to be friend rather than master, father, or lord (John 15:15).

The egalitarian covenants are structures for a life lived among citizens. Our equality as citizens arises not from any natural attributes we may have but from the covenant we have made to treat each other according to the categories of law and constitution; that is, to treat each other as subjects of justice. This is the essential covenant of civil life. From it emerges a framework for the many smaller covenants of marriage and association as well as the many contracts that sustain our daily living.

Even egalitarian covenants have a kind of hierarchical dimension inasmuch as our equal participation also rests on some commitment to a more transcendent source or purpose that relativizes our own hierarchies and levels us. There is also a hierarchical quality to the way the covenants of earlier generations are received by future generations. Our lives are shaped by covenants we receive through our bond with our parents, with the land of our birth, and with the society that passed on to us the achievements of earlier generations in science, technology, law, and the arts. They are handed down to us as the presuppositions of our early life. We are dependent on them like children on their parents. We live these covenants out before we even recognize them. It is important that we acknowledge them as sustainers of our common life.

At the same time, by recognizing these as received covenants rather than as a static form of "nature," we affirm our capacity to reshape them, to augment them with new promises, and to bring to an end received covenants that are no longer able to sustain their intended fruits, that stifle the dynamic of publicity, or that even contradict the wider covenants of God with the whole creation. Thus, these received covenants need not be stone tombs in which to bury ourselves but invitations to live out a free relationship with our Creator.

As an example, in our own time we are struggling to reconstitute our received covenant with the land, water, and air. We have assumed that they would be "faithful" to us no matter what other changes we wrought. Now we have to enter into a renewed covenant with the land, air, and water if we are to sustain a fruitful life for us all. Otherwise, the inexorable imperatives of ecological equilibrium will finally take their vengeance on us. This is a normative question not only for our formal legal constitutions but also for the informal cultural and social covenants binding us together on the land.

Political Federalism

The political concept of federalism has both informed and been informed by the covenantal tradition. At its minimum it consists of an order of governance constituted by treatylike relations of mutual obligation among polities that are in some degree self-governing. These federating partners, while retaining a certain degree of autonomy, also constitute a larger political entity that has legitimate claims on them.[4] The set of agreements that constitutes the federation almost always has to take the form of a written constitution in order to specify the distribution of power and authority entailed in the founding compact. There are, in fact, a range of federal forms, from the relatively centralized federalism of India, which devolved from a former imperial unity, to what is usually called a confederal form, such as that found today in Switzerland.[5]

Federalism, with its dependence on a written constitution that specifies the relationships of the partners, requires a strong and relatively independent judiciary to interpret this basic compact. Inevitable conflicts among the constituting polities need to be adjudicated peacefully if the federation is to preserve its compactual character and not disintegrate into civil war or a pyramid of coercive command. Thus, this study will concentrate on the way federal-republican structures interact with religious structures in the development of constitutional form or in the adjudication of disputes under the existing constitution.

This distinction between government and judiciary required by the constitutional form of federation further implies the distinction between the act of legislation and its execution. Law, in a federative polity, must always transcend in some way the political process. Thus, the making of law must be separated from the executive power, yielding our now familiar constitutional "separation of powers." The underlying ideas of governance through covenantal obligation and transcendent law thereby lead to an internal differentiation of government as well as to a distinction among the polities making up the federation.

Finally, this differentiation of polities implies that citizens hold allegiances both to their local polity and to the more expansive polities of the federation. This dual citizenship, when infused with democratic values, means that they have a right to participate both locally and in these wider publics in forming policies and electing officials. This dual citizenship is necessary if the federation itself and not merely its constituting polities is to be "republican," that is, enabling persons to participate in the formation of public policy.

Finally, federations require a principle of representation so that the interests of the constituting polities can shape their federation itself. Both citizens and federated polities require a voice in the general policy making of the federation. How a particular federal republic handles the inevitable tensions between these two requirements can vary greatly, just as the way citizens organize to affect politics can be shaped variously by family, kinship, religion, economics, and voluntary association. In any case, a federal republic cannot exist without clear principles of representation.

The inevitable complexity of federalist theory, with its dependence on the historical agreements of a people or peoples, robs it of the clear intellectual profile we can attribute to the pyramidal theories of monarchy, the classical business corporation, or the socialist state. However, its capacity to preserve the local liberties of peoples while also integrating them into a large whole has given it the power to become the increasingly dominant political form of our time.

The Concept of Covenantal Publicity

Covenant points to the theological roots of federalism, just as the ecclesial dynamic of the church points to the theological roots of publicity. These two conceptual orders are intertwined with each other. They have arisen in concert in that tradition we know today as federal-republicanism, especially in its democratic forms. The dynamic of publicity demands the bonds of covenant. Covenant, in turn, needs the dynamic of publicity lest it become introverted, rigid, and closed. Covenant is for the sake of publicity, and publicity is for the sake of covenant. It is this intrinsically reciprocal dynamic that we point to with the term "covenantal publicity."

Covenantal publicity is a bridge term between the religious language of covenant and ecclesia and the political language of federalism and republicanism. It points us to the way these two families of terms and practices can, do, and should inform each other. It is both a normative term that indicates the direction we should take in our common life and an analytical term that identifies ways we do or do not pursue these values in our actual behavior.

Publicity bears with it values of participation, plurality, persuasion, and concern for a common good and common world. The values of publicity demand that we ask about the nature and quality of people's participation, the forms of their plurality, their patterns of persuasion, and the common basis by which they adjudicate their disputes and search for the common good upholding them. "Publicity" generates a normatively informed analytical task.

Covenant reminds us of the network of promises among the people, God, and the land. While there can be many covenants, each with slightly different forms, they ultimately must take into account these three parties in order to be a "full" covenant. Moreover, covenants need to take account of the hierarchical and received dimensions of our common life as well as the compacts arising out of negotiation and agreement among equals. These are the covenantal reference points for our value-shaped inquiry.

Covenantal publicity involves not only the reciprocity between these two component elements but also reciprocity between its theological and political domains. The ethical values embedded in the theological roots of these concepts have penetrated the political ethics connected with federal-republicanism. Moreover, over the centuries the values developed within the political tradition have also deeply affected the ecclesiology and ethics of the churches. For instance, in Christian tradition, the ecclesia of Christ exists only on the basis of the web of covenants among the people and with Christ, who draws them into God's covenant with all of creation. Moreover, the gift of the Spirit in the ecclesia continually leads the people into ever-expanding covenants with all peoples—Jew and gentile, slave and free, male and female. The church is thus, in this normative vision, an ever-expanding constellation of publics linked in covenant. It is a federal structure in terms of its root relationship with God as well as in terms of the relationships among the ecclesial communities.

Similarly, republics, joined in covenantal relationships, can remain vital only if they include the dynamic of public expression, debate, compromise, and agreement. This activity of publicity can be maintained only if the covenants underlying their formal constitutions are continually remembered, rehearsed, critiqued, and renewed. Moreover, each public must find adequate federal linkage with other publics in order to survive. People's struggle today to establish and maintain vital publics within a federal framework is a theological as well as political question. For many peoples around the world this task is the earnest of our ultimate hope. Political longing finally expresses itself in religious hope, just as religious aspiration requires political form. How to steer the engine of covenantal publicity between the twin perils of religio-political fanaticism, on the one hand, and cynical apathy, on the other, is a central question for both politics and religion.

From a religious standpoint the nurture of these covenantal bonds and this openness to wider publics rests finally in the power of God. From a faith standpoint, we recognize that God is both the pivotal party to covenant and the One who empowers us to publicize our lives. Both partners in this dynamic of covenantal publicity need to be open to the transcendent power of God. From a Christian standpoint, it is through the Spirit of God that we can enter ecclesia. It is through God's spirit that we can have the courage to speak of the source of our life (Matthew 10:26–33). Preaching and public witness stand at the center of the Gospel's impulse. This publicity is not merely a matter of words and preaching, but of all the forms of human expression—the visual arts, dancing, music, and film.

God's creative spirit is also critical to covenanting. Without openness to the transcendent power of God, covenants can become closed, narrowly nationalistic, or arrogant.[6] God is always at work reshaping the covenants and constitutions of our lives. not simply the dead hand of past agreements but the living spirit of human relationship. When we seek to imprison people in them, God breaks them open and calls us to new covenant (Jeremiah 31:31; Isaiah 43:19, 65:17; Luke 5:36–38, 22:30; Galatians 6:15).

Simultaneously, God is the Spirit that calls us out of our unconscious bondage to lesser powers—whether they are parental, ethnic, religious, national, or scientific—and asks that we expand our little publics to be open to God's ultimate republic. There we will express our lives and not be afraid, we shall trust others and not be betrayed. We will listen to others and find the invitation to create a new world with them. We will encounter total strangers and they will be our friends. In short, God will be the foundation that we can trust to uphold our covenants and the final proclamation of our lives with God.

From a political standpoint we seek to resolve conflicts without resort to war. We also seek ways to enable people to cooperate to enhance their common life without destroying the natural world we inhabit together with future generations. This demands not only an enhancement of public participation to express one's sense of wrong or one's hopes for a better world. It also demands a clarification and strengthening of those common assumptions that inform both our deliberations and our deportment in the public realm. The federal-republican heritage has always rested on the cultivation of civic virtue as well as the constitutional machinery of government. While much attention has been given to the mechanics of political science, only recently have we begun to recover attention to the roots of civic virtue, mutual bonds of commitment, and the interaction of political order with deep cultural roots that can sustain the everyday operations of government. That is to say, just as a theological sense of covenant and ecclesial life lead us to questions of political order, so do those questions in turn lead us back to religious questions again. At the center of this relationship stands the question of legitimation.

Religion and Political Order in Sociological Perspective

Legitimation

One of the classic roles of religion has been to legitimate political orders and indeed entire patterns of authority in a society.[7] Religion is usually bound up with the establishment of cultic activity, which in turn provides the paradigms of action, value, and orientation that shape a culture. The models of relationship with the Ultimate that are rehearsed in cultic life become the foundational reference for judging the rightness of social relationships, especially those involving power, authority, and personal sacrifice. We have only to think of the impact of biblical notions of vocation, Hindu conceptions of *dharma*, and Islamic values of submission to see the enormous impact these religious conceptions can have on the construction of political and social order.

Just as these basic images and models of action can legitimate ongoing social orders, they can also create countercultural models that challenge and delegitimate the existing order. A relationship that has been projected into the transcendent realm can come crashing back to earth and call into question all existing orders that do not conform to those ultimate patterns. This has been the impact of utopian and millennialist religious movements throughout Western history.[8]

In the interaction between the cultic rehearsals of religion and the cultural patterns of authority there arise bridge symbols and concepts that carry values back and forth between the two spheres. In this study covenant has been one of these powerful symbolic bridges. In the Jewish and Christian West the symbol of covenant has enabled people to carry values from the sphere of cultic memory into the political world of constitutions and the economic world of contracts, creating a kind of cultural glue to help people hold their social world together in a coherent, consistent, and dependable way. Similarly, in India conceptions of caste conceived in terms of ritual purity became the ordering principle for all social life.

Bridge symbols can also create contradictions. The bridge symbol of "kingdom" held together the ritual life of Christianity and the governance of Europe for 1,500 years. Today the symbol of kingdom stands in a puzzling contradiction to the republics and democratic assemblies that are the symbol of legitimate order for many, if not most, Christians. Some interpret the distance of kingdom language from the symbols and values of republican culture as a kind of transcendence limiting the pretensions of secular government. Others see it as a source of outright rejection of liberal democratic orders, the root of a fundamentalist return to patriarchal order in family and government. Still others see it as a purely psychological symbol legitimating our personal struggle to control our passions and instincts for the sake of a public life among equals. For them, a psychological monarch makes a democratic citizen possible. All of this is to say that religious symbols can stand in an ambiguous relationship to the wider culture. They can be seedbeds for legitimating both the standing regime and alternative regimes. Moreover, the way they exercise their authority can move in different ways.

Clearly, one of the ways this root authority is exercised is through the socialization and character formation that takes place as people grow up in a religious community. Their participation in regular rituals, their study of ancient scriptures and stories, and their exposure to artistic expressions of that tradition all work to shape their outlook, responses, desires, and relationships. Basic conceptions of ourselves as persons, individuals, and members of a larger body deeply affect the kinds of institutions and relationships we value and validate with our participation. Legitimation is mediated through the kinds of people we are or are willing to be in light of our religious education.

Finally, the religious institutions we form in order to live out these basic values—churches, synagogues, monasteries, councils, and the like—can themselves be prototypes or antitypes of social and political institutions. That is, our ecclesiologies are political experiments. models for wider social life. To the extent people who assemble around cultic rehearsals of memories and hopes also form enduring institutions to express and inculcate those values, they also create mini-orders that can be imitated in other institutional arenas. In the late Middle Ages monasteries nurtured many of the values indispensable to the economic life of the factory.[9] Church councils to resolve doctrinal and liturgical disputes were also models of town governance and later parliaments.[10] In the eighteenth century, meetings of the Society of Friends became models of democratic consensus formation.[11] These are only some of the historical ways religious practices could become not merely sources for cultural paradigms but models for actual social institutions.

How religions might legitimate or delegitimate federal republics in such ways is a central concern of this book. With historical examples of this function, I will assess how these relationships of legitimation and delegitimation might function in contemporary cultural and political contexts.

Differentiation

The second critical relationship between religion and political order concerns the degree of differentiation of religious organizations from political institutions as well as from other institutions, such as family, economy, and education. One way of understanding Western history is in terms of the development of increasing differentiation between religion and other social institutions.[12] The distinction between prophet and king in ancient Israel became the distinction between church and kingdom in Christendom. The shift in the meaning of vocation from being a religious call to holiness to being an economic call to frugality, honesty, and industry also legitimated the differentiation of economics from religion and politics. The baptismal sanctification of church membership independent of family and state further differentiated these institutions from each other and from the educational institutions that worked out the implications of baptism and Christian vocation.

Much of this differentiation is possible only because the religious life already is taken up into a self-governing institution distinct from all others. Whether for the sake of the purity of the cult and its priesthood or of the holiness of its members, a "church" develops that understands itself not first of all as a part of the society but as a transcendently grounded institution with its own purposes and loyalties. As a separate institution, often with its own professional associations, it gains distinct interests over against other institutions. It can then become to some degree a countervailing institution in the society. The distinctiveness of "church," like the distinctiveness of Jewish communities or religious communes, becomes the entering wedge of social and cultural pluralism, one of the prime elements in our conception of public life itself.

Ancient and traditional religions were not only the seedbeds for forces of differentiation and voluntarism. They also contained models and values of social integration that tended to fuse these institutional spheres together. Thus, both the individualism of modern societies and the religious reaction against it have religious roots. For some, the crises of modern republics lie in their individualism, whether fostered in the marketplace, the media, or the schools. For others, the crisis lies in the rise of religious fundamentalisms that seek to return republics to a fused society where religious values directly govern family, economy, and politics. Both of these are religious views. In this study I will examine how the process of differentiation or reaction against it affects the drive for federal-republican life. Is there any optimum degree of differentiation necessary for a federal republic? If so, what shapes might it assume?

Mediation

Because religious traditions usually contain impulses toward both differentiation and legitimation of entire social orders, they inevitably serve as mediators among the various institutions, classes, and groups in a society.[13] Churches reach into the heart of family life and open up families to responsibilities in neighborhoods and wider political units. Synagogues seek to inculcate values of philanthropy and service even as they reinforce the values of literacy, learning, and industry essential to personal economic success. Universities founded by religious institutions struggle with the mediation of traditional religious values and innovative genetic and medical technologies fostered in their research labs.

These practices of mediation are both horizontal, as between groups, neighborhoods, and regions, and also vertical, between smaller spheres of authority, such as the family, and wider spheres of economics and government. They mediate not only through their impact on individuals who act in all these different spheres but also as institutions themselves, seeking to coordinate the various expressions of their values in hospitals, schools, social service agencies, and their congregational cultic and educational life.

The way religious institutions perform these mediating roles in the wider society is directly related to the degree of differentiation and the patterns of legitimation present in that society as well as to the core values of that religious tradition itself. Some religious traditions long for a close integration of a society around a common cultural core. Historic Anglicanism comes to mind. Others, at least theologically, are adamantly opposed to such integration, even if in practice they may be deeply intertwined with a particular culture—Baptists in the southeastern United States provide a striking recent example.

In looking at the relation of religion to some actual federal republics, I will be concerned with the kind of mediating role they play. Between what institutions are they mediating? How do they carry out this mediation? What values are at stake as they do so? How does mediation relate to the processes of legitimation and differentiation that are at work in these contexts?

Mobilization

Finally, religious institutions, especially because of their traditional proximity to family and personal life, can mobilize people for wider purposes than daily routine. This is one aspect of their function of mediation. Their very cultic life often mobilizes people for collective rituals, pilgrimages, festivals, ordinations, funerals, and weddings. These patterns of mobilization can then easily channel people into political and national campaigns, forms of economic cooperation, and community action.

These occasional mobilizations for wider purposes can then be institutionalized into religiously based political parties, factions, labor unions, cooperatives, and community organizations. Such organizations are the heartbeat of large-scale public life. Thus, the religious capacity to mobilize people for wider purposes can be indispensable to the maintenance of any federal republic.

At the same time, religiously based forms of mobilization can also undermine public life by restricting entry, by absolutizing claims that would otherwise be the subject of compromise, or by reducing the capacity to form flexible coalitions around specific interests. In short, they can reduce the capacity for ordinary politics even as they mobilize people for political action. This can create an explosive conflict between religious expectations and political possibility, as we see in recent religio-political conflicts in India.

Thus, how religious institutions mobilize people and how they mediate this mobilization into the wider society is crucial to the processes of public life. The degree to which this mobilization absolutizes political issues deeply affects the possibility for genuine persuasion and appeal to common values. Whether people are mobilized as whole communities or along lines of special concern and interest shapes the kind and degree of pluralism that this mobilization brings to the public order. Whether this mobilization replicates the structures of authority in the church or operates under the authority patterns of the general public also deeply shapes the kind of participation this mobilization engenders. Are the religious leaders also the leaders of the public interest group or is this a lay leadership? Are political leaders using religion to mobilize the people or is this mobilization being engendered by the religious institution? These are questions that return us to the other themes of mediation, differentiation, and legitimation. Together they form a background checklist to guide our inquiry into the relationship of religion to the development of federal-republican life.

Summary

The struggle for authentic public life within a federal constitutional order is the primary form of the longing for a more just and peaceful political order in our time. It inherits the traditional Christian and Jewish longing for the Kingdom of God. As in the earlier linkage of legitimation and critique between the transcendent kingdom envisioned in religion and the earthly kingdoms, this modern struggle also has to find its peculiar relation to religious forces if it is to survive and find continual critique and renewal.

The religious notions of covenant and ecclesia can be seen as the religious counterparts to federalism and republicanism in our own era. The idea of covenantal publicity can be a terminological bridge between the religious and political dimensions of this struggle. It can help us draw connections not only between the values and theories on either side but also among the forms of organization they develop. It can be a conceptual bridge between ecclesiology and political order as well as between faith and political theory.

The religious traditions behind covenant draw us to the wider context of ultimate loyalties and ecological responsibility within which federalism needs to exist. The ecclesial notion of a public into which God seeks to call all peoples stands in judgment over against all the ways both religious organizations and republics seek to secure themselves within the narrow boundaries of ancestry, gender, and race. Conversely, the political traditions of republic, federalism, and constitutional democracy continually reawaken religious traditions to the wider import of concepts, values, and practices that easily find a merely private expression in individual piety and closed communities of absolutized beliefs. Just as covenant and publicity need to correct each other, so do federalism and the democratic struggle for public life need to shape each other.

The idea of covenantal publicity is both an analytical concept that opens our eyes to critical dimensions of the contemporary human struggle for public life and also a normative concept that directs our attention to appropriate political as well as religious values within this struggle. However, these values and orientations never float in the air. They have specific historical form within peculiar cultural contexts. Thus, to explore the relation of religion to federalism and public life, we need to examine it in various cultural environments. Out of this comparative study the key components and dynamics of covenantal publicity in our own time might emerge. That is the task of the following chapters.

Two

The Churches and Germany's "Peaceful Revolution" of 1989–90

In 1989 the citizens of the German Democratic Republic overthrew the Communist regime in a "peaceful revolution." The churches, especially the churches of the Federation of Evangelical Churches,[1] played a leading role in this remarkable "turning point" *(Wende),* as it was popularly called. Although the effort by reformers to build up a new democratic republic in the GDR was buried in the unification with the Federal Republic in the West, the experiences, questions, and perspectives at work in this process remain crucial for our understanding of the dynamics that can emerge in the involvement of religious organizations in the struggles for new publics and new constitutions.

This overturning of Germany's divided political order was not merely the result of contradictions within a Cold War tyranny but had roots in Germany's complex history of church-state relations. Moreover, the revolution's impulses toward democratic participation and federalism were not spontaneous imports but had been developing within the confines of crown, kingdom, and empire for centuries. To grasp the significance of this struggle for a new order of justice we have to identify some of its key historical roots.

Key Historical Considerations

Federative and Monarchical Unity in German History

Federal practices are deeply rooted in German political history, but within rather than over against structures of monarchy, kingship, and nobility. The commercial confederation of the northern merchant cities in the Hanseatic League of the fifteenth to eighteenth centuries is the most notable example of self-governance under a compact or charter. Bremen, Hamburg, and Lübeck have long histories as city-states within a world governed until the twentieth century by monarchs and princes. These princes themselves constituted leagues and confederations, whether to protect themselves from the monarchical ambitions within and without Germany or from the occasional threats posed by democratic movements.

Thus, the actors in federational arrangements were not based in democratic election but in the hierarchical structures within each region. Federation and federalism tended to be cut off from democratic impulses. Federalism and democracy were separated from each other to safeguard the traditional structures that cared for and protected individuals and families like a good father (the "*Landesherr*").

Efforts to unite the various German-speaking regions through confederations grew throughout the nineteenth century, dominated by Prussia and Austria.[2] In 1867 the northern states formed their own federation, the Norddeutscher Bund, which was later absorbed under Bismarck's leadership into the Prussian-led state. Austria was separated from this development at that time, and gradually the other German states came under Prussian dominance but with many federal elements and an increasing democratic element in the constitution of representative parliaments over against the councils of representatives of the confederating states. All of this, however, continued within the overall tradition of monarchy.

With the collapse of this order in 1918, monarchy was abolished and steps taken to separate the church from the old order of princely and governmental control. Democratic and parliamentary governance of the former German Empire led to a greater centralization of government in the Weimar Republic, especially to consolidate these republican gains over against a possible recrudescence of conservative elements in the individual states.[3] It was this government that the Nazis took over in 1933, completely eliminating the federal as well as democratic elements for the sake of imperial conquest and unity.

In the wake of the Nazi defeat, the three western Allies encouraged a more robust federal structure for the provisional constitution of an eventual unified Germany. Both widespread commitment to democratic principles and processes and a vigorous federalism would protect Germany from a new imperialism as well as from a fissiparous distintegration. This provisional Fundamental Law (*Grundgesetz*) was ratified by the three western zones in 1950 in anticipation of an eventual ratification by the Soviet zone, at which point it would become a full-fledged Constitution (*Verfassung*) for the German nation. It would be 45 years before this would become a possibility.

Church Governance

It is impossible to understand the dynamics of the revolution and the churches' role in it without seeing some of their institutional history. Since the Reformation the Evangelical churches in Germany had experienced a long and complicated history. Their theology and liturgy is still deeply permeated by their Lutheran heritage. The Calvinist strands—along with those of Zwingli and Bucer—have also been interwoven with them over the centuries, especially in terms of synodal structures of government. The ecclesiastical structure of the regional churches, however, was basically formed under the influence of the German princes and monarchs who championed the independence of the churches over against papal control.[4] The regional form of church life itself, whether Evangelical or Catholic, was the outcome of the Peace of Westfalia (1648), which brought an end to the terrible Thirty Years War to determine which church would control all of Germany. Thus, the federal differentiations of church and civil life are rooted in deep ecclesiastical divisions.

This regional autonomy for the churches did not mean, however, a general fostering of self-governance for Christians in the political sphere, nor did it mean that the newly independent Reformation churches were self-governing. The democratic and voluntarist impulses triggered by the Reformation led by Martin Luther were curbed by the princes as well as by Luther in response to the so-called "Peasants' Revolt" of 1525. Christian freedom was to be focused on the inner freedom of the individual believer. To protect this spiritual freedom from democratic excess as well as Roman intervention, church leaders after Luther sought external governance by princes and monarchs—the "*Landesherrliches Kirchenregiment.*" Like the parental God who seeks to nurture and protect our inner spirit, the prince would care for the church's (that is, the antipapal Evangelical church's) external form.

In spite of the widespread practice of federation and the struggle for wider public life in the emerging commercial cities, German Protestant theology, especially on its Lutheran side, never developed concepts of covenant or ecclesiastical associationalism to any significant degree.[5] The work of Zacharias Ursinus and Johannes Koch (Cocceius) in the sixteenth century stayed largely within a religious conception and failed to affect wider social developments.[6] Covenantal concepts focused on the individual, and the concept of a public sphere remained tightly bound to traditional governmental orders. Thus, it was difficult to develop a religious culture that would legitimate the recurrent efforts to secure a wider public life within a federal order.

From State Church to People's Church

Because of their peculiar position under the care of the princes, the churches from the sixteenth to the nineteenth centuries were actually a part of the structure of government. At the same time, in a typically medieval way, they could also occasionally come into conflict with the princes, although still within an essential unity. Because of this hierarchical and monarchical structure, the congregations could never develop their potential as independent and voluntary associations. They remained objects of princely care and pastoral ministration.

With the advent of the modern nation-state in Germany in the nineteenth century, the churches in the various German states became by and large "state churches." They passed from tutelage under the princes and monarchs to being parts of the emerging state bureaucracy of the late nineteenth century. At the same time, the churches gradually and cautiously won or were forced to assume a degree of distance from monarchs and the emerging state structures. In the process people came to advocate a popular church (Volkskirche) that would reclaim the church for the people. The Volkskirche idea did not dispense with the assumptions of government paternalism through the church but tried to establish the church on a more popular basis.[7]

With the breakdown of the old imperial order under Prussian hegemony in 1918, the regional churches gained greater independence from the state, in terms of both self-governance and reception of a protected status in finance, education, and social service. While many voices argued for episcopal or state controls over the church to protect the freedom of faith of individuals within the church, the desire for greater ecclesiastical autonomy largely prevailed.[8] The importance of more democratic forms of governance within the church largely overrode the defense of confessional purity lifted up by defenders of parentlike control in church and state.

In the struggle over democratic self-government and the differentiation of church from state, we see both an ambivalence about the nature and extent of democratic values and the desire for a federal system that protects regions and the churches within them from imperial or central control. We see, on the one hand, a deep commitment to personal autonomy springing from central values of Lutheran theology, but, on the other, deep suspicion of extending this into church or civil governance. The deep suspicion of mass movements of democracy has its symbolic root in Luther's attacks on the "enthusiasts" of the Peasant's Revolt. However, the spiritual values of personal faith have continually nourished impulses toward direct democracy—a major theme in both the rhetoric of centralized democracy under the Communist Party and in efforts to reform this regime by leaders of the 1989 revolution. These historic tensions fed directly into the effort to find a new relationship of democracy, federalism, and religion after World War II in the western sectors and in the whole of Germany in 1989–90.

The first step toward republican governance and a new relationship of church and state occurred in the wake of World War I. The Constitution of the Weimar Republic established the pattern of church participation in the public sphere that exists to this day. Article 37 declared that "[t]here is no established state church." This process of separation, however, has still not worked its way through to completion, because even earlier mechanisms for independence, for instance the "church tax" (Kirchensteuer), which sought to replace direct support from the state, now are seen as means of accommodation to state structures.[9] The movement for a purely voluntary and independent church continues to strengthen in the wake of the unification of 1989–90, not only because of the exodus of members but because of the conviction of many theologians that such independence is necessary for the church's prophetic mission.

This more critical stance toward the relationship of church and state was fostered most especially by the experience of the "Confessing Church" growing out of the Barmen Declaration (1934) and questioning the church's acquiescence to Nazi ideology. It received its most cogent and lasting apologia by Dietrich Bonhoeffer, whose martyrdom in the final days of the war seared its tenets in the minds of a younger generation of theologians.

This historic tension between a church of the lords from above and an independent and critical church from below shaped the history of the Evangelical churches into the postwar era. The collapse of the Nazi regime gave the churches the possibility of constructing new structures, procedures, purposes, and conceptions of their mission in order to overcome their passivity in the face of the Nazi terror. However, the churches did not seize this opportunity and largely reestablished the earlier structures. During the Cold War these new structures eventually developed somewhat differently in the two German states.

Church as Public Corporation and as Voluntary Association

The form under which the former regional churches preserved some of their privileges while also gaining some autonomy from the state was that of the public corporation *(Körperschaft des öffentlichen Rechts)*. As a public corporation the churches—and here I mean the Evangelical Churches and the Roman Catholic Church—could use the tax system to raise funds, carry on instruction in government-run schools, operate essentially public hospitals and social services, and place representatives on the boards of public radio and television networks.

Other churches, such as Methodist and Baptist, were certainly free to form and carry out their work but not as public corporations. They were private associations *(Vereine)* that had legal standing but no more special relation to the government than a brewer's association or a sports team.[10] As a symbol of this differing public status, they could not ring church bells as did the "public churches."

While these two types of organizational forms—open as well to non-Christian religions—differed vastly in their relationship with the government, their members were all equally protected in their freedom to pursue any or no religious path and to proclaim and propagate their faith without censure or hindrance. The only differences lay not in the rights of their members but in the privileges of their institutions. The enormous contributions of the churches to the rebuilding of Germany after the Nazi era further secured their position in government policy as well as public opinion, in spite of the relative lack of voluntary participation in church life itself.

The Development of the Two Germanies, 1945–69

The Federal and the Democratic Republics

With their victory over the Nazi forces, the four Allied nations temporarily divided control of Germany among them, pending an eventual reunification. The three North Atlantic powers promoted the establishment of a government governed by a provisional federal-republican Constitution (the *Grundgesetz*).

Almost immediately the Russian sector established its own independent constitution and government under control of the Communist Party. It took on the form of "democratic centralism," in which the powers of the states and other smaller governing bodies were sharply curtailed or eliminated. Thus the party (the Socialist Unity Party of Germany) could control every aspect of governance directly. Each individual was equally related to the central control of the government dominated by the party. This was the meaning of democracy within the socialist framework. The radical democratic impulses rooted in Luther's teachings broke through to the political realm but within an overall structure of parental care exercised by the party through the state. This new, bureaucratic monarchy succeeded in largely eliminating the federalist differentiation rooted in German history.

While the pretense of temporary zones of occupation was never entirely given up in the subsequent 45 years, the process of separation into two distinct states was underway decisively by the time the two different constitutions—one a Fundamental Law, the other a Constitution—were ratified in 1949.

The One Church in the Two Germanies

Shortly after the war the Evangelical churches in all four zones of Allied occupation joined in a federation—the Evangelical Church in Germany (EKD).[11] The internal structures of the church were reconstructed according to the patterns of the prewar era. In the western sectors the Fundamental Law had legally confirmed this restoration by taking over from the Weimar Republic the constitutional provisions pertaining to church law.[12] In addition, the Fundamental Law contained important guarantees of human rights, especially freedom of belief and religious organization, that strengthened the position of the churches in the society and in the new republic.[13]

Although the 1949 Constitution of the GDR also guaranteed the freedom of the church, this freedom was sharply curtailed in the revised Constitution of 1968.[14] Nevertheless, the member churches of the EKD remained together throughout the 1950s. However, with the Communist Party's introduction of the "Youth Dedication" ceremonies in the GDR in the 1950s, the churches experienced a sharp attack on their most important sacramental and popular basis—confirmation. At the same time, the churches were ordered to register all their nonworship activities with the government. They were unable to resist the first attack. With the second, they found more success and were able to defend control of the free space within the church.[15]

With the construction of the Berlin Wall in August 1961, the regime began to exert increasing pressure on the eastern churches in order to divide them from their western partners. In the wake of the more repressive GDR Constitution of 1968 the eastern members of the EKD formed their own federation, the Bund der Evangelischen Kirchen (BEK), in 1969. Nevertheless, they remained in a "special communion" with the churches of the EKD.[16]

The Roman Catholic Church and the so-called Free Churches, primarily Methodist and Baptist, comprised only a small percentage of the church population in the GDR. Their basic stance, especially among the Catholics, was to "hibernate" through the Communist winter.[17] The Evangelical churches, because of their historic role as primary religious partners of the state in eastern Germany and their relatively greater size, could engage the regime in a more open way as an alternative public institution. They continued to conduct their synods according to democratic forms and parliamentary procedures. Relatively open preaching, small group discussions, and seminars preserved the experience of public discourse. The experience of the Confessing Church and the writings of Dietrich Bonhoeffer played a crucial role in legitimating this course of being the public representative and voice for the voiceless. Despite its decreasing numbers, the church, as the only institution not fully controlled by the state, gained the trust of many people as an independent organization that could be their advocate.[18]

As the GDR regime began to lose credibility with its citizens in the later 1970s, it gave up its effort to divide and dominate the churches. In exchange for giving the churches more free space it asked for more cooperation in pursuing common goals.[19] The churches gained increasing freedom to participate in international conferences, while the state gained a certain degree of international recognition and internal legitimation.

With this unwritten agreement, the churches soon took up an open discussion concerning peace, military policy, human rights, and environmental conservation. The Helsinki Agreement of 1975, to which the GDR was a signatory, became the kernel of this legitimate discussion. The biannual regional and national church conferences *(Kirchentage)* demonstrated a kind of public debate and decentralized federalism that presented a vivid contrast to the state and Communist Party policies.[20]

As a consequence of Mikkail Gorbachev's policy of glasnost and perestroika the regime lost its military support. Governance was increasingly forced back to open debate and persuasion as the primary means for resolving problems. With the increased pressure to open up the process of governance, the GDR entered the "turning point" of revolution in 1989.

The Church in the Revolution of 1989–90

The revolutionary events of 1989–90 can be organized into seven phases:

- The development of activist groups in the churches in the years before 1989.
- The Conciliar Process for Justice, Peace, and the Preservation of Creation in 1988–89.
- The demonstrations in the cities of the GDR in the fall of 1989.
- The creation of the round tables.
- The rapid unification with the Federal Republic in 1990.
- The resulting efforts to change church structures and transform the Fundamental Law of the Federal Republic into a genuine Constitution for the new Germany.
- The emergence of the struggle to come to terms with the Nazi and Communist past in the period after 1990.

The Rise of Activist Groups under the Church's Roof

The union of the regional Evangelical churches into a federation legally independent of the West German churches gave these churches the possibility of carving out their own space within the socialist conditions of the GDR. As the only remaining institution that possessed relative independence from the state, the churches could gain a certain freedom not only in worship and internal education but also in the internal discussion of matters of public ethics and policy. Their position as the only independent public in the society provided the basis for their crucial role in the political changes at the end of the 1980s.

In those years a variety of groups used the church as a place of refuge and rehearsal where they could claim their own voice and cultivate their own convictions. These groups were diverse in their makeup, purpose, and connections to and consequences for the established church institutions. In the early 1980s some small groups began to gather on a weekly basis in various cities to pray for peace. Other groups concerned with conscientious objection to military service, human rights, and environmental preservation gathered alongside them. In addition, increasing numbers of people seeking to emigrate came to the church for protection, support, and assistance. These groups developed a kind of public life under the protection of the institutional church. These groups wanted neither to be evangelized nor to join the church. They simply wanted to be partners in the struggle for justice, peace, and ecological renewal.[21]

These groups were an indispensable part of the church's witness for peace and justice, especially at the local level. At the same time, they were a thorn in the institutional church's side. Their spokespersons were often called "running board pastors," those who used the church but never climbed inside. At one point, at the Leipzig Kirchentag of 1989, they formed a "counterconference" to discuss more openly the burning issues of reform in the GDR.[22] Joachim Garstecki, a longtime participant in church peace efforts and an analyst of church affairs, observed that the churches "maintained in general an overwhelming distance from the emancipatory groups. . . . It was the people whose wisdom and impatience pressed the church into the center of renewal activities. Church doors opened for this purpose simply because people pushed them open from outside."[23]

Ehrhart Neubert, a research colleague of Garstecki's, saw in the tension a deeper underlying dynamic in which a process of differentiation within the society was seeking to find expression. The manifold problems of an increasingly technological society demanded a more pluralistic and open debate in the search for solutions. Since the formal governmental processes would not accommodate this need, the churches and groups, even though often in tension with one another, became the outlet for this normally public dynamic.[24]

Though small in numbers,[25] the groups were a critical threat to the state's effort to monopolize public discourse and organizational power. The state considered them "counterrevolutionary," "negative," and "inimical to the state," and began to exercise extraordinary measures to co-opt or suppress them.[26]

Church leaders often found themselves standing between the groups under their roof and the state, especially its security apparatus, the Stasi (*Staatssicherheitsdienst,* the State Security Ministry). This delicate tightrope walk between maintaining orderly and sometimes fruitful channels of communication with the state and protecting the groups played itself out in various ways, depending on the local constellation of ecclesial and governmental structures. The church was often caught between preserving its identity, on the one hand, and its social purpose, on the other.[27]

These tensions and alliances cut clear across all the structures and activities of the churches and groups, producing a very mixed picture. Perhaps the words of Rudi Pahnke, one of the activists, might best sum it up: "The groups were the source of democratization in the GDR. The churches have helped steer this process for good or for evil. Both were present—sympathy and action, skepticism and faintheartedness."[28] As events came to an explosive denouement, the groups and the institutional church found their most productive cooperation in the Conciliar Process for Justice, Peace, and the Preservation of Creation in 1988–89.

The Conciliar Process, 1988–89

Since its inception, the BEK and its member churches had tried to foster concern for peace and human rights.[29] Even in 1965 the church leadership of the future BEK had pronounced conscientious objection to war to be a "clearer witness" to peace than military service. In its Synod of 1982 the Federation had declared its "renunciation of the spirit, logic and practice of the system of terror [nuclear deterrence]."[30]

In the 1980s, the ecological destruction of eastern Europe began to come to light. At its Greifswald Synod of 1984 the BEK confessed the complicity of Christians in this destruction and appealed to its members, not only as Christians but as citizens, to take on responsibility for the preservation of the creation.[31]

In response to a petition brought by the BEK to the World Council of Churches meeting in 1984, the WCC called for a conciliar process to give expression to the church's responsibility for justice, peace, and the preservation of the creation. In this process, which the Roman Catholic Church also came to support, churches, congregations, and activist groups were stimulated to pursue these questions in their own context. In this way the covenant with the Creator, with one another, and with the earth could take on a concrete though not foreseeable form.

The process began in the GDR under the initiative of Heino Falcke, a leading church official and theologian in Erfurt, and Christof Ziemer, the church superintendent in Dresden. The initial meeting took place in Dresden in 1988 on the anniversary of the February 13, 1945, firebombing of Dresden, thus legitimating itself in terms of the memory of terrible destruction and the determination not to see it repeated.[32]

Congregations, groups, and individuals were invited to submit their suggestions for themes to be discussed in the process. This process of building up from the grass roots was expressed in the conciliar slogan "a hope learns to walk" *("Eine Hoffnung lernt gehen")*. Out of this request they received over 10,000 responses, which were then organized for discussion by the 150 delegates.

The most stirring report at the first assembly concerned the long-term devastation produced by the uranium mines in Thuringia. The discussion of this long-concealed environmental destruction exposed the desperate need for factual information, without which no public can function. The destruction of the land was intimately tied to the destruction of public life itself. The demand for adequate information became a burning central theme of the conciliar process.

The governmental officials, though very suspicious of this "counter public," reluctantly let it continue as a legitimate process within the carefully secured free space of the church. However, after the first assembly, the regime prohibited all public reports either in the state-controlled or church media. Even a prayer for the "turning around and renewal of our country" was censored before it was delivered. Old party bosses like Werner Jarowinsky and Stasi chief Erich Mielke saw in the Conciliar Process a direct attack on the state, on the "leading role of the Party," and on socialism itself.[33]

Debates over the themes and proposals of the Conciliar Process took place throughout the GDR in congregations and groups in 1988. In these encounters the participants began to overcome the mistrust generated not only by the security state but by old religious and regional divisions. In the words of the final document:

> We have taken the newly experienced community of nineteen churches and church communities as a precious gift from God. The ecumenical dynamic of our assembly is irreversible. We have experienced it as a sign of hope for the ongoing way of our churches. God's spirit leads us all together as his people. We have spoken with many tongues, but in the end spoken one language. We dare not return behind old walls and into old divisions.[34]

In bridging the strategic and confessional differences among the churches, the Conciliar Process helped overcome the party's strategy to divide and dominate the churches.

The assembly set forth its resolutions as "covenants" *(Bundeschlüße)*—a fitting expression of a covenantal process aimed at repentance and renewal. In the concluding document we find a call to conversion that applied also to the whole society:

> Since the time of the Old Testament prophets the biblical preaching of conversion has been directed not only to individuals but to the whole people, to its representatives and social classes (for example the rich). This call to return to God is realized in military, economic and social policies. The call to conversion is aimed at hearts and behavior as well as relationships. Conversion has a historical as well as a biographical hour.[35]

With these words the assembly was able to build a clear bridge between theology and politics, church and state, that not only called the party's monopoly into question but also demanded radical changes in the course of the GDR ship of state.

This appeal concerned not only the policies of the Communist state but also the public processes in which the goals and means of policy would be determined. In its resolutions the assembly called for "the cultivation of nonviolent means for dealing with conflicts and for the cultivation of a culture of public disputation and active citizen co-responsibility for their own country."[36] This was a call not only for reform but for a complete overturning of the political structure as a whole.

These covenantal resolutions were sent to the various synods for debate and adoption in the late spring and early summer. They were also taken up by the concluding assembly of the European Conciliar Process in Basel in June, where Heino Falcke was a major speaker. By the time the BEK Synod took them up in September, the process of political change was in high gear. Through the Conciliar Process the churches in the GDR engaged in a worldwide ecumenical process that was rooted in the experience of the GDR churches and that in turn also affected them and their society profoundly.

Most important, the "covenants" of the Conciliar Process became the main theses of the reform movement in the fall of 1989. They formed much of the framework of proposals for a new Constitution for the GDR that was laid out by a commission of the Central Round Table in Berlin. The participants in the assemblies became leading figures in the demonstrations that burst out of the churches that fall and in the formation of a new political order.[37]

The Outbreak of Demonstrations

The little publics in the churches broke out into the streets in many cities simultaneously. With prayers and petitions, with posters and pleas, thousands of people baptized in the spirit of nonviolence from Gandhi and King marched out in front of the security police.

These public encounters and demonstrations had their roots in earlier marches and demonstrations. In 1987 church peace movements had participated in the three-day Olaf Palme Peace March. At the same time police seizure of an environmental action library housed in Berlin's Zion Church had precipitated vigorous church action and public demonstrations to defend those who had been arrested.[38]

On January 9, 1988, groups in Leipzig tried to join the annual Rosa Luxemburg–Karl Leibknecht March in order to lift up their democratic values in the face of the hypocritical democratic facade maintained by the party. The government reacted with arrests and detentions that further aggravated the tensions between church spokespersons and governmental authorities.[39]

In May of 1989 citizen groups monitored the local elections, which were seen to be a litmus test for real democracy in the GDR. When the party trumpeted its usual claims to an overwhelming victory, the observer groups countered with claims that the elections had been systematically falsified. People's experience of elections in the church could not find a reflection in their civil life. The revelation of these deceptions further undermined the legitimacy of the government.

Church leaders openly protested against this sabotage of the elections and petitioned in vain for a response from the government. At the same time, however, they spoke out against "exaggerated actions or demonstrations" as appropriate "methods for the church"—a position heatedly attacked by Falcke and others.[40] And so with one foot on the brake and one on the accelerator the church bus loaded with fellow travelers lurched through the papier mâché wall of party democracy. The Communist state began to buckle.

In the wake of the bloodbath in Beijing's Tiananmen Square in June of 1989 every arrest of a demonstrator took on a threatening meaning. Violence lay in the summer air. Church concern to protect but also to restrain the groups grew with the tension in the streets. With the opening of the Hungarian borders a surge of emigration began, posing the question with human feet: Can this regime really change? Is there still any possibility for reform?

In Wittenberg, on June 24, 1989, Pastor Friedrich Schorlemmer—like Luther before him—distributed a paper with 20 theses with the admonition: "The time of silence is past and the time to speak has come."[41] The theses emerged from the resolutions of the April Ecumenical Assembly in Dresden and brought them to public debate. The growing protest thus sought to legitimate itself by appealing to the heritage of the Reformation—celebrated only four years earlier with lavish state support. The state's response to this expression of the Reformation spirit was to put further pressure on church publications to censor their coverage.

In the summer months more and more applicants for emigration began to visit the peace prayer services to find a room where they could express their anxiety and hope as well as find concrete help for their difficulties. The reformers as well as church leaders had to pick their way between sympathy for those who "wanted out" and those who wanted to remain in order to reform the system.[42]

In Dresden in early October the spark of protest became a roaring fire as state police attacked people trying to get on the trains headed for the West.[43] The facade of legitimacy had fallen away altogether. The church—the last publicly recognized legitimate institution—began to advise the police in order to protect the people in the streets. The police, realizing the government had lost its legitimacy, began to take its directions from key church leaders like Christof Ziemer.[44] On the night of October 8 the two sides reached an agreement to renounce violence and work with a group of 20 citizens to ensure a peaceful administration of law and order in the city.[45]

In Leipzig the Monday peace prayers in the Nikolaikirche began ending with long processions circling the old section of the city.[46] With pastoral admonitions to nonviolence in their ears, they carried candles as diffuse but powerful symbols of peace and of a new light in the society. This "Revolution of the Candles" manifested itself in other cities as well.

The confrontation in Leipzig between the demonstrators pouring out of the Nikolaikirche and the police in the streets came to a climax on October 9. The city authorities restrained the police. Another Tiananmen Square was averted, and authority began to flow from the regime to the disorganized but determined people. The most basic form of mass democracy was prevailing against established structures of control. The Communist Landesherr was yielding to "the People."

In Magdeburg people placed candles in the form of a cross in front of a sculpture by Ernst Barlach created in protest of World War I. After the prayer service, regular open discussions took place. The cathedral preachers—Waltraut Zachhuber and Giselher Quast—mediated between local officials and the people.[47] After October 9, when it was clear that police were not going to respond violently to demonstrators, an artisan distributed green armbands to the demonstrators at the cathedral, saying "These armbands are 40 centimeters long. After 40 years of unending red now we take the soft green of hope that we have learned in the cathedral."[48]

The prayers for prisoners and emigrants had brought the desperate condition of the GDR to light. A resonance between the suffering and the sympathetic reverberated against the fortress of the state. In this resonance people gained the power to move out into the streets despite their fear and anxiety. The cry "*We* are the people!" soon led to "We are *one* people!" The people who had found their voice in prayers and petitions now broadcast their messages on banners and placards as well as through chants and responses.

The activist groups began to leave the protection of the churches in September and October in order to form their own independent parties and movements, thus challenging the government even further. Many, if not most, of them were led by pastors and lay leaders from the churches. Their programs, values, and procedures were strongly shaped by their origins in the churches. The core of their leadership was constituted by church activists and pastors. "New Forum," "Democratic Awakening," and "Democracy Now" began to create the basis for a new political order. On their heels came branches of the western parties. Political pluralism was soon in full swing. Within two months these groups moved from persecution to partnership in the reconstruction of the East German state.[49]

The leading reformers in church circles wanted to create an improved but still socialist state and society. They presumed the survival of a separate German state. With the opening of the Berlin wall on November 9 all these aims were put in question. The emigrants had reached their goal. Now, not only the western media could penetrate the border but the German mark as well. Without being able to anticipate the repercussions of this opening the new political forces set about trying to reconstitute the GDR according to new values. They established "round tables"—a lesson from Poland's Solidarity movement—to bring the people together on an equal basis.

The Round Tables

The pressure for participation permeated the whole upheaval in the fall of 1989 and found its strongest expression in the formation of the round tables.[50] Their most immediate parent was the "Group of 20" in Dresden, with its progeny in other cities, that took up the task of representing and cooperatively advancing the common interests of city, nation, and even the environment.

As it became clear that the state was losing its legitimacy, the round tables constituted a new kind of conciliar process. Around them gathered the spontaneous "councils of the people" that Hannah Arendt has identified as the core of every "revolution of freedom" in the modern age.[51]

The round tables in cities, towns, villages, and suburbs were almost always moderated by experienced church leaders. Having been nurtured in the buried public of the church, they were the only people experienced in democratic process who could constitute these new, provisional publics. In the synods and parishes one did not even need a table, only the express equality of the participants, openness to conversation, and—the most difficult—the courage to express one's opinions honestly and openly. Without being able to exercise force, one had to reach common agreements rooted in mutual trust. The round tables nurtured a whole political culture of democratic process. In the words of one participant:

> For me, those round tables were the best. Even things we didn't know everything about could be discussed and decided openly. It took place in church space, but it was more like an island. I never would have thought that I would be able to express myself freely in a place where the SED/PDS and even the military were present. Everyone was heard, nobody's word was denied to them. The [church] superintendent there, Mr. Riebesel, led the round table and did

it really well. The moderator was a Catholic woman who executed this task brilliantly.[52]

The round tables, which had to discuss and resolve questions arising in numerous areas, also had to develop a structure of representation—something the direct-democracy groups could not do. Different groups showed up at each meeting demanding a voice. It was almost impossible to develop a principle of orderly representation in the four short months of their existence. This was due not only to the short time and the general political chaos but to the special function of the round tables, namely, to represent the ongoing interests of the whole society and thereby help ground a new political culture, if not system.[53]

In Berlin the reformers brought together a "Central Round Table" in November in order to deal with the common problems of the whole republic. In particular they had to bridge the gap between the Communist Party's surrender of its "leading role" (decided on December 1) and the new elections in May (later advanced to March). Secondly, this group was to develop a new Constitution. The Berlin round table arose out of talks between Bishop Gottfried Forck, Consistory President Manfred Stolpe, and General Superintendent Günter Krusche on the church side and Berlin Mayor Erhard Krack and SED party secretary Günter Schabowski from the government's side. The moderators of the table were Martin Ziegler, secretary of the BEK; Dr. Karl-Heinz Ducke, a Catholic priest; and Martin Lange, a Methodist pastor and ecumenical leader. Here not only the people's general confidence in the church but also a new collaboration among the churches came to expression. With these round tables the party's monopoly on public life broke apart and a public plurality of parties received new legitimation.

In the discussions and debates of the round tables almost all of the elements of the "peaceful revolution" came to the fore: free and almost ecstatic expression of opinions, a deep sense of common values and goals, a commitment to nonviolent democratic procedures, and the delegating of representatives from free associations to the round tables. These values then sought permanent expression in a new Constitution.

Members of the Berlin table struggled to draft a new Constitution and bring it forward for debate. The result was a proposed Constitution incorporating the rediscovered democratic values and procedures within the context of ecological responsibility.[54]

In this way the round tables, like the churches themselves, were a "school of democracy."[55] They were the midwives of a potential new republic. In spite of the subsequent miscarriage of the effort to reform the socialist system of the GDR, the round tables remained important symbols of public life that needed to find a prominent place in the symbolism of the political culture of a new Germany.

The noninstitutionalized "effervescence" in the streets and around the tables lasted almost a month before being dissipated by the centrifugal forces created by a multiplicity of interest groups as well as by increasing economic and diplomatic pressures. The reform movement was overrun by stronger powers inside and outside the GDR. The hopes for a better satisfaction of life's necessities and the growing number of emigrants strengthened the desire to join the world of the German mark as quickly as possible.

The Rapid Accession to the Federal Republic of Germany

At the end of November 1989 Chancellor Helmut Kohl offered to form between the two German states a confederation that rested on the assumption of mutual equality. But the strain toward full unification increased so quickly that by the first free elections in the GDR on March 18 the parties of the Christian Democratic Union's "Alliance for Germany" won the elections with its promise of reunification. By May 18 representatives of the GDR and the FRG agreed in principle that the states of the old GDR would join the Federal Republic. Monetary unification began on July 1. A treaty for full unification was signed on August 3. Legal accession was completed on October 3, 1990, and in December the first free all-German elections were held. The chance of developing a new constitution in the GDR or of formulating a federation between equal partners had disappeared within a year.[56]

The treaties were concluded between a republic that had only a Fundamental Law, but which was far and away the stronger partner, and a republic that had a Constitution, but which was clearly the subordinate party. The treaty of May 18 began with gratitude "that a peaceful and democratic revolution had taken place in the German Democratic Republic in the fall of 1989." It then committed the parties to realize the unity of Germany within a peaceful European order and to pursue a "social market economy" with "social equalization [between East and West] and social security as well as ecological responsibility." Furthermore, the parties pledged to bring about their unity according to Article 23 of the Fundamental Law in conversation with the World War II Allies and to introduce federal structures into the old GDR.[57]

The old GDR joined the FRG without their first developing a new common constitution arising from their disparate experiences (the option presented by Article 146 of the Fundamental Law). People felt they lacked the time for such an extended process due to the intense economic pressures and the fear that the Communist Party and its security apparatus might return to power. Indeed, reports of such plans among the Stasi forces circulated widely in the winter and early spring of 1990.

The churches were taken into this accession process step by step. At a special meeting in Loccum on January 15–17, 1990, delegates and bishops expressed the fervent desire to reunite the former members of the all-Germany EKD. They recalled the "special communion they had experienced for decades in countless connections." This communion had shown itself to be a "strong bond between people in a divided Germany. This has had political consequences. The consciousness of the common membership of Germans in both states is an important basis of their mutual action. We have strengthened this feeling, we sense it ourselves. We want the two German states to grow together."

While respecting the diverse development of the two states, the delegates wanted "to give to the special communion of the whole of Evangelical Christianity in Germany an organizationally appropriate form in one church. We want to carefully deal with the experiences and differences that have grown up during the separation."[58] Since the churches in both parts of Germany had been joined together for more than 20 years (1948–69), it was easier to speak of their *re*unification within a common constitution than one could in the political sphere, where no common constitution ever existed.

Although the participants at Loccum had "considered" the differences between the two partners, others, especially theologians, felt these differences more keenly. In a "Berlin Declaration" four of these theologians expressed their fear and hesitation in the face of a rapid unification.[59] Instead of emphasizing a "special communion," the churches, they held, should exercise their "special responsibility" in a representative fashion to preserve the political separation a little while longer. This would help prevent the weaker party from being swallowed up into a revived German nationalism.[60] Only in this way could the German people work through the "emotional nationalism that has already worked itself out so fatefully several times in German history" and do justice "to their common bonds with other peoples in the one People of God."

By putting German unification within this wider horizon, German Christians could emphasize their "communion in the one Body of Christ and the God who has struck a covenant with us and the whole creation." This sense of global humanity could lead them further to recognize the multicultural character of German society itself.

Such a pause in the unification process could also help clarify the churches' task of helping people see this new political order as part of a global reordering. It would provide time for the grief work and reevaluation of the past as a new basis for reconciliation among the peoples of the region. All of this would provide a sounder basis for the new kind of order intimated in the Conciliar Process of 1988–89.

In the tension between these two declarations we see two sets of basic questions. First, are we dealing with the coming together of a people, in which the church participates, or with a manifold and multiethnic reality in which the church plays a representative role over against "the German people"? Will the new political order be part of a wider federation or will it simply fall back into a new version of German nationalism? Will it be grounded in the kind of new covenants enunciated in Dresden, Basel, and Seoul or will it simply rest in the traces of the past?

Second, how are we to understand these new relationships—as community, treaty, alliance, confederation, or federation? What are the rights and obligations of the participating political units? What conception of individual rights—including the rights of refugees and stateless persons—will prevail? These questions pervaded the consequences of the accession of the eastern states and churches to the Federal Republic in 1990.

The Struggle for Structural Reform

The swift accession of the former GDR to the Federal Republic made reform within the old socialist framework impossible and excluded creation of a new federal arrangement between independent states. The churches and political groups on both sides had to turn to questions of possible internal reforms in light of the GDR experience and the new situation. How could they transplant the experience of the past 40 years into the new soil of a united Germany?

Internal Church Reform

Because of the legal and economic structure of the old GDR, the BEK churches had created several structures that still held theological importance. This legacy of the socialist era concerned several important aspects of church life: finances, education, ministry within the military, and the federal structure of the church itself.

CHURCH FINANCES AND THE "CHURCH TAX." The "church tax" had been abolished in the GDR, even though the state continued to pay "state payments" to the churches that were first established in the secularization process of the early nineteenth century. According to an estimate by Bishop Gottfried Forck, the Berlin-Brandenburg Church received 40% of its annual income from voluntary contributions, up to 40% from churches in the West (principally the churches of the EKD), and 10–12% from the state. A similar situation held for the other BEK synods, although the exact total sums were known to very few church leaders.[61] In short, the eastern churches were never financially self-sufficient. Ironically, even the voluntary contributions were still called "church taxes," thus undercutting the development of a culture of voluntarism in church finances. Nevertheless, the churches of the BEK posed the crucial question whether the churches could now move to a fully voluntary system of church finances in a united Germany.

To the disappointment of the reformers, the church tax system returned as an unavoidable necessity in order to put the churches of the former BEK on a sound footing and bring the salaries of church workers back up to a reasonable level.[62] At the same time, they were adjusted to reflect the pay scale of civil servants—the long-standing practice in the EKD churches.[63] Just as church reforms had been set aside in the postwar era, so they were once again buried by the necessities of economic and institutional reconstruction.

RELIGIOUS EDUCATION.   The second question concerned religious education in parish and school. In the GDR religious education had to take place in the parish rather than in the schools, since the party sought at every point to secure its monopoly on all truth claims in the society. In the Honecker era all questions from the churches about this exclusion from the schools were dismissed.[64] Pupils were subjected to the indoctrination of the state. After unification, the churches recovered their western status as "public corporations," which meant they were once again able to conduct religious education in the schools.

This new situation, however, required retraining and recertification of the parish catechists in order to comply with state educational standards. It also posed the danger that the church educators would simply replace the ideological indoctrination formerly imposed by the Communist apparatus, with the same response of mistrust and indifference. Most important, from a theological standpoint, it raised the question of the relation of belief to congregational life. What is the proper context for the internalization of faith? What role, if any, should the government play in Christian formation? Finally, the new situation raised not only the whole question of church-state relations (and separation) but how to treat small and large church bodies alike.

The desire to distinguish clearly between the church and the governmental sphere led to a distinction between Christian formation in the parish and information-oriented religious instruction in the schools. Within this framework of religious studies in the schools the various denominations could perhaps work together on a nonconfessional basis—a new opportunity for ecumenical cooperation.[65]

MILITARY CHAPLAINCY AND MILITARY SERVICE.   The question of church policy regarding the military came to the fore above all in the discussion about military chaplaincy. This question emerged not only from the central commitment to peace issues among the BEK churches and their desire for more independence in the society but also from the very history of the BEK's founding. In 1957 the EKD had entered into a military chaplaincy arrangement with the government of the Federal Republic without a public discussion within the EKD.[66] As member churches of the EKD at that time, the synods in the GDR fell under deep suspicion. This treaty was at the core of the GDR government's reproaches against the church and had led to the legal separation between the eastern and western churches.[67]

In the GDR years the churches were excluded from any kind of relationship with the military. The struggle for a legal recognition of conscientious objection consumed an enormous amount of the church's energy. In this exclusion the churches could develop a more pronounced peace witness than in the West. This found expression in the special military service option of construction work and at the end of the GDR in alternative civilian service—though still undertaken with significant career losses. Moreover, the BEK churches committed themselves to a "renunciation of the spirit, logic and practice of deterrence" and to a public advocacy of pursuit of nonviolent means to secure peace.[68]

The reunion of the churches in 1990 posed the question anew: How can the churches provide appropriate pastoral care to soldiers without becoming entangled in the structures of the military and the government? How can the churches, on the basis of their commitment to peace, uncouple the military chaplaincy as far as possible from the government and the structures of military rank and be anchored more in the congregations themselves? Such a step would preserve the church's peace mission as well as the newly rediscovered centrality of the congregation.[69]

FEDERAL STRUCTURES WITHIN THE CHURCH.   In the GDR the federal structures of the BEK churches stood in stark contrast to the centralized structures of the states. The federal structures that were eliminated from the life of the states found a kind of substitute existence in the synods of the regional churches. Here the structures of the churches themselves were a kind of witness for a just social order. Moreover, the financial structures of the BEK churches, which were more dependent on parish offerings, exercised a kind of strengthening of federal relationships. The churches tried to strengthen this federalism after the revolution in 1989–90. Crucial to this federal commitment was the distribution of income resulting from the reintroduction of the church tax system.[70] Only through a web of federal structures could the church adequately cultivate the activities and initiatives in local districts, groups, and parishes. Only through such a structure could it speak to the various power centers of the society on an appropriate footing.

This struggle for a strengthened federalism served not only the interests of the little publics in the parishes and districts. It was itself a kind of witness. In the practice of the churches people also could learn a vital spirit of federalism. The church was not only a school of democracy but a school of federalism. The churches provided to some extent a model of political practice for the society that now had to be developed further. Jürgen Moltmann put it sharply and prophetically: "If the new Europe is to take on a federalistic and democratic form, then a centralized church can hardly be a model or bring anything new to birth."[71]

In the discussion of church reorganization shortly after the autumn of 1989 any changes in the Constitution of the EKD were postponed. Rather than burdening the parties with the task of constitutional reform at the outset, they agreed to embark on a joint course whose experiences would lead to subsequent possible constitutional changes. From the perspective of EKD President Hartmut Löwe,

[I]t was simple realism and not an avoidance of possible changes, not to burden the new beginning with fundamental debates. Rather, after making indispensable modifications with our terse and tested constitutional text, to set out on a common path together in the expectation that a new and unified institutional history will lead to a deepening of communion which, when the time is ripe, can be given legal form.[72]

The history of the church in the GDR posed critical and continuing questions for the common history of the united churches. What the BEK churches had learned about alternative church practices and structures would have to be evaluated and worked out within the new common history in order to find expression in a revised Constitution.

When the time came for the reunification of the EKD and the BEK, however, the BEK, like the GDR, gave up its possible independent regional status and was reabsorbed into the EKD with only minor modifications. Unlike the GDR and the Bundesrepublik, this reunification represented a genuine return to an earlier unity, thus undercutting arguments for a new federation "from the ground up." Moreover, pressing financial crises as well as time needed to make administrative changes were cited as justifications for bypassing a process of refederation for the sake of simple reunion. While these moves were understandable, they meant that the churches could not at least institute the kind of full covenanting that could have served as a critical alternative to the political accession that left unanswered so many questions about the deeper bonds of covenantal mutuality that might sustain a new structure of federation.[73]

The Relationship of Church to Society

The whole history of the Evangelical Church in the GDR can be understood as a search for a new basis for the relationship between churches and the society in Germany, including its implications for church structure. The difficulties in securing this new stance found forceful expression in the failure of efforts of the various Reformation churches in the GDR to forge a common federation in the 1970s and 1980s.[74] This search for an appropriate relation of church and society also became a lens for viewing and assessing what the churches had learned in the 40 years of the GDR. In the words of Church Superintendent Christof Ziemer:

> We will have to newly define or become conscious of our task and role in society. We have a choice between following the path of the Federal Republic or pursuing the course we learned as church and tested last fall [1989]. In the '80s we were present as church in the conflicts of the society and had our place there. We defined ourselves in terms of our social engagement on behalf of those who had fallen as victims. Now we have to ask whether we want to be drawn into the structures of the society themselves. That is the fundamental decision.[75]

In a pluralistic society, where the state exists only as one special institution among others, this is a question not only of the "distance" between church and state but of the very self-understanding of the church—of the nature of membership in it, of its normative structure, and of its special task. In raising these questions in the course of reunion, the BEK churches resurrected many questions that had been buried after World War II.[76]

Behind all such concerns lies the old question concerning the church's character as a Volkskirche. At its heart this question is a controversy over the definition of the church in a "Christian culture"—one faced in various forms by churches in other western societies as well. In the GDR the historic popular (and state-connected) churches had become a minority church separated from the state but at the end became a genuine advocate for the people. This development reawakened the question whether some of the functions of the traditional popular church, which tended to reinforce a monocultural and nonpluralistic stance, could or even should emerge in new and more critical forms appropriate to a pluralistic society.

The constitutional issue here is whether the churches should continue to exist as public corporations or whether their purposes would be better served if they were recognized merely as one set of voluntary associations among others.[77] This question opens the way to manifold questions about constitutional changes not only in the church but also in the Federal Republic itself.

Constitutional Questions for Germany and Europe

In May of 1990 the GDR and the FRG signed a Unification Treaty regulating the economic and social relationships for the new unified Germany. In addition, the parties committed themselves to "guaranteeing the application of the rights of the European community" in the implementation of this new unity, so that it would be a "contribution to European unification."[78] Because the unification took place according to Article 23 of the Fundamental Law, the larger constitutional implications of the unification—both for Germany and for Europe—were put off to a later date.

The proposals for a new German Constitution that emerged from the round tables were passed on to others. The Board for a Democratic and Constitutional Federation of German States pressed for further debate.[79] On May 24, 1991, an EKD working group recommended discussion of these questions with a popular ratification according to Article 146 of the Fundamental Law. In light of an emerging consensus both houses of Congress resolved to develop a revised Constitution for ratification by 1993, with the Social Democrats favoring a popular ratification and the Christian Democrats a simple congressional vote.[80]

Forces for revising the Fundamental Law and presenting it as a Constitution for popular referendum emphasized the following points:

- Preservation of the democratic impulses of the "Peaceful Revolution" as expressed in the round tables, through direct accountability of the government and Congress to the people and through strengthened federal structures.[81]

- Thorough review of the mission of the military, especially its assignments within NATO, in order to pursue a policy of peace and disarmament, including a far-reaching protection for conscientious objectors to military service regardless of their religious or philosophical grounds.
- Openness for refugees seeking asylum from any country, in order to exercise Germany's mission as a home for refugees—a mission forged in Germany's own responsibility for creating a flood of refugees in World War II. Promoting this right in Germany would require ultimately a common policy in the European community. In this way this new dimension of Germany's self-understanding would become a benchmark for evaluating the emerging constitutional form of a united Europe.[82]
- Explicit provision for caring for the environment.
- Developing a common law on abortion out of the very different policies in East and West, so that the position of women, especially in the former GDR, is not disadvantaged.[83]

Besides these concerns stood the continuing question whether the social security system and the struggle for greater equality could be sustained under the conditions of a market economy. Could there be a middle way between Big Brother and the Robber Baron, or were these distortions inevitable outcomes of state socialism and a free market economy?

What was not a question for any of the proponents was that Germany's existing Fundamental Law had proved its viability and would remain largely intact. Questions largely revolved around changes that would absorb crucial elements precipitated by the experiences of the GDR reformers.[84]

Coming to Terms with the Past

The last challenge emerging from the revolution—certainly unanticipated in its immensity—was to disclose and work through the church's relationships to the Communist state and its security apparatus, the Stasi. Snaking over 120 miles, the Stasi files lay half submerged like a deep and dangerous unconscious underneath the new and uncertain consciousness of the churches and the people. Although Stasi officers had destroyed the most important files early in the fall of 1989, most of the files had been secured by intrepid citizen committees in Leipzig, Berlin, and other places in January 1990. These committees knew that the core of the Communist tyranny lay within these secret files.

In 1990 and 1991 a small selection of these files, especially from Leipzig, found the light of day.[85] In January 1992, on the basis of a new federal law, citizens of the former GDR could apply to see their own files. It then became clear how extensive and sweeping the tentacles of the Stasis penetrated every aspect of life—church, marriage and family, factories, schools, and the spirit of the people itself.[86] Moreover, the Stasis had sought to use the BEK to influence the World Council of Churches and the Ecumenical Assembly in Basel in 1990.[87] With its 100,000 employees and countless "informal" and "unofficial" collaborators, "the Firm" was the necessary means to accomplish anything important in the old GDR.

The destructive impact of the Stasi apparatus was not confined to institutional arenas but permeated the psychological and cultural spheres of life as well. The motives for collaboration or cooperation with the Stasi were quite various—including fear, anxiety, envy, compassion, revenge, and the need for a trustworthy companion. The Stasi agents were not only threatening bullies but also sympathetic friends. They were, in the fullest sense of George Orwell's *1984,* "Big Brothers," who take care of people as long as they behave like good children.[88] In this situation the Stasi sowed mistrust but reaped trust. Such a readiness for cooperation and such needs for friendship arose as much from deep patterns of parentalism in the socialization process in church and society as from the alienation produced by a traditional hierarchical structure of authority. In the face of this powerful heritage, cultivating genuine civil courage and true partnership required that people carefully work through this complex history.

In the months after the files were laid open a flood of accusations, media hunts, and name-calling, as well as earnest inquiry, poured forth, powered by a multitude of motivations.[89] In its wake came deep psychological trauma, divorces, and even suicide.[90] Manfred Stolpe, former consistory president of the Brandenburg Church and now minister president of Brandenburg, saw himself exposed to special recrimination, since he was seen by the old opposition in the GDR as a cautious appeaser and by the western media as a collaborator.[91] With the person of Stolpe the whole Evangelical Church was also addressed. Was the church a fellow traveler with the Stasis or the Communist state? In its struggle for some free space for itself had it also become part of the apparatus of oppression? If so, what does this involvement mean for an understanding and evaluation of its theology and ecclesiology in the GDR years?

These glimpses into the Stasi files and the consequent recrimination against people identified as collaborators produced myriad confessions, explanations, and declarations at all levels of the church and society.[92] The problem was, how could a veracious historical account be retrieved from the mass of self-serving data in the Stasi files in order to assess the events and persons and to render judgment on the perpetrators and compensation to the victims? How could anyone find the light of truth in such a fog of deception and mistrust?

In 1991 and 1992 church leaders pursued three different approaches for dealing with this past. First, synods and official church leadership tried to introduce a voluntary "review" of employees and leaders. But this voluntary review soon proved to be inadequate because many were not aware of being used by the Stasis or were afraid they might be made objects of false accusations and recrimination.[93] Therefore, many church leaders felt pressed to a second step of introducing a stricter obligatory juridical process, also with limited success.[94] The inclination toward a wide open obligatory review shattered on the realization that a juridical process would lead more to repression and mistrust than to enlightenment and the building of trust. Moreover, the Stasi files themselves were, in the words of Magdeburg's

Bishop Christoph Demke, "correct as far as correctness was necessary for the self-preservation of the Stasi. But only a more precise examination of the files with those they report about can somewhat more reliably bring the true history to light."[95] The problem was, how could a world of trust be built up out of a world of mistrust and lies?

The ambiguities and limits of a juridical approach opened the way to a third alternative—discussion in small groups and open forums. This might enable people to make personal confession and collectively work through their history. The first such attempt began in Leipzig in February 1992. It was initiated by the politically engaged church historian Wolfgang Ullmann, pastor Friedrich Schorlemmer, and other leaders from the reform movement. Originally advertised as a "tribunal," it was renamed a "forum" for clearing up the past and getting on with the future.[96] This undertaking also gained support from Joachim Gauck, a former pastor in the GDR and head of the agency responsible for the oversight of the Stasi records.

All these efforts resonated within the expanded EKD. The churches attempted their own process of clarification in order to promote "reconciliation instead of anger."[97] Almost simultaneously the Bundestag formed a similar commission under the leadership of Representative Rainer Eppelmann, himself a pastor and leading member of the opposition in the former GDR.[98] In all these cases people were trying to bring the events of the past to light. It was not so much a matter of judging specific accusations against persons but rather of introducing institutional reforms that might avoid possible future injustice.

All three approaches—the paths of voluntary review, obligatory review, and open discussion—did not exclude legal action for personal damages or illegal acts. To build up a new and just society, citizens needed not only a new kind of open public discourse but also a recognition of justice and injustice. It was not merely a matter of truth but also of justice. Here we encounter the considerable question of which statutes and legal procedures to follow. Legal process on behalf of the victims of the regime was unavoidable if the injustices of the GDR regime were not to disappear into the twilight of collective guilt. Whether the victims received justice and compensation through a judicial process or through direct talks, it was important that the victims gain new possibilities for their lives. In the pungent words of pastor Matthias Storck as he revealed a friend's betrayal of him: "It's become clear to me that the one thing we must not do in all this Stasi commotion is to keep silence. To throw a jacket of love over such things, as the church has been doing until recently, would be a renewed betrayal without love for the victims. . . . Therefore I am throwing this torch into the straw. . . ."[99]

Behind the contest between the smoke screen of denial and the single-minded pursuit of the light of truth lay critical questions of political culture, ethics, and ecclesiology. How best do a people start a new political order of openness in the face of a past of official lies? What role can or should the churches play in the creation of this new culture if they are also implicated in the deceits of the past? Where can the new order find legitimation in the swamp of mistrust and tangled hopes?

As we look at these dilemmas and try to evaluate the church's past in the GDR, we can see that the churches at that time stood before two alternatives. Either they could withdraw into a secure niche to hibernate through the Communist winter or they could try, as far as was in their power, to influence the social and governmental structures and gain some elbow room for their work. The Evangelical churches by and large took the second path illuminated by the Confessing Church and the Declaration of Barmen in the Nazi era. In the GDR that meant that church leaders had to deal with the Stasi on every hand. They were able to help the imprisoned and the would-be emigrants, receive and disburse West German marks, and protect the groups that formed the little publics in the churches, even when they tried in various ways to restrain them from what they thought might be excessive confrontation.

Before the revolution it appeared as if the GDR regime would remain in power indefinitely. In the framework of the Cold War one had to deal with the actual powers in one way or another. "When you are in jail you have to find a way to deal with the warden," as General Superintendent Günter Krusche succinctly put it.[100] The story of the BEK churches was in large part the intricate choreography developed by prisoner and warden in the GDR.[101]

After the revolution of 1989 it became clearer that the church might have done more to foster a genuine public life. The radical opposition groups, often disappointed over their subsequent loss of power, felt justified in reproaching the church for its timidity. In its ongoing dialogue with the state and the Stasi they felt the church had only stabilized the regime.[102]

At this point the great swamp of questions and difficulties threatened to swallow the legacy of the revolution itself. In the effort to disclose and work through the past the very identity of the church and of the people in their 40 years of GDR existence hung in the balance. Was it a church of hard-won "publicity" or a church of the shadowy fellow traveler? Was it a church of newly won trust or a church of mistrust? Was it a church of participation or an institution that had become a willing accomplice of the state?[103]

The effort to judge this narrow path "between accommodation and resistance" leads to the question of the appropriate status of the church in constitution and law, of the relationships of internal accountability within it, and of its cultural position—how the church conceives of its mission and pursues it in the context of popular Christianity. The questions about the Stasi past concern not only individuals but also the institutional form of the church itself. It generates questions not only about the history of the GDR but also about the whole development of the church in this century.

Key Issues in the German Experience

The experience of the churches in the revolutionary changes in East Germany not only challenges our customary theological concepts and theories but also raises important leads for rethinking our theology, ethics, and ecclesiology.

The Frame of Interpretation

In German history efforts to understand the political context of the church from a theological standpoint have revolved around various interpretations of the "Two-Realms Doctrine" *(Zwei-Reiche-Lehre)*.[104] This tradition has usually sought to clearly distinguish the institutional spheres of ecclesial and civil governance, drawing on the basic understanding that God governs the world through two institutional means. Sometimes it has meant that the two institutions have collaborated closely, as in the nineteenth-century "Throne-and-Altar" doctrine of Friedrich Julius Stahl; other times they have been in sharp contrast, as with the Confessing Church of the Barmen Declaration. Certainly these themes have continued to illuminate the crucial questions of church "distance" from the state—whether in assessing the problem of collaboration with the Stasis and the SED or developing policies concerning military chaplaincy and religious education. Moreover, it can serve to establish clearly the secular character of the state apart from the ultimate values of the religious sphere.

However, what this tradition does not illuminate is the question of normative order within any sphere of governance. The traditional formulation of two spheres arose in an epoch of patriarchs, princes, and monarchs. Both the church and the princely orders were permeated by this hierarchical and monarchical paradigm of governance. Focus on the distance between them or their interaction did not critically question the actual structures within them.

A decisive step toward modification of this somewhat static conception occurs when people emphasize that the two "realms" are better conceived of as the "two ages" sharply presented in the Gospel accounts. This eschatological approach stresses dynamic processes of institutional change in both church and state as we move toward a new creation.[105]

Certainly this sense of eschatology and almost utopian expectation was present in the intense experiences of 1989. Biblical stories of radical change resonated immediately with people's experience. The 40 years in the wilderness became the archetype for the 40 years of the GDR. The Berlin Wall fell down after the people of Leipzig—as in ancient Jericho—circled their old inner city wall seven Mondays in a row. The repristination of Jerusalem shaped a new vision at Wittenberg and the revolution itself represented an open door to the promised land.[106]

What is more important, however, are the particular struggles for new institutional structures that arose in this ferment of longing. Germany has seen too many chiliastic movements and idolatrous nationalisms. The crucial questions lie not so much in tasting the new wine of perfect creation but in seeing and living out new visions of faithful relationships. Here lies the theological key to these events. To unlock their ethical and ecclesial ramifications we need to remember what constituted the inner structure of this movement and then place it in an appropriate theological framework.

Themes in the Revolution

For most observers the recent German revolution was a struggle for freedom. But what did freedom mean in that context? First of all, it meant establishing a genuine public life in which people could openly and honestly deal with the problems of their common life. Second, but not less important, it meant the decentralization of institutions to cultivate a greater pluralism of initiative, whether in the economy, government, or cultural institutions. "Democratic centralism," with its suffocating bureaucracy, had to be dismantled not only for the sake of the people but for the sake of the polluted land and the wider European community. In short, the revolution was largely about the struggle for public life and for a renewed and expanded sense of federal order. Before proceeding to its theological meaning, a review of the events shaping this summary analysis will be helpful.

The Struggle for Authentic Publics

The small groups in the church were relatively protected spaces where people could find their voices and claim their subjectivity as actors. They could begin to break down the interpersonal walls of systematic suspicion and even the inner wall of dependency and repressed feeling.[107] They could begin to develop a spirit of civil courage over against historic tendencies to subordination.

In the churches they could find forms for public witness and confession, even if they were not believers. Through sermon, rituals, and the fragile glow of candles the church helped cultivate a spirit of nonviolent resistance that eventually delegitimated the state. In the round table discussions and debates, as at church and synod meetings before them, people were able to learn and preserve the arts of democratic persuasion and compromise. They could begin cultivating a civic culture for a new republic.

All of these developments were of course halting and often ambiguous. Both church and society were shot through and through with countercurrents. Yet the church was mother and midwife of the revolution, even if her children often rejected or did not recognize her.

In these events we see a vivid expression of the church as the seed of an authentic public assembly. It is a generative ecclesia. Rather than emphasizing the parent-child relationship that fed into state domination, participants became, for a transparent historic moment, a public assembly of people who share in the spirit of mature citizenship. This spirited life in debate through free prayer, round table arguments, and the search for covenants based in mutual agreement appealed more to the work of the Holy Spirit than to the obedience of a son to his father and lord. This is the theological and ecclesiological line of inquiry opened up by the experiences of the church in the Peaceful Revolution.

However, the dynamic of publicity here was not enough to sustain the emerging republic, just as it is not the full story about the church. Constantly accompanying and complementing the struggle for publicity is the struggle for proper federal order in which to establish and protect these publics and mediate them to wider public orders.

Constructing New Federal Relationships

The SED-Regime had established a "German *Democratic* Republic" over against its western counterpart, a "*Federal* Republic of Germany." This was in fact the symbolic expression of its policy of "democratic centralism," which overrode the dense web of federal distinctions for the sake of centralized control—a path explicitly rejected in West Germany in its effort to avoid ever again the centralized tyranny of the Nazi era. The revolution of 1989 was in many ways an effort to restore and improve a federal order to protect the freedom of a variety of publics, including the church. By vitalizing a federalist spirit within Germany, citizens could also participate in a broader spirit of European federalism, without which a united Germany would only return to its pretensions to hegemony and control over the continent. The vicious cycle of the last 150 years might return again.

From the standpoint of the concept of covenantal publicity outlined in the first chapter, we can see a rich interplay of covenantal themes in the German struggle for a more adequate public life within a federalist framework. We see the covenant theme most dramatically in the Conciliar Process of 1988–89. The public participation of thousands of people was made possible by meeting in small groups to evolve common theses, points of consensus and agreements. The process took seriously a grassroots federalism that respects the integrity of limited publics. These points of consensus then emerged finally as "covenants" ratified by delegates in a concluding assembly. They were then passed on to even broader assemblies in Basel and Seoul. Here the meaning of covenant as promisemaking and as "federal order" came together. The covenantal process not only began to develop a cultural consensus for future public debate and constitutional proposals but also strengthened the federal structure necessary for participative democracy.

The covenant metaphor bears a rich treasure of concepts and theories for ordering our life and understanding. How does this lens help us grasp the events of the Peaceful Revolution? They can be better understood through the idea of the three partners to a full covenant in biblical tradition—God, land, and people.

IMAGES OF THE DIVINE PARTNER IN COVENANT.   In the revolutionary period we can see a deep struggle about the image of God. In the spirit of the small groups and voluntary assemblies we see an image of God as a

Spirit of free and creative expression, of persuasion and eschatological renewal. God is liberator and president more than controlling parent and monarch. This image runs up against the inherited image of God as "*Landesvater*" or Landesherr—the lord of a distinct people on a distinct land.[108] This image helps legitimate parental control in economy, state, church, and school, whether this is realized in its feudal, socialist, or communist form.

In the struggle between these two images we see emerging a third—God as Victim. This "crucified God,"[109] deeply embedded in German piety as well, can be the counterpart either of God the Lord or of God the Spirit of the Assembly. As counterpart of the Lord this image tends to reinforce the hierarchy of parent and child, evoking obedience and submission—and thus "victimage"—in return for the bestowal of the lord's inheritance. It is the classic religious paradigm of patriarchal feudal society. As victim in the context of assembly, this image legitimates the voice of the voiceless, the call to persuasion rather than coercion, agreement rather than domination.

In short, these images of God can move toward legitimation of hierarchical as well as of egalitarian relations. Both are contained in the religious heritage; both are rooted in the original covenantal images. Which one comes to the fore is deeply conditioned not only by historical circumstance but also by whether people place a high priority on the church's character as a free public open to the Holy Spirit or on the church as a household of children cared for by parental figures.

We see such a dialectic between hierarchical and egalitarian covenants in the way the GDR states joined the Federal Republic. A senior and stronger partner absorbed the junior. Thus, the people of the GDR achieved a unified "Fatherland" of new security and anticipated cultural familyhood. Here God the Landesvater held sway. However, in not giving adequate due to the egalitarian aspects of this new covenant, the union leaves an enduring sense of subordination, tutelage, and resentment among the eastern partners. Having achieved mature citizenship in their old state, they often feel themselves reabsorbed into a new and larger familial hierarchy that increasingly lacks the social security of the old ideal. This is now the dynamic that must be addressed to fill out an adequate covenant in the new Germany.

We can also see this tension in the larger European context as Denmark lit a fuse of protest in 1992 by voting against the imposition of a new European covenant—a potential federal order—by the bureaucrats in Belgium. The new European covenant was emerging out of economic necessities rather than the free and argued consensus of the many publics of the continent.

Reconciliation of these three God images has a very specific and practical meaning in this context of creating new publics within a new federal order, not only in Europe but in other places as well. It is ultimately a problem of trinitarian order, in which we find traditional motifs of familial hierarchy as well as egalitarian-spirited assembly. Our image of God shapes our approach to the covenants by which we seek to live.[110]

THE LAND AS COVENANT PARTNER.   "Land" is a matter of boundaries among peoples as well as the common earth that sustains their life. Both as boundary and as ecology the importance of land in any adequate covenantal order came to striking prominence in the revolutionary events of the last few years.

The condition of the land and of the whole natural ecology of life in the GDR became a major rallying point for public debate in the Conciliar Process and subsequent efforts at constitutional reform. Respect and responsibility for the land became a fixed value in every proposed constitution and public policy. Without a renewed covenant with the land there could be no future for the people. Land as ecological partner became crucial to any new covenantal order.

Land also had its meaning as a bounded arena for a people. The revolution of 1989–90 was vitally concerned with tearing down old boundaries— the wall between East and West—and clarifying new ones—the Oder-Neisse line between Poland and Germany. These boundary changes had a viability and validity resting on a deep consensus that had been cultivated over the decades on both sides within the imposed understandings of the Cold War. This was in sharp distinction to the tragic dismembering of Yugoslavia where no new covenants had been nurtured under Communist rule to overcome the deep ethnic hatreds that have ruined the people and the land.

THE STRUGGLE FOR PEOPLEHOOD BEYOND RACISM.   Participation in covenant requires some enduring sense of identity and recognition as a people. At the same time, the drive for participation in publics continually expands and differentiates a people. Individuals, interest groups, ethnic and regional groupings, and nations struggle for appropriate public articulations. In the revolution we see several aspects of this dynamic. Germans from East and West had developed to some extent separate national identities that now had to find expression in any new covenant between them. Germans from beyond the two German states came as refugees from parts of the former Soviet Union and its satellites, seeking to be part of the new German state. How would they find a place in the new covenant of German public life?

Finally, as a result of immigrations over the past 40 years Germany was no longer (if it ever had been) a monocultural and monoethnic nation-state. It was ethnically pluralistic but without a well-developed heritage of pluralistic values. This ethnic pluralism could not be dealt with through any appeals to race, biology, or ancestry but through the arduous construction of an explicit covenant for living together. This was not merely a matter of developing a patriotism based on loyalty to the Constitution but of developing an even more wide-ranging commitment—a deep cultural covenant—that finds expression most clearly and most conflictually in a commitment to Germany as a home for refugees.

Thus, the vociferous debates over restriction of refugee law in the new Germany were debates about the identity of the people of a unified Germany. The imposition of restrictions on these laws of asylum in 1993, though justified by appeals to economic necessities, nevertheless severely wounded this emerging component of a pluralistic German identity within an expanding covenant with the nations around it.[111]

In short, a unified Germany was also seeking to reconstitute its identity on a new basis. This new basis of identity—one arising from historical experience, present reality, and constitutional loyalties—had to be as much a product of covenants as the basis for them.[112] This new sense of identity could not be part of a renewed nationalism but had to be welded to a new sense of "calling" or popular purpose. In the context of the revolution this sense of new purpose consisted in becoming a catalyst for European federation and economic interdependence—foundations for an enduring peace respecting human rights and ecological responsibility.

This reconstruction of identity and purpose was an indispensable part of the reconstruction of deep covenants that would transcend the ancient appeals to race, ethnicity, language, and birthplace. It pressed for a covenantal identity built primarily on promises about the future—of Germany, of Europe, and of the globe.

When we look at the biblical pattern of identity formation and covenant making, we also see one more indispensable dimension—the past. A people's identity is built up not only in its expectations about a common future but also about the memories and fears grounded in its past. Biblical covenant making always included recital of the history that had created a people's identity—a history of God's sustaining grace and of the people's sinful violation of the covenant. It is the struggle to come to terms with this past that has been a festering sore in the body of the new covenant coming to birth. I conclude my exploratory reflections on the revolution by placing this struggle within the theological framework of covenant and publicity.

Trust and Reconciliation in a Covenantal Public

One can understand the past 40 years of German history as an effort to come to terms with the evil of the Third Reich.[113] The GDR regime had never cultivated a process of public repentance and reflection because it claimed to be a liberator from Nazism and ipso facto purged of that guilt. However, many of the brown shirts were simply turned in for red ones. The Stasi apparatus was erected on the soil of the old Gestapo. The collapse of this tyranny unearthed the ghosts of the past once again—for West as well as East. Coping with the Stasi past required an equally painful review of the "reeducation" the western zones had undergone under Allied supervision.[114]

It was not only a matter of repentance for wrong but of grieving for what was lost. In recovering a sense of guilt for wrongdoing as well as rage in the face of betrayal, people could claim their own subjectivity. Not only could they be judged but now once again they could act as responsible human beings.

As we reflect on the process of coping with the past, we see two fundamental dynamics arising in the synergy between covenant making and publicity. The first involves the difficult effort to find appropriate public forms in which to bring the sin, betrayal, and banal complicities of the past to light. Finding human truth requires the construction of a public where every possible witness can corroborate or disconfirm each other's perceptions, memories, and values through open argument. Without this common truth people cannot cultivate mutual trust—the English "troth" and "truth" still bear this connection. And so people caught up in the whirlwind of Stasi files sought appropriate publics in small groups, forums, tribunals, courts, and confessionals.[115]

However, the very act of public truth-finding, because it still occurs within a world of clashing private interests and the lies they generate, can cut off the very trust it seeks to recreate. Publics are indispensable for creating the truthful basis for new covenants of mutual trust, but they can also provide a seedbed of weeds that choke those covenants off. The point is that the process of making things public cannot merely serve the purposes of retribution but must also foster reconciliation and the formation of new, more trustworthy covenants of civil coexistence. A new covenant demands publicity in order to produce agreement and understanding. Conversely, a public needs some kind of preexisting covenant in order to provide the minimal preconditions for the argumentation by which we secure greater truth. Both dimensions—new covenant and new publicity—have to be served. The dilemma lies in finding out how. It is a dilemma the German people are now working their way through slowly and painfully.[116]

The second dynamic lies in the tension between covenant's retrieval of the past and its basic disposition toward the future. Here is where the tension between retribution and reconciliation is lodged. Retribution and punishment consider our past actions. We try to bring them into the public light in order to test them and see whether and how we might go on living with those who wronged us or whom we wronged. In establishing guilt we try to burn away the false underpinnings of our previous common life. However, the forms of collective and systemic evil that we have encountered and perpetrated in our own time stagger our efforts to allocate guilt and innocence according to a juridical model. If this was at all true for the Nazi era, as Hannah Arendt tried to show,[117] it is even more true in the case of the SED and the Stasi era. When publicity is reduced to juridical process, it can have only a limited role in laying a new covenantal foundation for the future.

From a biblical perspective it is not the acts of judgment and condemnation that provide this new covenant but the gracious and creative act of God in opening up a new common future. It is on the basis of grasping such a new future that we can then deal with our past. Without the grace of this new future we simply repress our past in all manner of self-defenses, including projecting our own hidden evils onto others. The public search for truth becomes impossible because there is no covenant with the future. Entering into this future extended by God's covenant (the "hierarchical" moment) constitutes the first step in the acts of reconciliation that fill out this covenant with our fellow citizens (the "egalitarian" moment).

For many Germans the Wende was just such an act of God, so utterly unexpected and full of promise. Gorbachev was seen as an instrument of God's liberation. The Hungarian government, the suffering nature around them, and even the church appeared to be used by God to bring about a new step in history. Only in walking into this new future could they then begin to deal with their past.[118]

We see both of these dynamics in the struggle to cope with the past 40 or 60 years of German history. Sometimes the emphasis falls on juridical processes to establish guilt, as with the efforts to try Eric Honecker and Eric Mielke for the crimes of their regime. At that point the opacity and mendacity of witnesses and records obscure our perception and judgment. We often find no reliable truth. Certainly we find little with which to enter a new future. Other times people have concentrated on compensating the victims in order to help them enter this common future. They have sought to strengthen people's hope and self-esteem so that they might go about the process of living more reconciled lives within a new covenant. However, in erecting new standards of common justice and decency (the contents of a new covenant) we are driven to expose the failures of the past as well as the derelictions of the future. Our juridical impulses return in order to confirm the values emerging in our struggle for a new future.

Covenantal Publicity and the Partial Revolution

The themes of covenantal publicity developed in the first chapter play a rich and often conflictual role in these revolutionary events. Specific institutional peculiarities of Germany's patterns of religious and political organization shape the way they have played out in these tumultuous experiences. The historic establishment of the Evangelical churches and their tight connection socially and institutionally with government made it possible for them to carve out a free space within the otherwise totalitarian sweep of the regime's powers. Free publicity for resistance groups went hand in hand with this inherited establishment, thus necessitating the ethical compromises so clearly revealed after 1989.

The inherited culture of the Landesherr, which also served as a cultural legitimation for the all-embracing parental control and care of the regime, was also deeply entrenched in the culture of the churches. This contrasted sharply, however, with the emergent power of the small groups and congregations that formed the spawning ground for the leadership that emerged in the collapse of the old regime. Whether the symbols of this model of church as a critical public of people who hold a transcendent citizenship can prevail in the ongoing worship, education, and socialization of the churches remains a critical question, especially as these powerful memories are buried in the economic concerns of the ensuing years. The power of the church as a place for honest public dialogue can easily be dissipated in questions of the Stasi or Nazi past rather than harnessed to the development of covenants that might constitute a new future for Germany and Europe. In such a recovenanting within these publics questions of ecology and land use as well as of the interlocking character of ever-expanding federal relationships in Europe occupy a critical place.

Finally, the way these peculiar publics within the church relate covenants about the future with reconciliation about the past informs not only the church but the wider society. From the standpoint of covenantal publicity the question for the Evangelical churches is whether they can reclaim biblical patterns of covenantal hope as a framework for forging new patterns of trust or whether they will be drawn into the more legal confines of sin and forgiveness as the exclusive lens for handling the mistrust created by the experience of two totalitarian regimes within three generations of living memory.

All these dynamics—of judgment and reconciliation, of clarity about the past and hope in the future, of publicity and covenant—are essential elements in establishing a common life. How we go about them, what priority we set in pursuing them, and how adequately we establish new covenants and new publics will determine the quality of our common life in the midst of a pluralistic people. The recent German revolution forms a kind of laboratory from which not only Germany but all of us can learn.

Clearly these organizational forms and conflicts are not the only ways these values of publicity and federalism can develop. The way churches might cultivate deeper cultural covenants to sustain federal structures would inevitably arise in different ways outside the peculiar German context. My interest in this comparative study is to ask whether they can and do provide normative guidance for people seeking a more just political order in other historical and cultural contexts. What shape does such a struggle take when religious organization, belief, and political heritage differ markedly from those of the West? To explore this question I turn to some case studies from India's recent struggle.

Three

Religious Organization and Constitutional Justice in India

Recent German experience offers us a dramatic story in the present world struggle for more adequate public life and federal political order. The story of the revolution and the churches' involvement in it has helped sharpen our understanding of the underlying dynamics of covenant making and ecclesial publicity. I now turn further from a European orbit to some less known, indeed everyday, cases in Indian life to see what kinds of issues can be identified with the analytical lens of covenantal publicity.

Though seemingly minor from the standpoint of the national transformation I have just explored, these cases nonetheless lift up struggles relevant to millions of people around the world. They involve questions of redressing the inequities of past injustice to minorities in order to bring them into democratic public life, of insuring justice for women, especially in family relations, and of defining the relation of religious organization to the political order. Each of them illuminates struggles over participation in public life and the deeper meanings of federalism.

Throughout the twentieth century the people of India have wrestled with these dynamics within one of the world's oldest and most complex conglomerations of cultures. Over 900 million people are bound together in an often shaky federal structure consisting of over 25 states and jurisdictions, speaking some 15 official and over 300 local languages. All the major world religions swim here in a sea of customs, rituals, and philosophies we call Hinduism. "India," like "Hinduism," is a fiction created by foreigners—both Persian Muslims and European Christians—to encapsulate a land whose richness of culture, language, geography, and history otherwise defies our comprehension. The pungent smells of the streets, the cacophony of color, the bustling collision of its myriad peoples in the markets and alleys, the spices exercising tender palates—all of these have fascinated and bewildered foreigners for centuries. Despite its endemic pestilence and the crushing poverty of its people, it has brought imperialist and pilgrim, missionary and poet to its mountains, plains, and shores for millennia. If any country exhibits the plurality and possibilities of republican confederation, it is this palette of peoples we call India. India may come closer than anywhere else to being a laboratory for research into the struggles over public order that are occurring in other forms throughout the world.

In this century the peoples of India have managed to create a quilt-work of republican federation that continues to amaze both its fiercest critics and its most fervent supporters. With its diverse population and regional divisions, India requires some form of federal order to honor its plurality as well as its need for unity. At the same time, its tradition of monarchical and imperial rule frequently paralyzes the pursuit of genuine federation. Though its traditions of village councils and relative local autonomy press for a greater republican articulation, its traditions of caste and patriarchy strangle the very child seeking to be born.

In all of India's bubbling cultural stew the factors we call religion play an enormous role, whether it is the whole chicken of Hinduism, the vegetables of Islam, or the spice of Christianity. To get a taste of this complex recipe we first need to look at its historic setting. Since I am assuming that most readers will be less familiar with India's history, I shall spend a little more time presenting crucial background information for understanding these cases. I shall then trace the religious and constitutional strains leading to the Constitution of the present Republic of India. Then I will turn to the religious dimensions of this modern constitution and the specific cases where the fractious engagement between religion and government comes to a burning point. From that vantage point I can then explore the central issues of the constitution of public life within a federal framework.

The Ancient Matrix of Religion and Governance

The Religion of the Hindus

The concept of religion as a discrete set of ideas, organizations, rituals, and behaviors is a modern creation resulting from the differentiation of society into spheres of governance, family, economy, education and the like. Religion is one of those social "functions." This is a peculiarly unhelpful way to try to understand the peoples of the subcontinent. The notion of "religion" tends to separate aspects of life that for most Indian people are fused together, while it overlooks the plurality of traditions and possibilities within a supposed "national" culture. Nevertheless, we as well as the anthropologists are stuck with the term and so are the societies like India for whom the concept of "religion" has become part of their legal structure. What I want to look at here in light of this ambiguous term is a people's enduring patterns of governance and the way they are legitimated by conceptions of ultimate power and worth as well as by an articulated sense of "the nature of things." These convictions gain their public expression in symbols, rituals, and ethical norms.

"Hinduism," like "religion," is also a modern concept. While the Muslim rulers seemed to have first coined the term to refer to those living beyond the Indus river,[1] it required the revival of Sanskrit by missionaries like William Carey and Joshua Marshman in the early nineteenth century and the translation of early Sanskrit texts by Max Müller to constitute a "religion of Hinduism," with its own scriptures, rituals, ethics, and beliefs. It was this emerging cultural "object" that then provided the basis for the rise of both Hindu reform and Hindu nationalism.[2]

It is easy to make the mistake of assuming that all the peoples of India have shared this "Hindu religion." However, it is in fact only the Brahmanic tradition of the ancient Aryans. Like all other "victorious" religions (such as Christianity in Europe) it overlay a mosaic of earlier cultures—the so-called tribal peoples who generally escaped to the mountains and inaccessible territories, the Dravidian peoples of the south centered in Tamil land, who survived for a long time in pockets, and the lower castes and untouchables—remnants of the native peoples of the lower peninsula. Brahmanic religion in some ways absorbed them as part of its own amalgam or drove them out with the help of like-minded monarchs.

This subaltern religion of the non-Aryan peoples seems to have been largely based on agrarian fertility patterns, with prominent female as well as androgynous deities (such as the later Shaivite deity Ardhanari). The people's governance patterns probably included matriarchal elements, which survive to this day in the southeast and northwest. They were probably conciliar rather than monarchical and contained no notion of caste.

While the reconstruction of these people's life requires painstaking archaeology and relies on a healthy dose of inference, Brahmanic Hinduism presents us with a clearly articulated schema based in ancient texts and summarized in terms of *varna-ashrama-dharma*, that is, the rule of caste and stages of life.[3] The classic conception of *varna* (literally, "color") envisioned four orders of existence: *brahmin* (the priests), *kshatryia* (the warriors or rulers), *vaishya* (merchants), and *sudra* (peasants). Each caste is a hereditary community with strictly defined dependencies on the higher castes, prerogatives with regard to the lower, and prescribed spheres of marriage. They are communal compartments woven together not by appeal to some ancient covenant but by appeal to the metaphysics of things, that is, by appeal to the original "great self" (*mahapurusha*) from whose body came the varnas—the head, specifically the mouth, is the brahmins, the arms the kshatryias, the legs the vaishyas, and the feet the sudras.

Within this scheme of varnas each person, especially each male, exercises duties appropriate to his stage of life. The stage of the student *(brahmacarya)* demands celibacy in the pursuit of spiritual growth. The stage of the house-holder *(grihasti)* demands marriage, industry, and procreation, especially of a male heir. The stage of forest dweller *(vanaprastha)* returns one to the life of contemplation, a brahmacarya on a higher plane. Finally, the forest dweller can renounce life entirely (the *sannyasin*) in order to obtain ultimate release *(moksha)*. Whether or not many people followed this in a strict man-ner, this notion of the four ashramas—the four modes of life struggle—exercised a powerful influence on people, legitimating these four modes and delegitimating any alternatives.

There also has existed a well-developed conception of the four purposes of existence: *dharma, artha, kama,* and *moksha.*[4] Each of these, according to a systematician like Kautilya or Manu, yields its own science, or *sastra,* as well as norms. Dharma constitutes the field of right living in general. Artha is the arena of political power and political science. Kama is the realm of bodily pleasure. Moksha is ultimate release, the path to which is interpreted by the sannyasins.

The upshot of this ordering of existence is to construe life in terms of independent spheres of action that rest on their own logic. They reflect an overarching ethos in which everything has its place but there is little search for a coherent system binding them all together, as occurred with the west-ern logic of law and philosophy. Indian flower displays, clothing, temple towers, devotional practices—all reflect an ethos of prolix plurality without a dialectic of contradiction demanding intentional resolution through argu-ment, logic, compromise, and agreement.

Life within varna and ashrama constitutes a life within dharma—the eter-nal way of life. By being both the interpreters of dharma and the gurus who taught it to others, Brahmins occupied a central cultural position, although judicious kings could and did circumscribe their rulings and powers when necessary.[5] Because of the way caste and the ashramas are rooted in the routines of biology, varna-ashrama-dharma was peculiarly unhistorical and unable to adapt to change, though clearly it absorbed changes over the three millennia of its existence. Caste groups changed position in the hierarchy, temples and ritual practices evolved, and ethical norms shifted. On the whole, however, because these traditions were rooted in inherited orders, Hinduism was extremely unreformable. It never developed a public institu-tional order for self-correction through argument and negotiation. It never developed a sense of voluntary contract or covenant to legitimate intentional changes in human relations.

Finally, the very word "Hindu" indicates that these ritual and social tradi-tions are rooted in a specific geography—originally the watershed of the Indus river. Religion in India has a highly geographic specificity. Holy places, sacred anthills, rivers (the Ganges and the mythical Saraswati), boulders, and caves are central to people's religious identities. Traditional Indian religion is infused with a profound "geo-piety."[6] This geo-piety absolutizes disputes over land in a heavily populated country, leading to such conflicts as the violent destruction in 1992 of the Babri Masjid Mosque in Ayodhya, purported birthplace of Rama, the Hindu god-king. Moreover, it means that regional divisions and differences gain an enhanced identity, contributing to the sense of national pluralism, while tending to exclude religious groups not tied to that specific land. When combined with the "bio-piety" of family and caste, it creates a myriad of kinship pools resistant to outside manipulation and change. This, at least, is the historic cultural context within which the modern Indian republic has had to construct a secular federal state rooted in a pluralism of voluntary association, law, and public negotiation. These general cultural patterns legitimated governance structures, which I will now examine.

Governance Among the Hindus

India's two great literary classics—the *Mahabharata* and the *Ramayana*—are epics of monarchs and princely houses engaged in combat and conquest. Increasingly sophisticated analyses of archaeological sites in the Indus river valley and elsewhere indicate that this feudal world of Aryans overlay an ancient indigenous culture of hunters, gatherers, and farmers who were driven gradually southward. These darker skinned peoples became the subordinate varnas ("colors") in the hierarchy of rule by the lighter skinned Aryans.

This congeries of tribes and princes tended to come under the overlordship of great monarchs ruling from the central plains, beginning at least a millennium before Christ.[7] Monarchs like Harsha (seventh century BCE) and the Buddhist king Ashoka (third century BCE) began the development of state order, which was then given intellectual form about the third century BCE by Kautilya. For Kautilya rule was forged in skillful alliances and recognition of the appropriate spheres of action of princes, priests, merchants, and peasants. The king was to uphold dharma.[8] Here we find some echoes of the leagues and treaties that formed the ancient bed of Hebrew covenant, but we also find a concept of law that comes not from a divine command but from the cosmic necessities of natural order—rain, family generation, fertility, and survival.[9] Dharma is much closer to the ancient Egyptian concept of *Maat* than to the will of Israel's YHWH, who makes covenant with peoples and issues law as his word.

For historians like Romila Thapar the struggles within these epics can also be seen as struggles between emerging monarchs and the forest dwellers, tribal oligarchies, and other elements of ancient assemblies and republics.[10] Alongside simple chiefdoms, we find here governance through agreement, argument, and consent rooted in the conciliar experiences of the villages. In the *Ramayana*, for instance, we find not only King Rama's struggle to vanquish his archenemy, Ravena. We find also evidence that his real political foes were the little republics creating "disorder" in his imperial plan. While Rama may be the King David of India's history, Ravena may well be the Samuel, the priest and president of the ancient tribal council. Similarly, in the *Mahabharata* we find republican states confederated together, with Krishna as a kind of president over them.[11]

These same conciliar forms of village and ancient tribal groupings also appear in the congregations *(samgha)* of early Buddhism,[12] which can be understood as a form of cultural and therefore political protest against Aryan imperialism in the fifth and fourth centuries BCE. In its attack on caste and its religious grounds as well as in its relatively republican forms, Buddhism provided a clear alternative to hierarchical and caste orders. Buddhism favored elected over appointed kingship, including a kind of covenant of governance between ruler and people.[13] While Ashoka took up some of its concerns for legal justice and equity, his own empire took on traditional Aryan forms and then fell to successor empires, leading eventually to the extermination and absorption of Buddhism in India by its traditional Brahmanic foes.

From the eleventh century until the arrival of the British in the seventeenth and eighteenth centuries various parts of India were ruled by Persian monarchs who brought with them the religious culture of Islam. Islam, in its rigorous monotheism, its scriptural legalism, and its abhorrence of caste, was antithetical to the culture and social form of the established Brahmanic ruling groups. For over 600 years the Indian peoples swung erratically between periods of tolerant rule (such as with Akbar, in the sixteenth century) and repressive despotism (Arungazeb in the seventeenth).

With the incursion of English merchants in the late sixteenth century, India's Moghul empire began to fall gradually under a new imperium. This British Raj was not completed until the British Crown took over all aspects of governance of its territories from the East India Company in 1858. Under the Government of India Act of 1858, the country was administered by a governor general who included within his office all judicial, executive, and legislative powers. The secretary was responsible in turn to the Parliament for "the superintendence, direction and control of all acts, operations and concerns which in any wise relate to the Government or revenues of India."[14]

The governor general extended control to each of the provinces through appointed governors. These in turn had their own executive councils. In every respect policy pertaining to the British Raj was centralized and bureaucratically hierarchical. However, even this imperium, when taken for the continent as a whole, was a marble cake of treaties with over 300 principalities, whose acquiescence to British hegemony preserved their traditional forms of local rule.

The English brought not only their language but their legal and governmental forms. Under governors such as Lord Cornwallis (of American Revolutionary fame) in Madras, Warren Hastings, Thomas Babington MacAuley, and William Bentinck, they began a systematic compilation of laws, the creation of a rationally administered civil service, and public schools open to all castes. Through this thin overlay of an educated ruling class "India" became a national concept embracing the whole subcontinent. It was through this ruling class and its educated families that English notions of equality, social utility (versus caste obligation), parliamentary government, rationally codified law, and limited monarchy entered the genetic structure of emerging Indian nationalism. Crucial to this cultural transformation would be the impact of the non-Hindu religions—Islam and Christianity. I shall turn now to a brief look at their development and then to the Hindu Renaissance that intertwined with them to shape the cultural conditions for the new republic.

The "Historic" Religions: Islam and Christianity

Islam in India

Contemporary observers often find it hard to realize that the largely Persian Islamic culture shaped Indian life for over 600 years. In many ways, it differed strikingly from traditional Hindu belief and practice.[15] It shunned images in a land of gaudy and seductive idols. It reverenced a law that emerged from the will of a transcendent single God rather than from the manifold traditions of the people. It cultivated assemblies for common prayer rather than the individual *puja* of the devotee.

In other ways, however, it could fit traditional patterns. Its patriarchal ethos reinforced government by local monarchs. Like Hinduism, it did not create a religious hierarchy but rather a congeries of prayer leaders (the *imam* and *pesh-imam*), scripture scholars (the *hafiz* and *maulvi*), legal scholars (the *ulema*), judges *(khazi),* and others. Its typical institutions— mosques, schools *(madrasa),* and charitable endowments (*waqf*—were not well integrated institutionally. In these respects Islam is a comprehensive culture, well distinguished from other cultures but not internally differentiated on an institutional basis. Thus, after the fall of the Islamic dynasties, it could go on as a relatively self-contained culture within a larger culture it both resembled and differed from in many essentials.

In populous contemporary India, though Islam constitutes only 12% of the population, its adherents number over 100 million. Because of its rejection of caste, Islam remains a relatively separate and unabsorbed social form in India. This was a major reason for the rise of Islamic separatism, which led to the Partition of 1947, and for its troubled and often impoverished ghettoization within India today. This has also meant, however, that it has preserved some sense of cultural alternative to Hinduism, an alternative it has been able to transmit into wider Indian life only with enormous difficulty. Muslims who did not flee to the new state of Pakistan tend to support a secular state, just as do Jews in diaspora Judaism. From time to time, as we shall see, however, their fear for their collective survival drives them toward state protection for their religious laws.

Christianity in India

By the fourth century Christianity was established on the southwest coast of India, whether by St. Thomas (as Origen and *The Acts of Thomas* put it) or by Syrian missionaries, probably sent from ancient Persia.[16] In any case a Syrian Orthodox church has remained in that region to this day. Over the centuries it became an endogamous community, practically a caste to itself, which did not challenge Indian traditions but preserved its cultic separateness. Having survived both Islamic threats and Roman Catholic hegemony within its own structures, it has emerged in two forms today—a repristinated Syrian Orthodox church and a reformed Mar Thoma church. Their present superior educational level enables these Christians from Kerala to make disproportionate intellectual contributions to Indian Christianity and the wider society.

In the sixteenth century the Portuguese brought their own church to India's west coast (the modern Goa), partly by the sword, partly by persuasion. Whether through the sophisticated strategy of upper-caste assimilation practiced by Robert de Nobili in Madurai, church-controlled intermarriage, or the natural resonance between Catholic sacramentality and Hindu artistry, the Roman Catholic Church in India became thoroughly "indigenized," as we say today. The Roman Catholic Church to this day remains the most creative in adapting to "Hindu" forms, which means that it is less likely to take on the task of prophetic reform. However, it too has created a whole institutional panoply of schools, hospitals, social services, and parachurch action organizations that tend to break down the monopoly of family ties on social power.

By the end of the eighteenth century some Protestant Christian missionaries, most notably William Carey, were working in India, a number under Danish auspices. The British, who originally came to India through the ventures of their chartered trading corporations, prohibited any Christian missionary work under these arrangements until 1813, when the Parliament, in revising the East India Trading Company charter, permitted the entry of missionaries, recognizing that it is "the duty of this country to promote the interest and happiness of the native inhabitants of the British dominions of India."[17] The civilizing work of English missionaries then became the backbone of the missionary enterprise, though the government, aside from legal reforms based in English law, tried at every point to curtail any political impact this work might have.

Moreover, because of the large number of English militia in India, church chaplaincy had to be set up to minister to their religious needs. This religious establishment was in both cases dependent on foreign authority, as were, ultimately, the other national or independent missions that were allowed under British control. Christianity existed largely as appurtenances to the colonial governmental apparatus until the 1930s.

Within two generations, indigenous as well as missionary clerics began to relate their Christianity to emerging nationalist claims. Groups like The Bengal Christian Association for the Promotion of Christian Truth and Godliness, and the Protection of the Rights of Indian Christians (1868) and The Western India Native Christian Alliance (1871) became vehicles for articulating the hope of national autonomy as well as a truly indigenous church.[18] The British government responded with strict loyalty oaths requiring all missionaries to refrain from undermining the government in any way. Most missionaries complied, though C. F. Andrews, Mahatma Gandhi's close advisor, and E. Stanley Jones were notable exceptions.[19] Indian leaders like K. T. Paul and P. R. Saraswati, an early Christian feminist, had to carry the task of a national church. The strains between foreign and indigenous leadership, between nationalist and traditionalist, bound together in complex interdependence, persist to the present.

By 1921 the All-India Conference of Indian Christians, at the same time as it sought to negotiate a lifting of government restrictions on assembly and public freedom, issued a clarion call to place Christian work in India under indigenous leadership. In 1927 the British Parliament severed the Anglican Church in India from external control, making it an equal member of the worldwide Anglican communion.[20] The institutional church was gradually distinguishing itself from the colonial government. Some reformers would go on to try to find a way to anchor this national church in a new kind of Hindu-dominated establishment. Others, like Paul Devanandan and M. M. Thomas, would seek in a new secular state a clear institutional separation between church and state, at the same time as they realized special civil arrangements might have to be instituted to protect the numerically tiny Christian minority.[21] How the Christian churches would become truly indigenous without simply changing the robes of an established foreign church for the familiar *dhoti* of a communal or caste organization would become a virtual drone bass in the church's life for decades to come.

Both Islam and Christianity have been intimately tied to imperial regimes but also have preserved alternative values and customs that can imperil as well as support the rise of a secular republican state in the twentieth century. Both have a heritage of religious establishment as well as historical experiences that support a secular state. Both have some strains of covenantal thought and practice in their history that might support a federalist culture.[22] Though mosque and church are very different conceptions and institutions, they are places of religious public assembly that can mobilize and shape political participation. Both have had an impact on modern Hinduism, though Christianity played a peculiarly important role in the nineteenth-century movement known as the Hindu Renaissance, an understanding of which is crucial for comprehending the modern relation of religion and the Indian federal republic.

The Hindu Renaissance

In the same year that the English Parliament opened India to missionary work, Joshua Marshman, William Carey, and William Ward founded a college at the former Danish mission station of Serampore outside Calcutta, where Christianity was to be studied in terms of the ancient and modern languages of the people, foremost among them Sanskrit and Bengali. The college and its secular imitators opened the way to an educated class of Christians and Hindus who were self-consciously Indian. The influx of missionaries challenged the old beliefs, customs, and rituals of the people. In the crossroad of this challenge arose efforts to reform this melange of religious traditions into a coherent, modern religion—Hinduism. This was the Hindu reform, or Hindu Renaissance.

The colorful flowering of reform efforts by charismatic leaders like Ram Mohun Roy, Keshub Chendra Sen, Debendra Nath Tagore, Akkoy Kumar Dutt, and Dayananda Saraswati has already been richly presented by J. N. Farquhar and David Kopf.[23] What is of interest here is not only the way they created a "religion of Hinduism" that was coherent for westerners as well as for educated Indians but the way they created a "modern" ethic, a philosophy to support it, and institutional structures to advance it. In all of these they reflected the enormous impact of European-American culture on the Indian intelligentsia.

The ethic of these "Brahmos" rejected the caste system and the subordination of women in marriage and society. With the rejection of caste inequality came also a concern for the uplift of the masses of the people through education, medical care, and public health measures. With the rejection of caste solidarities came also a higher valuation of individual achievement—the beginning of a western work ethic. This new ethic of equality led Sen, for instance, to champion the introduction of a new marriage law in 1872 (written under the direction of Sir Henry Maine) for his followers, who were classified as "non-Hindus" for purposes of the law, even though they considered themselves Hindus by culture and nationality.

Roy, Sen, Dutt—practically all of the Brahmo reformers placed the emancipation of women at the center of their ethical program, though, as pioneers they often could not live out or see through the implications of this emancipation. Sen, for instance, was mightily influenced by two female Unitarian missionaries, Mary Carpenter and Annette Akroyd, who not only preached but lived a new ethic of equality. This emancipation completely undermines traditional Hinduism, for it calls into question the primacy of male progeny (and its attendant female infanticide or explosive overpopulation), the dependence of women on men in both private and public spheres, and the joint family system at the center of the agrarian landholdings. Female emancipation is the keystone of any Indian cultural revolution. Thus, Kopf can say, "the Bill of Rights in the present Indian constitution represents an extension to all Indian citizens of the rights accorded only to members of Keshub Sen's progressive Brahmo community under the Brahmo Marriage Act of 1872."[24]

Accompanying this revolutionary ethic was a universalistic and rationalistic philosophy that bypassed the ritual concepts of purity as well as the rootage of the whole caste system in the great self of the Brahman. Sen, for instance, replaced this patriarchal metaphysics with one of the Great Mother.[25] Most of the reformers, however, were purer mystics who based the equality of all souls on their oneness in the Godhead. This is the main stream that flows through the Tagores to Gandhi.

The Brahmo Reform movement did not remain at the level of ideas and sporadic legal changes. It took over the institutional patterns of the Christian churches and missions to spread its message and ethics. So pronounced was this development that some people refer to it as the "Semiticization" of Hinduism. In fact, however, the very concept of Hinduism as a distinct religion is itself dependent on this development. Whereas traditional Hinduism was embedded in the communal forms of the joint family, caste, and ritual custom, not to mention place, the reformers formed congregations, societies, and associations based on explicit commitments by the members.

Roy's Brahmo Samaj (Brahmo Society) was founded with a trust deed in 1830, thus wedding the English trust law with Hindu religious form.[26] Tagore based his Tattvabodhi Sabha (Association) on a "Brahmo Covenant" in 1840. Sen founded the Church of the New Dispensation in 1866 and fitted it out with appropriate symbols and rituals. Saraswati founded the Arya Samaj in 1875. The formation of a reform society in 1870 by Sen and his associate Sastri planted the seed for future efforts, most widely represented today by the Ramakrishna Mission. By 1872 there were 102 local Brahmo Societies in India.

With this new model of a voluntary association based on subscription to a written covenant and legalized in a deed of trust came also the polity of western congregationalism and association. The clash between the old principles of patriarchy, monarchy, and family control with the new principles of elective representation, conciliar process, equality of membership, and rule of law is vividly dramatized in the revolt against Sen's increasingly patriarchal and familial control of the Samaj in 1865. Liberals within the organization, led by Ananda Mohun Bose, appealed to the rights of a wider "Brahmo public" and to the terms of the trust deed of 1868 to counter Sen's illegitimate control and pushed through a new constitution in 1878 that provided for a crude separation of powers among various representative councils and a clearer dependence on covenant and constitution in initiating new members and commissioning of missionaries.[27]

These principles of covenantal association and cultivation of public assembly and accountability survived in constant tension with traditional appeals to the conditions of birth—family, caste, and mother tongue and its modern offspring, nationalism. The nationalism of a constitutional democracy championed by liberal Hindu reform struggled with its sibling, the nationalism of communal heritage.[28] The first road led to Jawaharlal Nehru, the second to the Hindu Mahasabha of V. D. Sarvarkar. In Gandhi we find a complex interweaving of the two elements, a matter to which I will return shortly.

The Drive for Independence and Constitutional Order

The Early Assemblies and the Struggle for Participation

Neither Christian missionaries nor British governors could escape the call to reform the structure of caste, the relation of the sexes, and the forms of religion they found in India. Some reforms eliminated offensive practices, such as that of widow burning, or suttee. Others, emanating from the revival of ancient culture and language in Bengal, reinterpreted and shaped Indian society from within.

To this end nothing was more important than the creation of an English educated civil service and the integration of Indians into the structure of British imperial governance and military life. In the Indian Councils Acts of 1861, 1892, and 1909, the British gradually expanded Indian participation in legislative matters. As the Act of 1892 put it, they sought "to widen the basis and expand the functions of the Government of India, and to give further opportunities to the non-official and native elements in Indian society to take part in the work of the Government." [29]

Finally, with the independent creation of the Indian National Congress and its companion the Indian National Reform Society in 1885, the forces of external and internal reform found a social vehicle. Here were found English and Indian Christians, Muslims, and people of varying degrees of Hindu self-consciousness. At the same time, we see the first expressions of caste organization in public forms with the Kayastha Conference of 1887, which led to the formation of the All India Caste Association. [30] While these associations were originally a means to form an Indian public in partnership with the Raj, they eventually became a government in nucleus. Here the dynamics of generating a public beyond caste and a new covenant beyond the British imperium were played out in great complexity and great anguish.

As the INC gained in public power, it also reached the limits of the covenant that underlay it. In 1907, in response to the increasing identification of Indian nationalism with a reformed Hinduism, Muslims formed their own Muslim League to remain true to their own interests and heritage. While this split emerged from ancient differences, it also was easily manipulated by the British as an element in their long-standing divide-conquer-and-rule strategy. In the Indian Councils Act of 1909 the British introduced separate electorates for Muslims, thus beginning the process that led to the partition of the country in 1947. Religion became a basis for political formation. Nevertheless, many Muslims remained within the INC as nationalists above religion. Indeed, in 1916 ("the Lucknow Pact") the INC tried to mollify league anxieties by agreeing substantially to the communal electorates introduced in 1909. But this was not enough. The league took form as a sectarian antagonist defined first of all by ancient religion rather than by nascent nationhood. The INC came increasingly under the influence of a militant Hindu nationalism, which only Gandhi's enormous prestige was able to constrain.

Between these emergent public assemblies and the empire then began a long series of conferences and negotiations leading to the emergence of an independent constitutional order in India. The ravages of World War I provoked in England a growing support for greater autonomy in India, leading first to the Government of India Act (1919), which carried out the purpose enunciated by the British in 1917 to increase the "association of Indians in every branch of the administration and the gradual development of self-governing institutions with a view to progressive realization of responsible government in British India as an integral part of the British Empire."[31]

Here began a devolution of powers to the provinces through a principle of dyarchy, in which certain subjects were under the immediate control of the provinces, with other matters (military, foreign policy, overall fiscal policy) being reserved to the governor general. At the same time, the central legislature became bicameral, with both appointed and elected members, roughly following the British model. Since the authority of the provinces had devolved from the center it could be recalled at any time through veto and legislative act by the central government. Thus began the halting development of a more egalitarian covenant among the jurisdictions within the hierarchical order of the Raj. At the same time, by extending the principle of religious or communal electorates, the act bound the developing publics to the old orders of Islamic governance and caste separation. The emerging public was growing up deformed between the boulders of ancient rivalries.

The Movement toward Federation, 1931-35

Out of an official evaluation of these reforms in 1930 came the Round Table Conference of 1931, which was attended by appointees of the Crown, including INC leaders like Gandhi, and representatives from the Indian states as well. In this regard the round table was a far cry from the round tables of the German Revolution, with their democratic basis. Here, in resulting debates, were hammered out the main form of the Constitution that was to be carried over into the Indian Union in 1950.

The conference proposed a federal form of government in which each participant state would have its own limited sovereignty according to a list of legislative powers defining the jurisdictions of the states, of the central government, and of them jointly.[32] Even within this federal scheme the governor general could intervene in provincial affairs on a limited basis. The Crown could also veto repugnant legislation. The central government worked directly with tribal territories, another pattern carried over into the Constitution of 1950.

The princely states were then invited to join this federation on an equal footing. They refused to do so, however, most likely in order to protect their own prerogatives, which were greater under their treaties with the Crown than under the proposed federation. Moreover, the federation would also entangle them in legislative reforms, a common legal system, and creeping democratization.[33] For these states the forms of hierarchy and monarchy could not give way to a new covenant of expanding provincial publics. In passing up the federal scheme, the principalities foreclosed, in effect, on their survival after independence, when they were eventually swallowed up in the new republic.

The Act of 1935 required the drafting of constitutions for the participating states as well as for the center. That is, India was eventually to become a dominion, like Canada or Australia at the time. In the meantime its constitutive states would all have a direct relation to the Crown in terms of their constitutional status. Some of the act's proposed changes were implemented in 1937, but the progress toward a federal constitution of republican states became enmeshed in the cataclysms of World War II. Under the exigencies of the war the British government, through Sir Stafford Crips, pledged rapid movement toward an independent India, including the princely states, and a federal constitution based on an indigenously elected assembly. Here, too, the British (as well as most of the INC) struck upon the congealing resolve of M. A. Jinnah and the Muslim League to have a separate Islamic state. This the British were not prepared to support. Despite repeated efforts at negotiation the League and the Congress could not come together, forcing in the end the bloody rupture of partition. This the British finally acquiesced to in 1947 in order to hand over its authority to some constituted governmental order in India, even if fractured in crucial ways.

Communal Representation and Democratic Nationalism

All through the 1930s the vexing problem of minority representation continued to gnaw at the feet of the negotiators, threatening to undermine negotiations between the INC, the Muslim League, and the Crown. In 1932 the British government further extended electorates based on caste, religion, and occupation—in short, "communalism." Many Indian participants at the Round Table Conference, including the Christian delegates, S. K. Datta and K. T. Paul, opposed any communal electorates. Gandhi's fast in protest brought about some compromise on this issue (the "Poona Pact" of 1932), but in this he was increasingly confronted by the former untouchable from Maharashtra, B. R. Ambedkar, whose remonstrances against a caste-blind electorate at the Round Table Conference had been rejected in favor of territorial electorates.[34] The Poona Pact refrained from special communal electorates but agreed on having reserved seats for certain categories of historically oppressed groups.

In this way the nationalist struggle for a citizenship based solely on the configuration of the land was increasingly threatened by a concept of citizenship restricted to biological descent and its communal forms. From the side of Ambedkar, a nationalist equality had to be subordinated to the need for substantive equality for the former untouchables and lower castes. From the side of the Muslim League, it had to be subordinated to the need to provide a land where Islam was the common faith of the majority.

Thus, the Indian people claimed their republican aspirations only by maiming the chances for forming a covenant that might hold them together across the chasms of ancient cultural and dynastic differences. The people of the subcontinent faced the task of forming their separate constitutions in a land split along communal religious lines.

The Federal Constitution of 1950

The Constitutional Structure

In negotiations leading up to independence, the participants envisioned a constitutional assembly composed of delegates elected from the provincial assemblies and appointed by the princely states. This arrangement was unsatisfactory to Jinnah and the Muslim League, leading to their withdrawal from the process and the tragic Partition of India in 1947. In the complex negotiations among the ultimate delegates a federal state was created that was more concerned with national unity than the autonomy of the local regions. Creation of a modern industrial state took precedence over the possibly disastrous consequences of enhancing local and communal interests. Thus, in Ambedkar's words, "the federation was not the result of an agreement by the States to join in a Federation, and the Federation not being the result of an agreement, no State has the right to secede from it." [35] Ambedkar called this a "dual polity," perhaps harking back to his American exposure. Granville Austin, an early and astute commentator on the Constitution, called the system a "centralized, cooperative federalism." [36] The trauma of Partition and the national models provided by the Soviet Union and the United States worked together to create a federalism rooted more in "hierarchical covenants" between the ghost of empire and the children of nationalism than the compactual federalism of well-formed states seeking a broader unity. While the princely states could entertain and to some extent pursue the making of covenants among themselves and with the emerging state, this product of their situation could not infuse the dynamic of the whole process. They were, after all, not republics but principalities. Ultimately even their newly covenanted status was obliterated in the Reorganization Act of 1950. [37]

The values of democratic participation and national unity permeated the new Constitution. In order to cultivate this new democratic nationhood the Constitution sought to create a secular state that guaranteed religious freedom for all. Second, it committed succeeding governments to the eradication of the vestiges of caste. Third, it directed the government to create a uniform civil code that would place men and women on an equal legal footing in domestic matters regardless of the religious traditions that had governed them in earlier times, usually to the gross disadvantage of women. In subsequent years each of these commitments has encountered enormous resistance. Moreover, each effort to pursue these purposes has created in turn a host of unforeseen and nearly intractable problems. One of the primary sources of these difficulties is the conflicts among the traditional religions and between them and the new republic. Though committed to a secular state, Indians have had to seek to accommodate it to religious traditions in order to secure its legitimation.[38] While many of these issues will be taken up in the following case studies, let me turn for a moment to the core of the debate over the religious sources for the legitimation of the 1950 Constitution.

The Legitimation of the New Republic

Three figures epitomize the divergent tendencies underlying the struggle over legitimation of the 1950 Constitution—Mahatma Gandhi, Jawaharlal Nehru, and B. R. Ambedkar. Gandhi represents the reformist Hindu tradition anchored in the Hindu Renaissance. Nehru represents the secularist effort to privatize religion, and Ambedkar represents the rejection of traditional Hinduism in favor of a religious alternative rooted in the aspirations of the "Dalits," the former untouchables.

Gandhi was steeped in the *Ramayana* and the *Bhagavad Gita,* key Vaishnavaite texts that infused his understanding of *"Ram-raja"* and *"Dharma-raja."* Right governance occurs through figures that exemplify virtue (King Rama) within an order in which everyone is governed by a law rooted in the cosmic order of dharma. That is, he never rejected the fundamental bio-piety of Hinduism, which connects one's biological place in life with social duties. Thus, Gandhi's first task was to govern himself through ascetic discipline and to advance a social order in which each person could practice in an immediate manner a way of life compatible with dharma. While Gandhi sought to reinterpret this dharma in a way he felt compatible with the civil order he learned through British law, he never moved far beyond the village and handicrafts as the normative social and economic unit for a just society. The Gandhian-inspired notion of India as a federation of "village republics" was rejected by the Constitutional Assembly not so much as a political idea but as an impractical response to the need for large-scale industrial development.[39]

Both his ascetic discipline and devotion to a sense of dharma came together in the ideas of *swa-tantra* and *swa-raja*—that is, self-rule. The self-rule of the ascetic would be mirrored in the self-rule of the nation. It was this notion of swa-raj that Hindu nationalists would take up to advance a conception of the new nation as a Hindu state. Their appeal to Mother India combined the bio-piety of Gandhi's tradition with the geo-piety that would essentially exclude or subordinate "foreign" religions. It was these religious nationalists who eventually assassinated Gandhi, whose faith always sought to embrace other religions, albeit within the overall framework of central Hindu traditions.[40]

Ambedkar did not believe that Hinduism was capable of the egalitarian inclusiveness necessary for a democratic order. The crux of this antimony between Hinduism and democracy lay in the concepts and practices of caste. Ambedkar, who was the principal author of the Constitution, was himself a former untouchable (a "Mahar") from what is now called Maharastra state. With the support and patronage of a local maharaja, he was educated under John Dewey at Columbia University and he went on to secure a degree in law from Oxford University. His American and English training and his rejection of the system that would have ordinarily prevented him from exercising his enormous abilities led him to clash sharply with Gandhi, who remained loyal to the essential components of Hindu caste.[41] In 1935 he was prevented from giving a speech repudiating Hindu traditions as a viable religious basis for a future democratic state.[42] In 1956 Ambedkar converted to Buddhism, which he saw as the authentic Indian religious alternative to Hinduism, taking with him several hundred thousand followers.[43]

Although Ambedkar repudiated Hinduism as a viable religious source to legitimate a democratic republic, he did not repudiate the importance of religion in the government's necessary role to root out the destructive vestiges of caste. For the sake of fuller democratic participation, the government would have to take positive action to advance the interests of former untouchables and the Constitution would have to use religious categories to do so. This position was already presaged in his defense of some communal electorates at the Round Table Conference and then later in his oversight of the drafting of the new Constitution.

Nehru was a committed secularist who felt that religion, at least organized religion, stood for "blind belief and reaction, dogma and bigotry, superstition and exploitation, and the preservation of vested interests."[44] In this he was not very different from Jinnah, who willingly used religious motivations for political purposes but who otherwise was contemptuous of it. In Nehru's case this rejection meant that religion should be a strictly private matter of belief, leaving the state to operate on quite different bases to create a public order devoid of the markings of religion. Industrialization and economic development would create the conditions for democracy that would in turn make the new Constitution a viable political reality.

The three approaches—reformed tradition, religious progressivism, and secularized privatism—found uneasy compromise in the creation of the new Constitution. However, they also sustained significant tensions that continue to shape India's living constitution.

Redressing Past Inequities: Compensatory Discrimination and Soosai the Cobbler

The Constitutional Directive to Redress Caste-based Inequalities

The Indian Constitution of 1950 directed the state to "promote with special care the educational and economic interests of the weaker sections of the people, and, in particular, of the Scheduled Castes and the Scheduled Tribes, and [to] protect them from social injustice and all forms of exploitation" (Article 46). The former "untouchables," whom Gandhi called "children of God" *(Harijan)*, were now called members of castes "scheduled" by the government for advancement. The Constitution also extended such provisions to "other backward classes," who needed assistance to overcome historic inequities (Articles 16(4), 46, 340). Article 46, along with additional articles (330-42, 366), orders (1950), and statutes, has formed the backbone for ongoing governmental efforts to grant special privileges to these disadvantaged groups by providing reserved seats in national and state legislatures, educational privileges, and other advantages to compensate for entrenched and long-standing practices of discrimination. This constitutes what Marc Galanter has called the government's policy of "compensatory discrimination."[45]

Both Gandhi and Ambedkar, though from very divergent standpoints, had recognized casteism's religious roots, thus ultimately reinforcing the use of religious categories to decide who would be "scheduled" for compensatory discrimination benefits. This course was already prepared by earlier decisions to create Muslim electorates (1909) and reserve legislative seats for the "depressed classes" (1919) or, as the Government of India Constitution (1935) put it, the "scheduled castes."[46]

The first list of beneficiaries ("Scheduled Castes Order") issued by the newly constituted government in 1950 stated that ". . . no person who professes a religion different from the Hindu or Sikh religion shall be deemed to be a member of the Scheduled Caste." Only those known as Hindus, for whom caste was a part of their religion, would be able to avail themselves of these privileges. Non-Hindus, having left behind the caste distinctions embedded in Hinduism, were supposedly unencumbered by their caste disadvantage—not only in their own eyes but in the eyes of others.[47]

Immediately, excluded groups began to mobilize for recognition. Pressure from Sikhs had already led to the inclusion of some of their former untouchable castes in the first order. Further pressure then led to a blanket inclusion of all Sikh groups in 1956. Buddhists, led principally by Ambedkar's neo-Buddhist followers, were unable to attain this status until 1990. Within the last few years Christians and Muslims from low-caste origins have pressed their claims to be included, arguing that not to do so is to discriminate against them on the basis "only of religion," which is prohibited by Artcle 15(1). The case of Soosai the cobbler brought to poignant expression this struggle to reform and democratize Indian society, especially by relieving it of the burden of religious identification as a prime criterion for state policy.

The Story of Soosai the Cobbler

Soosai had belonged to the Adi-Dravida caste of cobblers in Madras before his conversion to Christianity. As a leather-worker he was deemed untouchable by the caste Hindus. His caste, whose very name points to its origin in the "original Dravidians" who were overrun by the Aryan invaders more than 3,000 years ago, was listed as a scheduled caste in the Presidential Order of 1950. Soosai exercised his craft at a hot and dusty street corner in Madras. While possessing a few basic tools he had virtually no place he could call his own. As part of its general program of uplift for this caste the Tamil Nadu Khadi and Village Industries Board allotted free bunks to some members of this cobbler caste in 1982, but they excluded Soosai because he was not a Hindu or Sikh.

Suit was brought on Soosai's behalf on the grounds that such exclusion violated Article 14, guaranteeing equality for all citizens before the law, and Articles 15 and 16, which forbid discrimination "on grounds only of religion. . . ." In addition, Soosai's advocates appealed to Article 25, which guarantees "freedom of conscience and the right freely to profess, practise and propagate religion." Soosai, they argued, was not free to practice his faith, because he was being tempted by government policy to reconvert to Hinduism in order to claim the bunk that was denied to him solely on the basis of his Christian affiliation.

In its ruling on September 30, 1985, the Supreme Court[48] held that it did not have to decide whether caste conditions continue upon conversion to Christianity. It was ready to concede that point for purposes of this case. However, Soosai would have to show that Christians of his caste "suffer from a comparable depth of social and economic disabilities and cultural and educational backwardness and similar levels of degradation *within the Christian community* [my emphasis] necessitating intervention by the State under the provisions of the Constitution." More specifically, he would have to show that "the disabilities and handicaps suffered from such caste membership in the social order of its origin—Hinduism—continue in their oppressive severity in the new environment of a different religious community." Since this was not proven, he could not argue that he was eligible for provisions to ameliorate these conditions. He had not been discriminated against. He had simply not fulfilled the conditions for application for special relief. His petition was therefore denied by the court.

The Key Issues

Citizenship, Religion, Community, and Caste

Soosai's tiny but fundamental claim was crushed in the collision between the culture of the Constitution and the traditional culture of India. The Constitution addresses people as citizens—individuals with the capacity to reason, to express themselves in public, and to secure their claims through due legal process within a fundamental constitutional order. The categories of traditional Indian culture, however, consider people as members of all-encompassing communities. "Religion" does not really attach to an individual but to a "community" that embraces economic, familial, social, and cultural aspects of life. To speak of "Hinduism" is to unite "religion" with "community" and social order. Since religion can mean both communal embeddedness and personal persuasion, the court can move easily between talk of Christianity as a "religion" to its being a "religious community" separate from "Hindu society," using whatever definition fits its decision in a particular case. In his case Soosai had to show that his continued degradation based on caste discrimination was "within the Christian community," thus severing his civil claim from his status in the society generally. His religious category prevailed in defining his civil rights.

In this situation it is difficult to set out the economic aspects of discrimination from the category of "religion," or for that matter family, language, place, and occupation. The progressive reformers of the 1970s and 1980s in India tried to restructure the whole system of compensatory discrimination so that it would rest entirely on economic conditions. The categories of religion used since 1936 and 1950 would be superseded by assessments of economic position generation by generation. Compensatory discrimination would become one aspect of the effort to pursue the socialist vision first articulated by Nehru and pursued by his daughter Indira Gandhi and grandson Rajiv Gandhi.[49]

While finally being governed by a communal definition of religion, the court also used this argument, for it agreed that if Soosai could have shown, through scientific research, that he suffered the same degradation in his "community" (we assume here especially economic disadvantage) as Hindus of his caste suffered in theirs then he could apply for relief, making the religious classifications of the scheduled caste law moot if not invalid. However, the court was completely unwilling to address the central question of whether the use of religious classifications in scheduled class law was itself contrary to the religious nondiscrimination provisions of the Constitution. It tried to have it both ways. It spoke the language of the Constitution's social democracy (and liberalism) as well as the language of traditional Indian communalism, but in the end came down on the side of communalism.

In doing so the court only reflected the original ambiguity in the Constitution, which had to set forth the values of constitutional democracy within the culture and language of traditional Indian life—what westerners called "Hinduism." The concept of religion was a hinge pin between these two normative worlds. With Soosai's case we see several dilemmas in this effort to found a new constitutional order.

First, we see a conflict between the underlying social compact of citizenship, which seeks to treat individuals on the basis of personal merit, and the historic communal character of Indian society, which treats people according to their membership in status groups, that is, castes.[50] While setting forth a list of fundamental rights, the Constitution expressly allows for deviation from them to promote the social and economic base necessary for all people to exercise these rights. But in allowing the category of religion to be used to advance these underlying conditions for democratic life, it jeopardizes the civil rights themselves, primary among them the freedom to be a citizen without regard to religion, whether religion is seen as personal persuasion or communal membership.

The argument that the civil equality of democracy requires the socioeconomic equality of socialism as its precondition opens the door in the Indian context to the repristination of religious and caste categories as the basis for the society generally, thus in the end overturning the civil substance of the new constitutional order. The contractual and covenantal culture indispensable for constitutional governance is swallowed back up into organizational patterns whose ultimate appeal is to biology and tradition. The public order of constitutionalism is reabsorbed into the private world of kin and caste.

The use of religious-communal categories within the constitutional order to promote a kind of socialist democracy leads us to a more fundamental dilemma, namely, the overthrowing of the secular character of the constitutional order itself. This is the threat posed throughout the century by Hindu nationalism.[51]

Clearly one decisive political support for this approach to compensatory discrimination has lain in Hindu fears that unless Christians and Muslims are excluded from these benefits, there will be mass conversions of low-status citizens to Christianity or Islam.[52] This, of course, is an argument that proceeds from the belief that caste hierarchy is essential to Hinduism. On the other hand, progressive Hindus, instead of excluding Christians, turn to the reform of Hinduism as a way of stemming conversion. They, however, run up against yet another force, namely Hindu nationalism, whose focus is on the maintenance of the cultural ascendancy of Hinduism as the basis for an Indian state. Both Hindu traditionalists and Hindu nationalists join together to push other religious groups to the margins.

This coalition is fraught with contradictions. The nationalists, in order to gain widespread political followings, have to overcome caste at the same time that they focus popular anger against "foreign religions" such as Islam and Christianity. However, the traditional Hindus drawn to them reawaken caste consciousness, thus reinforcing Brahmanic leadership of Hindu nationalist groups like the Bharatiya Janata Party (BJP). This, however, can disenchant the subordinate caste groups. The effort to reground the Indian federal state in "Hinduism" will eventually founder on its internal contradictions or undermine the national state itself.

Secularity between Separation and Equal Protection

We return, then, to the claim that the only way a national state can exist in India is as a "secular" state. But what shall "secular" mean? Does it mean "atheism" and "antireligion," as the Urdu newspapers translated it for Muslims when the Constitution was promulgated? Does it mean institutional separation of "religion" from government? Does it mean the grounding of the Constitution in "nonreligious" traditions or claims? Does it mean strict "separation," barring any involvement in religious matters, or does it mean "equal treatment" and "equal protection" of religious groups, thus allowing state interference in and utilization of religion?

This last interpretation has been a powerful one in Indian political culture, even shaping some court rulings. The secular-democratic commitment to pluralism easily begins to justify the maintenance of historic communities and traditions. Each religious community should be guaranteed a right of survival. While it can propagate itself, this ought not to be in such a way that the survival of another religion is threatened. At this point we have to ask what the benchmark for survival is. "Equal protection" can be used to counter the Hindu nationalist groups who destroyed the mosque in Ayodhya, which is part of the existing Muslim community. But should we see the present mosque (or church for that matter) as the result of an earlier attack on Hindu survival? Should we now engage in compensatory action to recreate the status quo ante? Here questions of law and rights devolve into murky contests over pre-constitutional history and ancient communal claims.

Even barring interference with organized religion, can the state still use religious categories to advance its secular purposes? Can the notion of "religion" merely be an instrument of state policy or does it inevitably devour the secular constitution itself? These are all questions familiar to American readers, but they take on different meaning in the Indian context, where religion is often communal and noninstitutional rather than individual and associational.

Ultimately the question of government's secularity is decided not merely by the interpreters of law and politics but by the religious traditions themselves. Some religious traditions allow a clear distinction between sacred and secular that gives room for an independent state. Others seek to cement every aspect of life into a seamless whole rooted not in the conventions of some type of covenantal or contractual order but in the ontological claims of birth, gender, race, and place. The debate is not merely between different theories of government, say between monarchy and democracy, but between different types of religion as well, in this case between those with some sense of covenantal relationships open to historical creativity and those rooted in categories of origin and return.

These two fundamentally different approaches to life underlie the question of whether people should be addressed in public policy in terms of their membership in some involuntary grouping like caste, kinship, race, or even religion, or whether only individuals, organized in associations, can be the subjects of public policy attempts to overcome discrimination. Where religion is defined communally, the question presses to a group-oriented solution. Where it is seen individually, then the question moves to an individual solution. This difference between communal and individual subjects of political participation also affects the way covenantlike religion might function in a society. Covenantal types of religion, whether Christian or Islamic, that stress the immutable will of the divine partner over human respondents can also stress cultural fusion over differentiation, thus undermining the voluntaristic values necessary for genuine public life. These differences in type of religion and approach to political participation have profound implications not only for public policy on domestic matters but also on conceptions of religious organization and its relation to the public order and the state.

The Church between Competing Equalities

This situation also poses critical questions for the church and Christians, not to mention those who know themselves as Sikhs, Muslims, Buddhists, and Hindus. Should Christians press to be included among the enumerated religions in scheduled caste orders or should they press for exclusion of religious categories from these laws altogether? By becoming scheduled caste Christians under the law, they may be advancing a form of justice but at the same time forfeiting their faith in a church that transcends the social boundaries of caste and the legal categories of the state.

Some observers have already pointed out how the indirect restrictions on conversion posed by these laws have greatly reduced conversion among scheduled caste people. On the other hand, since tribal groups are seen as *ethnic* rather than *religious* groups, members of scheduled tribes can still benefit from laws and policies favoring formerly oppressed groups. This circumstance has resulted in tremendous recent gains in Christian mission work among tribal groups.[53] This contradiction between Christian policies with regard to tribal and scheduled caste groups presses the church to find a consistent path, namely, to put members of scheduled castes on a legal par with scheduled tribes. However, this path to consistency immediately puts the church in conflict with the "higher road" of castelessness. Compensatory legislation practically forces Christians to reconsider caste as a possible social form for Christians (ironically, in the name of democratic leveling). Julian Saldanha, for instance, has argued that "a Christian can remain within the framework of the Hindu society whilst being fully committed to Jesus Christ."[54] Since "being a Hindu is not a matter of creed, but of social and legal status," Christians can preserve their "faith" (a matter of conscience and creed) while fitting into the categories of Hindu society (a pattern of external behavior). Unfortunately, this then violates a Christian theological commitment to the unity of spirit and matter that makes it difficult to divide life into an internal faith and an external practice.

The alternative, which Soosai's advocates pursued, was that dominant in the Dalit Christian movement, which sees the essence of Christian faith in the life of "brokenness" *(dalit)*.[55] Those who are broken, whether "scheduled" or "unscheduled," must unite to achieve a society in which people are related on the basis of their personhood, that is, their potential for citizenship. While the Dalit movement can also be pressed in a communalist direction, its basic thrust is in line with the struggle for a constitutional order founded in voluntary covenants and public argument.

Christians in India stand between a Hindu communalism that is ultimately rooted in a biogenetic (and cosmic) understanding of social order and a Muslim communalism that rejects all such distinctions (except those of patriarchy) in favor of submission to God's universal will as made known in a comprehensive legal order *(Sharia)*. It is this all-embracing Sharia that can be drawn on to define the communal boundaries of Islam in a particular context such as India.[56]

Christian struggles for a third way between a mere individualism and some brand of communalism have generally sought to hold together both the individual and collective dimensions of life, but within a different social theory.[57] Rather than drawing the line between interior and exterior (between belief and practice), they have distinguished between the church and the social order and between this era and the new creation yet to be fulfilled, but that is already anticipated within the church. Thus, the crucial questions of social ethics for Christians tend to revolve around questions of ecclesiology. In India these ecclesiological questions reflect the tension between communal and individual interpretations of religion. To explore the questions of religion's communal nature in the context of India's Constitution I will turn to the difficulties confronting efforts to develop a uniform civil code. To take up the questions of individual religious freedom as they relate to ecclesiology I will then turn to the case of the Basel Mission.

From Religious Tutelage to a Common Civil Code: The Case of Shah Bano

The Struggle for a Uniform Civil Code

The framers of the Constitution did not confine themselves to creating the structures and procedures for government but also established a number of constitutional "directives" to guide government policy in creating the cultural, social, and economic basis for a viable democracy. Article 44 of the Constitution instructed the government "to secure a uniform civil code for the citizens." Such a code would replace the patchwork of customary religious laws governing marriage, divorce, adoption, inheritance, and family support. While a contemporary observer might emphasize the way such a code would secure basic human rights for all citizens, the idea of human rights, at the time, was still in its Indian infancy. What was more compelling then was the need for national unity once the British were gone. A uniform civil code would help neutralize the divisiveness of the multitude of domestic laws that reinforced caste consciousness, parochial religious loyalties, and the subjugation of women. However, reeling from the catastrophic conflicts of India's partition and its religio-communal massacres, the Nehru administration did not proceed to implement this directive—precisely because it would itself imperil the national unity it sought.[58]

In the mid 1950s Nehru did get Parliament to pass various "Hindu Code" bills drastically reforming Hindu practices of marriage, divorce, and inheritance. While this move was hotly contested by Hindu traditionalists, the Nehru administration rammed it through, reinforcing the old tradition of princely control over religious practices, even as it claimed only to be separating out the "secular" aspects of family law from its religious and sacramental aspects.[59]

The Nehru administration also created the Special Marriage Act (1954), under which couples, especially those entering mixed religious marriages, can register to take advantages of certain civil provisions. In essence, these two steps formed the nucleus of a uniform civil code, one that even some Christians felt should include them. However, no further steps were taken. A proposed Christian civil code pitted Roman Catholics against Protestants, a tangle Nehru did not wish to aggravate.[60] With the consolidation of the Hindu components of the directive, the other religious groups were left to fend for themselves, almost as if the true national task of reform had been accomplished.

Without this civil code, the traditional religions continue to shape the most crucial aspects of people's lives—especially women's lives—and deny them effective citizenship and civil rights. Specifically, Christians, who operate under "personal laws" dating from British rule,[61] and Muslims, who operate under the British-era Shariat Act (1937) and the Muslim Marriage Act (1939), are marginalized as premodern backwaters of family law compared to the Hindu Code and Special Marriage Act.

The state's failure to develop a civil code rests in its fear of antagonizing the religious leaders who have otherwise supported Indian independence and national development. It does not want to appear as a Hindu majority intervening in the internal affairs of minority religious groups. "The trauma of Partition" paralyzes any efforts to bring the various religious communities under a common law of domestic relations.[62] Thus, the minority religions have been largely left alone to do their own reforming. However, they either lack the organizational power to do so (as in Muslim groups) or are unable to reach a consensus (as with Roman Catholics, Protestants, and Orthodox).

In fact, the state and the courts are not always reluctant to intervene in religious matters, either for political gain, as we shall soon see, or when the religious matter at hand can be construed as a problem of "minority group rights." At this point the dominant Indian ethos of communalism easily rides roughshod over the claims of individual citizens.

The case of Shah Bano dramatizes the difficulty in bringing marital and family law, including the law of inheritance, under a common civil code. It also illuminates the conflicts and relationships between religious organizations, the law, and the state, including political parties. Finally, it opens up the profound conflict between male dominance and the principles of a democratic republic.

The Shah Bano Story

Shah Bano Begum was married to Mohammed Ahmed Khan in 1932 in Indore, Madhya Pradesh, according to Muslim law.[63] They had three sons and two daughters by this marriage. In 1975 her husband "drove [her] out of the matrimonial home," in the words of the Supreme Court.[64] Because she was illiterate, her sons helped her secure legal counsel and in April 1978 she applied for maintenance, not under any Muslim law but under the British-developed Code of Criminal Procedure of 1872 [Rev. 1898, 1978] (Section 125), which requires proper maintenance of indigent family members. Her husband then instantly divorced her in November 1978 using the short form "*talaq al-bida*" usually rejected by Muslim legal scholars.

Khan claimed that according to Muslim law the husband is required to support a divorced wife for only three months after divorce, the period of *iddat*. The court, however, bypassed claims based on Muslim law and imposed a court order for maintenance based on the criminal code.[65] Though allegedly earning some 60,000 rupees annually as a lawyer, he refused on principle to pay even the court-ordered sum of 179.20 rupees monthly beyond the three-month period. He appealed the case to the Supreme Court.

In its ruling of April 23, 1985, the court held that Section 125 of the criminal code is entirely secular in nature, "founded upon the individual's obligation to the society to prevent vagrancy and destitution." As a criminal law it overrides any religious laws, which have the status of civil laws, though it does not displace them. Shah Bano should therefore be entitled to support as an "indigent family member." Here the court appealed to the terms of the criminal code itself, holding that as long as she did not remarry, she was, for legal purposes, still the wife of Mohammed Ahmed Khan, whatever Muslim law might say to the contrary.

However, just to seal its case in response to claims from Khan's advocates, the court then sought to justify its decision also with respect to the Qu'ran, which does not place a limit on the period of maintenance. In conclusion it issued a ringing plea for the state, not the individual religious communities, to develop an effective uniform civil code according to Article 44 of the Constitution.

The court's ruling provoked an explosion of resistance from conservative Islamic groups, even as it gratified the proponents of change and introduction of a uniform civil code. The otherwise largely dormant Muslim Personal Law Board charged that the court had interfered with its rightful administration of Muslim law and began to set up special Shariat courts throughout the country to enforce its prerogatives. The Mullahs and other Muslim leaders, exploiting the fears of the Muslim minority in the face of resurgent Hindu communalism, attacked the court for trying to interpret the Qu'ran. They then led a massive drive to pass legislation exempting Muslim law from the application of Section 125 of the criminal code.

By November 2 the poor and illiterate Shah Bano, under pressure from Muslim religious leaders, endorsed with her thumbprint a letter requesting the Supreme Court to withdraw its decision in her favor because it contravened the Qu'ran and unconstitutionally interfered in the Muslim personal law.[66] In the same month mobs in the hundred thousands protested the ruling and stoned those organized to support it.[67]

By December Prime Minister Rajiv Gandhi, in order to bolster his relations with conservative Muslim leaders, agreed to support a bill that would effectively exempt Muslims from the jurisdiction of Section 125 of the criminal code.[68] With enormous pressure from Gandhi and the Congress Party, the bill passed Parliament in May as "The Muslim Women (Protection of Rights on Divorce) Bill."

Despite its high-sounding name, it was actually an act depriving Muslim women of most of the rights they would enjoy in Islamic countries. Not only did it limit payment of maintenance to the iddat period, but it insulated the former husband from any further obligations and made the woman's relatives and the local Muslim community trust fund *(waqf)* responsible for ameliorating her indigency.[69] Moreover, children would be supported by the father only for a period of two years—a transparent effort to transfer their custody solely to him even before the customary ages when children revert from their infantile custody by their mother to their adolescent custody by their father. As a result of a last-minute amendment the act allowed women to sue under the provisions of the criminal code only if they receive prior permission from the husband to do so, hardly a likely event.

On the surface the act looked like it gave women (but not children) the right to extended maintenance, but by throwing them on the entangled resources of relatives or the nonexistent resources of the waqf, it effectively exposed them to direct impoverishment, not to mention humiliation. In fact, even if it had the funds, as a trust fund the waqf could only be used for the purposes designated in the trust charter. It could not be an omnibus treasury for "the Muslim community." Here again the legal structures conflict with the communalist perspective.

The act did not effect reconciliation between Muslims and others. Rather it heightened communal sensitivities, exposed the tensions within the Islamic population, and further splintered the fragile efforts toward a national consensus that might underlie a uniform civil code. Without following these developments further, let me turn to the implications of this case for our analysis into the relation of religion to the development of a democratic federal republic.

The Key Issues

Religion, Patriarchy, and Communalism

At the outset we must remember Shah Bano's illiteracy, shared with the majority of women in India and especially Muslim women. The encouragement toward literacy found in any religion of the Book is countervailed by excluding women from the central tasks of public religious life. Added to this is the general poverty of much of the Muslim population. Because of this illiteracy Shah Bano was dependent on men for action regarding the law, that is, any action exercising power. Her sons were her first advocates but then their efforts were finally overturned by the resurgent power of the religious leaders, who controlled the gates of public acceptance or ostracism—the final sanction for illiterate people who must depend entirely on personal communal supports for their life.

Underlying the entire affair, as many observers pointed out, was the desperate attempt by conservative factions to preserve patriarchal domination among Muslims—an interest shared by many Hindus as well. But since democratic culture undermines these patriarchal claims, their proponents must inevitably attack the foundations of the democratic political order itself, not by attacking democracy as such but by upholding the rights of distinct communities to preserve their special customs, namely, customs that prevent women from exercising the full powers of citizenship. It is the combination of religious communalism and patriarchy that works to undermine the rational universalism of law in a constitutional democracy.

Citizen Rights and Religious Rights

Beyond her experience of illiteracy and male domination, Shah Bano was captured by appeals to the religious freedom of a particular community to control its internal affairs. Here religious freedom does not mean individual freedom of conscience and association but the autonomy of religious communities governed by traditions mediated through the elders. The notion of freedom of conscience rests in a voluntaristic understanding of religious organization, signaled by the religious centrality of congregations rather than communities. The communal interpretation of religious freedom draws on an involuntaristic understanding of religion that does not know of a thoroughgoing distinction between the religious sphere, represented in a separate church, samgha, or temple, and the ordinary daily life of marriage, family, work, and government. Indeed, at one time an Indian high court held that "freedom of religion" was the freedom *not* to be converted, that is, to remain within ascribed statuses.[70] While this extreme "equal protection" view has not prevailed in the courts, it reflects a deep underlying conviction among many traditional sectors.[71]

The problem with this version of religious freedom is twofold. First, it does not share with the environing democratic order an analogous structure for decision making, whether in judicial proceedings or in general consensus formation concerning policies affecting the community. Thus, the citizen rights enjoyed in one sphere do not translate into the other. This incommensurability produces an intractable inequality with respect to a universal legal order in the nation. People can equally exercise the right to belong to a religious community but not an equal right, based on the Constitution, to divorce, adopt, or inherit, due to the claims of their separate communities.

Second, there exists no clear way to establish who represents the community to the wider legal and governmental order. On what basis does the wider order recognize the claims of the minority community's purported leaders? In the parliamentary debate swirling around Shah Bano's head, why were certain leaders heard and not others? Was it, as some members of Parliament said, merely their respective willingness and ability to create violence, thus turning the parliamentary debate into a matter of "internal national security"?[72]

Without a principle of representation the community cannot be an actor in a wider political process. It cannot enter agreements with other groups or with governments. It is simply a pool of recruits for charismatics and demagogues, for whom a "community," shorn of its traditional constraints in the villages of natural order, is only a potential mob in the streets of change.

Secularity, Minority Rights, and Human Rights

In her personal struggle Shah Bano was caught between the claims of a secular state and those of a religious community. Parties on all sides appealed to secularity but, as with religious freedom, attached very different meanings to it. For the reactionaries of the Muslim League and Muslim Personal Law Board secularity meant that the state must hover above the separate religious communities like an umbrella, sheltering them but not interfering in their internal affairs. It should offer protection but not interference. At the most, changes within the claimed jurisdictions of these "personal codes" should come only with the consent of the affected community. This underlying covenant between government and religion undermines the earlier constitutional directive (itself a profound kind of covenant) to pursue a uniform civil code. However, this could not be a code imposed from the top, as were the Hindu Code bills of the 1950s. It would have to arise from below through a kind of religious federalism culminating in a national consensus.

For Shah Bano's supporters secularity meant that the legal conditions attaching to the secular realm of everyday life that peoples of all religions share should take precedence over the purely parochial and idiosyncratic claims of particular religious groups. The secular sphere should be controlled by common universal laws and the religious sphere by its own peculiar laws, whether these are revealed, traditional, or charismatically inspired. Change should flow from the national covenant embedded in the constitutional directive to create a uniform civil code, because it is a covenant with individual citizens whose rights must be elaborated in all the spheres they share in common.

Clearly, these notions of secularity themselves rest on fundamental conceptions about the relation of transcendent order to everyday life—conceptions that are not shared among the world's religions, either in their root convictions or their institutional elaboration. Moreover, these differing conceptions undergird very different understandings of the way law should operate and which priority of group and individual rights should shape it.

Competing Federalisms

Finally, Shah Bano's case raises the question of the character of Indian federalism generally. In sharpening the debate over the rights of communities versus the rights of individual citizens, it raises the question of which legal entities actually constitute the Indian federation. Federalism rests on clear principles of representation whereby territorial collectivities can enter into treaties that bind their members or constituent parts. Indian federalism has by and large arisen within the body of the British empire, for whom the constituent parts were not brought together in treaty (though the princely states were) but by jurisdictional ordering from the center.[73] Thus, there has been no adequate development of a culture of federal association that could legitimate the relative autonomy of groups as well as bind them to common commitments.

In the absence of such a culture of federalism, Indians are thrown back on the involuntary communities of tradition and insularity. The two components of this involuntary culture are caste and religion. These are the involuntary, implicit federalisms of Indian life, against which the centrist federalism (some call it "cooperative federalism") of the constitutional era is a bold but fragile combatant. The question of which kind of federalism shall prevail addresses the fundamental dilemma of Indian constitutionalism and nationhood.

Behind this question of federal order are the profound issues of what constitutes the religious. In particular, what are its institutional forms and what kind of autonomy should they exercise? In order to penetrate these questions further I turn to the final case, that of the United Basel Mission Church and the Church of South India.

Ecclesiology and Constitutional Order: The United Basel Mission Church Case

While Hinduism has always lacked a clear organizational form, Christians in India have worked out elaborate versions of classic Christian ecclesial forms—congregational, presbyteral, and episcopal. The first gives primary authority to the congregation, the second to the elders or ministers, and the third to the bishop. To these basic forms Indian leaders added efforts to reshape the church in terms of the classic Indian notion of the *ashram*—the retreat community for religious development.[74] The Church of South India attempted to integrate these three traditional forms into its constitution of 1947 when it brought together Anglican, British Methodist, and Presbyterian churches. Emerging at the same time as the modern Indian Republic, it has mirrored many of its partner's struggles to develop a truly federal order and viable democratic processes. This struggle for new forms of association and leadership erupted into open litigation when some of the churches founded by the Basel Mission decided to join the CSI in 1961.[75]

These churches had emerged from the missionary efforts of the Basel Mission, founded in 1815 by German and Swiss Protestants on a nondenominational basis to spread the gospel in foreign lands. The mission disavowed "the intention of establishing an Ecclesiastical union resting on a new confession of faith superseding the articles of established churches" and had "no wish to impose upon the congregations collected in heathen countries, by the preaching of the word of God, the creed of any European Church."[76]

The mission began its work on the Malabar coast of India south of Bombay (present Karnataka) in 1834, eventually giving rise to three churches (despite its original intent) that were related to each other through a common synod. In 1905 the Malabar unit of this United Basel Mission Church merged with the South India United Church, which subsequently became a part of the Church of South India in 1947. The Bombay Karnataka unit then joined the CSI. On May 9, 1961, the remaining unit in South Kanara and Coorg voted to join the CSI. This vote was immediately challenged in civil court by a suit brought by four of its members, who claimed to represent the other members of the church.

In order to understand how this ecclesiastical decision could be contested in civil court one must know something about Indian civil law, which was largely taken over from the British. The Code of Civil Procedure (1908) permits temporary injunctions when it is claimed that an action will cause "injury to the plaintiff in relation to any property in dispute in the suit. . . ."[77] Such injury can also encompass the right to worship, including having an unwanted priest forced upon "a section of the community" or a temple.[78]

Though these rules clearly originate in disputes involving Hindu worship, they can be easily extended to other religious groups even though their organization is vastly different. The court accepted the claim that this was a case involving injury to the right to worship. The question was simply whether the action of the church in uniting with the CSI had injured the rights to worship of these four members. The basis of their suit lay in their claim that the liturgy and organization of the CSI were so different from that of the UBMC that they could no longer worship and carry on their religious life as they had in the past.

Specifically, they held that the creedal basis of their church had been altered by excluding Luther's Shorter Catechism from the central role they felt it had had in earlier worship and instruction. Second, the introduction of an episcopal office contradicted their historic commitment to a priesthood of all believers, which entailed a congregational and synodal organization. Third, the vote of the South Kanara and Coorg District Church Council that approved the merger violated its own constitution, since, they held, the district council has no authority to dissolve itself. Finally, the action, in turning over properties to the CSI, violated the purposes of the trust holding them, which were to advance the faith and doctrine of the UBMC.[79]

In its ruling on December 18, 1968, the high court in Mysore ruled against the plaintiffs. After reviewing the documents presented by the parties, the court found that the doctrines and polity of the CSI were not substantively different from those of the UBMC. The plaintiffs appealed to the high court twice before receiving a ruling in 1974 in their favor that indeed the doctrines and order of the two churches were different enough to represent an injury to the right to worship of the aggrieved parties. The defendants, representing the CSI, then appealed this ruling to the Supreme Court, which delivered its judgment in 1988 in favor of the CSI claims and against the original plaintiffs of whom only one was living by the end of the 27-year process.[80]

While unusual for its length and cost, this case is only one of hundreds that have been filed in recent years to block the actions of church bodies and officials, whether in elections, liturgical changes, or policy dispute.[81] These eruptions of litigation originate deep within the legal and religious culture of India. Tracing them out can tell us much about the connection of religion, law, and culture shaping the lives of one-sixth of the world's population.

Clearly, there are always many factors present in church disputes in India—conflicts over language, region, caste, and social status certainly fuel most conflicts to some degree. Within the resolution of such conflicts, however, the courts play a central role. My focus here is on the way the legal system mediates between these social forces as they come to expression in religious struggles and national structures of governance.

The Key Issues

The conflicts underlying the UBMC case centered on the nature of worship as a civil right, on the legal status of the church, and on the conflict between episcopal and democratic orders of governance. From each of these issues radiate ramifications that extend far into Indian life.

Freedom of Worship as a Civil Right

How is it that the right to worship is a civil right in India? Understanding this fact requires further investigation into the popular meaning of religion and the social functions of law. Hinduism and Islam have very little specifically religious organization, whereas Christianity, especially in the Latin forms that arrived beginning in the sixteenth century, has an enormously complex organizational history. For most Indians religion is both all-encompassing—the communal customs of family, caste, and village—and restricted to the ritual actions of the individual. Though these ritual actions (*puja*) are highly traditional, they are usually carried out in an individual fashion in the myriad temples, shrines, and holy places that dot the land. The ability to perform these actions is an inextricable part of one's membership in the community. Failure to perform these acts, especially those revolving around preservation of the male family line, is tantamount to excommunication, to use a western term.

Moreover, freedom is understood in terms of becoming part of an embracing whole—a value rehearsed pervasively and profoundly in family life.

Psychologists like Ashis Nandy and Sudhir Kakar have explored in detail the way children are raised to move from being isolated infants to being part of the extended family, though this is worked out quite differently for boys and girls.[82] Little wonder that one's right to communal membership, when translated out of the communal context into a legal one, becomes a "right to worship." People turn to the courts in order to defend their status in their communal enclaves.

The right to worship thus means the freedom of individuals to maintain their traditions as they appear in the individual worship acts of those within the tradition. It is a kind of "communal individualism" quite different from the associational or institutional individualism characteristic of western religion. The prince or the state exists to maintain this communal order, with its religious dimensions, but this order has historically had very little voluntaristic character.[83]

In Anglo-American culture this freedom of religion has been understood in the context of the idea of voluntary association. Individuals are free to create religious associations, which are in turn free to conduct their internal business, including worship. If members do not abide by the rules of this association, then they can leave it to join or create another more suitable one. In the Indian context of "ascriptive solidarities" freedom of religion is first of all the freedom of the communal groups to maintain themselves in the face of voluntaristic forces. When the legal structure of this argument is severed from its original context, it is then available for use in church struggles that may not have a distinct communal basis, as in the UBMC case.

The British model of religious establishment did little to undermine this pattern in a direct manner. In this respect Anglican and Indian cultures meshed harmoniously. The uniformity of civil law brought by the British ironically enabled these communal needs to be expressed beyond local communities. Translocal organizations such as the church could be the field for claims that originated in the communal culture of the village. Where once the local princes had handled this oversight of the relation between worship and communal status, now the civil law and civil governments had to take over this function. This pattern was further reinforced by the near necessity of civil intervention to reform domestic law and Hindu temple practices (especially to admit former untouchables, though not, it seems, non-Hindus). While governments have generally been wary of intervening in the internal affairs of minority religions, the judges who make up the courts are often steeped in this tradition of benevolent intervention in religion for the sake of public order, which means upholding traditions meaningful to individuals as part of their communal existence. Their jurisprudence is a constant struggle between the ideals dominant in the Constitution and the values of traditional solidarities. Both the Shah Bano and the Basel Mission cases illustrate the major difficulties inherent in this tension.

This function of the law is analogous to the way the political process, especially elections, has transmuted and reorganized the always latent conflicts among caste and religious groups. The political "faction" replaces the commune as the unit of power.[84] The voluntary association becomes the form in which traditional solidarities of caste, kin, and religion can gain a voice in the public processes supported by the Constitution. Whether or not this transformation of biologistic relationships into public coalitions will be able to tame the violent forces of communal warfare or whether these forces will destroy politics is the question of the hour in India.[85]

In the case of the church in India, this combination of religious individualism, communal solidarity, and civil litigation threatens to undermine the church as an institution. Not only do the courts willingly entertain suits enjoining all manner of church actions but these factional conflicts engendered by cultural change also cultivate the spirit of civil litigation of church disputes. In order to remain a self-governing institution the church has to begin cultivating its own internal public life, whether in the way it organizes and conducts its elections or in providing prominent means of internal arbitration and adjudication that members must use as a condition of membership in the church. Rather than assuming an external civil culture that trains its members for church life, it must create an internal civility in the face of intense external forces undermining it. How it is to do this leads to the question of internal governance.

Episcopacy and Democracy

Indian Christians have a love-hate relation with the episcopal forms developed in Europe. One the one hand, these forms appeal to the patriarchal and monarchical forms of governance deeply rooted in Indian culture and history. On the other hand, they are inimical both to the religious individualism of Hindu traditionalism and the culture of democracy developed in the modern era. Though Indian history can attest to some experience with democratic, conciliar, and republican forms of government, most of Indian history has been shaped by monarchical patterns, whether Aryan, Islamic, or European.[86]

Shaped by traditions of raja, Crown, and guru, leaders in both government and church have had to carve out new models for their roles. The traditional roles always assumed that one male "head" must hold all authority in a collective relationship. While the organic model for social relationships militated against a totalitarian monarchy, it did mean that within any social relationship monarchical hierarchy prevailed. The democratic ethos of both Buddhism and modern liberalism is locked in struggle with these traditions of patriarchal monarchy even as it also partakes of them by often restricting access of women to public life.[87]

With this conflicted heritage, leadership roles in the new India were marked by a profound ambiguity in their original constitutional formulations for both the government and the CSI. While both professed allegiance to presidential authority within a council, both have tended toward a centralization of powers in the head. In the civil realm the Nehru-Gandhi dynasty replaced the British Crown. This has included defacto exercise of power as well as ritual ceremonialization. In the CSI the role of bishop has at times tended toward a monarchical episcopacy, only to be undermined by synodal politics and stalemated elections.[88] Formal commitments to conciliar, consensual, and collegial leadership are often overwhelmed by deep parental and monarchical cultural patterns in government as well as religion. In reaction against monarchical centralization, governance in church and state nearly collapses in stalemated factionalism among the lesser heads.

These headship models have often seemed necessary to ensure unity in the face of fissiparous tendencies. At this point, however, both institutions face the task of developing presidential models that evoke local creativity, participation, and decisions rooted both in deeper covenants and in public argument. The Basel Mission struggle was symptomatic of this deeper struggle for appropriate leadership models within a democratic order.

When the CSI formed in 1947, it took over the "constitutional episcopacy" of modern Anglicanism and rejected any of its historic claims to doctrinal status. The plaintiffs from the old UBMC claimed, rightly, that the CSI had taken on episcopacy. This violated their historic commitment to the "priesthood of all believers"—that is, ecclesial democracy. The CSI could claim with equal validity that it did not hold a doctrinal episcopacy, which they thought was the real concern of the UBMC plaintiffs, but a constitutional one embedded in congregational and synodal frameworks. Behind the UBMC suspicions of doctrinal episcopacy lay resistance to the monarchy and hierarchy historically associated with it. In this respect, we do not have a conflict between doctrinal and constitutional episcopacy but between monarchical, patriarchal, and hierarchical forms, on the one hand, and democratic-federal forms, on the other. Both are equally doctrinal and constitutional, but they rest on different theologies and ecclesiologies.

The court ruling, of course, does not touch the wide-ranging cultural issues of governance that are hidden behind episcopacy and democracy. Its purpose was to distinguish between the "religious" dimensions associated with the right to worship and the secular organizational issues. The distinction between doctrinal and constitutional forms of episcopacy gave it the wedge to rule against the UBMC plaintiffs.

Autonomy in Church and State

Both the peculiar communal-individualistic claims to "right to worship" and the way the courts approach church-related litigation threaten the autonomy of the church. With regard to worship rights, the court, indeed the whole society, must thread its way between the volatile fusion of religion and biologically rooted community, on the one hand, and the legitimate claims to institutional religious freedom in a secular state, on the other. If it grants too much autonomy to "religion," it risks reinforcing the religious communalism that can ultimately undermine the separation of religion and government essential for a secular state. If, however, it undermines the self-

governance of religious institutions, it also collapses the institutional pluralism in which separation makes sense. To avoid these perils it must develop
a keener distinction between community and institution, so that religion
becomes primarily an institutional rather than a communal matter. For this
to be effective the peculiar mixture of devotional individualism and communalism behind current theories of the right to worship must be supplanted
by a concept of personal religious freedom, which means the right to join
and to leave religious associations independent of one's communal heritage.
The Constitution promotes an associational individualism quite at odds with
traditional communal individualism, and court rulings express the tension
between them.

The right of these religious associations to govern themselves means that
they must gain some relative independence from state interference. They
need to be able to make decisions according to their own voluntarily
adopted constitutions. When the courts, defending the right to worship of
individuals, contravene their internal decisions, they actively undermine this
capacity for autonomy.

This defense of each individual's right to worship is part of a general
tendency to carry forward the ancient tradition of royal patronage for popular religion. Thus, rather than follow a model of absolute separation, the
state has pursued a pattern of "equal protection," which entails control in
the case of Hinduism and selective interference in the case of the church or
Islam. In both cases the courts and the governments seek to control religious
institutions in order to preserve the traditional religious devotions of the
people.

In light of this traditional conception of religious freedom as the right to
worship as a member of a community, the first step in securing religious
autonomy for institutions has not been to establish a clear case for the independence of religious associations from their communal contexts but to separate their form of religious governance from questions of "faith and doctrine" altogether. Thus, they can be insulated from attack under the right-
to-worship codes.

In the UBMC case the courts could not deal with the question of episcopacy in terms of church governance per se, because this would violate the
scope of their jurisdiction, which was to look only at the "religious" questions of "faith and doctrine." By putting their claim to ecclesial democracy
under the term "priesthood of all believers," the plaintiffs had already sym-
bolized this governance issue as a doctrinal one. While the courts accepted
the attack on episcopacy as a matter of faith and doctrine (thus agreeing
with the original plaintiffs), they then found that episcopacy in the CSI was
indeed not a doctrinal question in the religious sense but a "constitutional"
matter, thus ruling that the right to worship of the plaintiffs had not been
abridged. This argumentation produced at best a conceptual muddle, at
worst a time bomb threatening to explode the institutional meaning of religion necessary to a federal republic.

In the court's jurisprudence questions of religious governance become secular rather than religious questions and therefore cannot be addressed by the court under the civil code. Under the code, the churches do derive a peculiar kind of insulation from intervention by the courts. The unfortunate result of this approach, however, is to weaken the claims for autonomy by religious organizations under doctrines of religious freedom and separation of church and state. The church's claim to autonomy is not a religious claim. It must be taken up under the secular laws of trusts.

Within the trust law the Indian legal system inherited from the British, conflicts over church property have to be adjudicated in terms of their original charters. Thus, conflicts can arise between honoring the charter and honoring the constitutionally authorized decisions of the church for whose use the property exists. Without a strong sense of church autonomy the balance of court decisions can tip in the direction of a strict interpretation of the trust. In the UBMC case, where this was central to the dispute, the outcome of the court ruling ran in favor of the church, but only, it seems, by claiming that no violation of the original trusts could be shown. How the law of trusts and the protection of the autonomy of religious organizations as such will be worked out remains to be seen.

Critical Issues in India's Struggle for Covenantal Publicity

In Europe and America democratic constitutional government in the federal and republican tradition could draw on deeply rooted religious notions of covenant, of church, and of the individual soul. Thus, strong links could develop between religious culture and political structures. The question before us is whether in India an analogous religious culture can be identified that can play a similar role in the development of federal republicanism in that country. Would such analogs exist in Hinduism or in some synthesis of its historic religions, or would it have to rest on the development of a modern "civil religion" rooted in the experiences of the past century? Without some kind of deep legitimation by India's complex and pluralistic religious heritage the Indian political experiment will ultimately fail.

Three critical themes linking the Indian case studies might be able to throw light on this fundamental question. They concern the nature of religion, the form of federalism, and the conception of "the individual" essential to the democratic ideal of citizenship. Exploration of these three themes leads to questions of reconciliation and trustworthy participation linked to this study's underlying concept of covenantal publicity.

Religion: Communal, Associational, Institutional

All three cases are affected decisively by the conception of religion informing the protagonists and the structure of constitutional law. But "religion" is clearly not a homogeneous phenomenon nor an unequivocal concept. As a term it is first of all an abstraction that focuses on certain common traits in human behavior and thought. As a collection of practices it takes as many forms as there are histories of the groups displaying a "religion."

These cases lift up the importance of making distinctions among religions in terms of their institutional form. In particular, these conflicts stress the difference between religion as an associational, an institutional, and a communal pattern of group life. Associational religion is established through the voluntary compact of believers. It produces what Americans call "denominations." Institutional religion has associational aspects but depends as much on support from endowments, governments, and other long-standing institutions in the society. The religious "public corporations" in Germany represent this kind of religion. Finally, in India we have seen religion as one dimension of a total community. Usually and most importantly, this is a local community, bound together in bio- and geo-piety. Derivatively, however, it comes to take on a nongeographical form as members migrate to other places. It then moves in the associational or even institutional direction.

Each of the forms of religion, then, constitutes an ecclesiology—a pattern of religious organization. Each carries with it quite different implications for the structure of a federal republic. Both federal republican constitutions and secular democratic publics give priority to associational or institutional ecclesiologies. Only then can the state be differentiated from the ultimate loyalties conveyed in religious belief and practice—for the good of public persuasion as well as for the integrity of religious faith. The challenge to traditional Indian religion is to develop institutional forms that can carry the devotion of the past while minimizing its diffuse communal attachments.

For each of these three types the constitutional right to religious freedom or autonomy carries different meanings, as manifested in the three cases. Communal autonomy subordinates individual or even institutional religious claims for the sake of the survival of the community. Taken far enough, it reinforces the religious community as a partner in the federal structure itself, leading to communal representation, constitutional status, and personal religious law. Associational autonomy emphasises the right of the individual as well as the right of the specific association to carry out their religious aims. It claims the right to conversion and proselytization for the sake of the right of individuals to join an association that is "saving" for them. The institutional form, as we saw in Germany, carves out certain prerogatives with government in order to exercise that religion's God-given mission in education, social service, communication, and rituals of the life cycle like puberty, marriage, and death.

Each ecclesiology carries with it a different constitutional claim to its own integrity. Sometimes this may be expressed as "separation" from government, other times as "equal protection," and other times as privileged liberty and access. The federal-republican project itself does not settle the question of how these three expressions of religious autonomy are to be put together.

However, in pressing the claims of public participation, equality, public persuasion, and free association, it does stress the priority of associational forms over the others—a prioritization that will emerge in peculiar form in the American case studies.

The Nature of Federalism

Republican government also requires an adequate federal order so that the many smaller publics required for democratic participation can be linked together in a way that maintains local self-government but also wider economic, military, and political unity. But what kinds of units will constitute this federal order? The traditional Euro-American theories of federalism assumed that it was territorial units that would be represented in broader publics. However, in the Indian situation we see a parallel indigenous "federalism" of caste, commune, language, and religion. That is, the treatylike voluntary agreements of federalism are challenged by relatively involuntary units bonded together by traditions, genetic makeup, and communal identity. This indigenous or instinctive "federalism" cannot be simply ignored, but neither can it become the actual frame for republican order. These two orders of federalism have to be carefully distinguished if the republican experiment is to flourish.

More specifically, how shall the relatively communal partners to this indigenous or informal federalism take on appropriate public forms so that they can be represented in constitutional publics? How can the constitutional order require procedures of election, civil discourse, equal voting rights, and free association of them without infringing on their strictly religious autonomy? How, finally, can the civil process of public argument press communal groups to move from bonds of ascription, kinship, and bio-piety to bonds of compact, covenant, contract, and constitution without destroying the cultural glue that holds citizens together in the habits of their daily interaction? Not only do the two orders of federalism have to be distinguished but they also have to be integrated for the sake of the formation of wider publics and more embracing constitutions.

Indian federalism has always been faced with the question: Can republicanism and its federal order take root through imposition from the top? This top-down, or centrist, federalism is the heritage of British rule incorporated into the Constitution of 1950. In order to incorporate the democratic impulses in federalism, that is, federalism from below, people have to gain political identity and participation. At the beginning of this process their politicization takes the form of received caste, communal, and religious orders. The question before us is whether the dynamics of politics within the federal frame can transmute these patterns of group action into a more voluntaristic political life in which overlapping memberships in various interest groups cancel out the communal patterns.

Relating these two forms of federalism within a constellation of publics finally requires, as Donald Smith intoned 30 years ago, an appropriate civil religion. From the standpoint of the framework of covenantal publicity it means that the emerging public life of India has to create increasingly dense webs of covenantal obligation among the people in order to sustain their republican aspirations. Taking up the formula set forth in chapter 1 we need to see how the classic partners of God, people, and land might figure in such a deep covenant.

The intense religious plurality of India originally led people like Nehru to emphasise even more the necessity of a secular state. The kind of reference to God that appears in the Preamble to the German Fundamental Law, contentious as it may be in the new Germany, would have been constitutional suicide in India. However, a pure secularism has also proven to be impossible, both because of the mechanisms of compensatory discrimination and because the republic needs religious legitimation. Hindu nationalists have appealed to traditional bio-piety and geo-piety on a grand scale, with their invocation of "Mother India" and the bond between people, land, and their god of origin. The symbol of "Mother India" can be transmuted to help legitimate the deep ecological concerns within an increasingly polluted and exploited environment. The problem with this tight bond is that there is no covenantal freedom for others to enter "the family" voluntarily or even to associate for the sake of alternative ultimate visions. The god of land, biology, and parental care must be augmented or civilly contested by the gods of law and covenantal association. One reason Indian political life may be so contentious today is that this contest for an underlying civil covenant, with its religious roots, is taking place in the ordinary publics of legislation and election.

Finally, in the struggle over a deeper Indian covenant we see the contrast between hierarchical and egalitarian covenantal dynamics. A more hierarchical covenant, led by a transcendent and immutable God, may emphasise the unity of the people but imperils the plurality of public association out of which comes the web of "horizontal covenants" typical of a more confederal polity. Both dimensions of a full covenant are needed, but without fuller development of public life the covenantal dynamic itself will be drawn back into the pieties of land and kinship.

Concept of the Individual

Voluntary patterns of association require the development of individual autonomy. But what kind of individual does this mean? The individual as citizen lies at the center of the federal-republican tradition. While autonomy in the West is often reduced to merely expressive or private individualism, it also sees the person as one capable of promissory commitments—as covenant partner or associationalist. In India, however, this ideal competes with that of individual as devotee and as member of a community. At the voluntaristic end of the spectrum it competes with the individual as entrepreneur. We are familiar with how the entrepreneurial individualism of the market competes with citizenship ideals, but the communal individualism of the devotee and the saint is less familiar to us. It is this latter kind of individualism that lies at the heart of the defense of the right to worship and its associated invasion of any institutional conceptions of religion.[89] How Indian constitutionalism can steer between the extremes of entrepreneurial and traditional individualism is one of the crucial issues raised in this study.

The status of women as citizens emerges at the center of this cultural struggle. Without their exercise of public voice and vote the democratic features of the emerging Indian polity will never find full flower. This is not merely because a vast number of adults will not be able to participate in public life but because the patriarchal orders at the heart of much of Indian communalism will be strengthened in their nondemocratic control of the basic units of Indian society—family, community, village, and religious life. Both the federal as well as the democratic dimensions of the republic will be seriously undermined. In Germany public life and the conception of federalism had to move beyond the classic image of the Landesherr. In India the same struggle must move beyond the image of the raja who reigns as a god in the family and as a lord in the wider household and empire of the land.

Toward Covenantal Trustworthiness

Winding through these three themes is the question of how to build a broad enough pattern of mutual trust to enable public debate to function in order to achieve points of consensus and agreement. How can people from various castes be reconciled enough to enable them to participate in a common public life? How can men and women find a public reconciliation as equal citizens? How can different groups, regions, and communities be reconciled in a common constitution? These are the kinds of questions that press us to the underlying religious questions of covenantal culture and public participation.

Reconciliation of estranged groups is necessary for a federal republic that seeks widespread democratic participation. Clearly, men and women have to struggle along tortured paths—both conscious and unconscious—to find a new pattern of reconciliation in light of their age-old patterns of dependency and subordination. Likewise, and more explicitly, members of castes, tribes, and language groups need to come to terms with the past injustices that have created the present disparities hindering democratic life. The project of compensatory discrimination begun in 1950 has tried to re-create some "original position" of equality through policies of job and electoral reservation, scholarships, and aid to minorities. However, in many cases these policies have simply created a framework for win-lose interest group politics or intracaste inequities in which only the "advanced classes" of the backward groups can gain any benefits. The process of redeeming the past by creating a new future demands more than a vast system of entitlements and state patronage. It also means raising the welfare of the whole, that is, attending to the common good, whether it is literacy (especially for women), clean water, ecological conservation, or land use policies.

Without this broader conception of reconciliation between historically aggrieved groups and the heirs of their oppressors, the results will not be a new common life but a descent into sheer conflict among ancient adversaries. Here the questions of justice posed by Ambedkar return once again to the concerns of Gandhi and Nehru for a holistic vision and a sense of shared resources in order to lead India out of its bondage into a new order of participation and mutual obligation.

We have seen in the Indian cases some themes already raised by the German experience, though with new facets, as well as themes quite foreign to the West. With this refined focus we may now be able to move to the American experience with somewhat new eyes to explore what is both one of the oldest and also one of the youngest struggles for public life within a federal order.

Four

Sacred Lands and Religious Assemblies in America

Germans and Indians have struggled for a more adequate federal formation of their public life within an ancient heritage of monarchy and traditional order. Their experiences have lifted up for us the importance of independent ecclesial forms for generating the dynamic of publicity, the need for reconciliation of past injustice in order to cultivate trust and participation, and the power of deep images of divine agency and order for shaping the cultural basis for constitutional order. The constitutional forms and the implicit covenants underlying them are laced by geography and gender. Relationships of peoples to their lands and of men with women powerfully shape the kinds of publics and covenants that can emerge beyond the boundaries of household and parentage.

It was in America that a federal-republican order first unfolded apart from a momentous struggle with traditional orders.[1] This was the New World that was for John Locke the social clearing in which a contractual social order and state could emerge.[2] For many newly constituted peoples in the past two centuries the United States Constitution and American governmental experience have served as a model for their own new world of popular governance, not only in contemporary Germany, India, Vietnam, and Russia but earlier in the federated South America of Simon Bolivar's dreams.[3] However, just as their world could not be reconstructed de novo, so also the American development has not been without its old worlds and its internal contradictions.

The old worlds of Germany and India can already alert us to the deep power of biological appeals and ancient injustices in polluting the waters of new covenant and wider publicity. They also alert us to the delicate interplay between parental care and personal freedom in the sustenance of communities and peoples. As we turn to the American struggle to found and preserve its federal republic, we bring these sensitivities to the effort to understand anew the dynamics of covenantal publicity among a people who have walked for two centuries with talk of biblical covenant, congregational vitality, and federal polities.

Not only do our ideas and forms of faith arise in our histories but our histories also form the way these convictions take root and grow. The plastic of past freedoms congeals in adamantine forms that mold the habits of today. The struggle for covenantal publicity is no exception. The people of the United States have been molded by the dynamics of immigration and slavery as well as by the peculiar voluntarism and mobility possible in this New World. I cannot here dissect with detail and precision the complex history of this republic, even with regard to its pattern of governance. As with the inquiry into Germany and India, I can only identify the key factors shaping the struggle for republican governance within a federal form in this context. I can then proceed to some selected cases where these factors come to focus in our own time.

The Molding of the American Experience

Settlement, Invasion, or Coexistence?

Daniel Elazar has argued that covenantal political orders flower where people have to construct a political order in a new land.[4] This is archetypically true for ancient Israel and, as Donald Akenson has pointed out, continues to play out not only in America but in Northern Ireland, Israel, and South Africa as well.[5] From the standpoint of the covenanting newcomers these are lands to be tamed and settled. For the original inhabitants, who were present in all these cases, the settlement is invasion, dislocation, and extermination. The American case was no different.

On the one side we can see the flourishing of social experiments based on compacts, covenants, contracts, and charters. New polities exploded among a literate people related to each other more by achievement than inheritance. On the other side we see the decimation of over two million native people dispersed among some 700 tribes, lacking common language, literacy, and a technology to match the settlers.

Many of these aboriginal peoples did share, however, long traditions of conciliar governance and confederal organization—the Iroquois Confederacy, an inspiration for the colonial constitutionalists, being only the best known.[6] Kingship apart from military leadership seems to have been limited in scope. Entering into treaty with the newcomers was no departure from ancient custom. With these first agreements, whether for land use on Manhattan or mutual aid in Massachusetts, began the long trail of broken treaties, misunderstood contracts, and changing federal relationships that constitute the history of the relationship between aboriginal and immigrant peoples in America. Covenants and broken covenants are the language of this tragic and brutal encounter. The immigrants' failure to honor agreements with the native peoples constitutes the first of what Robert Bellah has called the broken covenant constituting American history.[7]

The encounter between Europeans and aboriginal Americans also had a religious dimension. European Christians oscillated between respectful admiration of the Americans' customs, so bonded to land and tradition, and a mad zeal to Christianize these "heathen" peoples. With Christianization, of course, at least among the majority of Northern European missionaries, would come literacy, agriculture, and, in short, civilization. This ambivalence has characterized their relationship to the present day and has been parallelled by an equal ambivalence about the nature of the treaty and federative relationships between their governments. The second case study will examine this religious and constitutional legacy through the lens of recent court decisions.

Slavery and Racism

The enslavement and massive importation of Africans overlay this tangle of broken treaties with the aboriginal peoples. The palimpsest of international treaty underlying immigrant relationships with the original inhabitants was reflected in the brutality with which slave masters incorporated Africans into the household economies of plantation and family firm—often under an ideology of paternal rule. The broken treaties on the land mirrored the patriarchal domination of the household of slavery. John Locke's two key ideas of antipatriarchy and solemn compact were both grasped and throttled in the early years of the emerging American people.

Both forms of relationship—treaty and domination—became increasingly embedded in an ideology of racism in the nineteenth century. Plantation slavery was often interpreted by slave owners through the metaphor of the household and parental control, with its parental care as well as abuse. Both the parental discipline, often expressed by the Christian missionary, and the physical abuse, exercised by soldiers, police, masters, and frontiersmen, were soon overtaken by an ideology of racial superiority and destiny nurtured by European cultural leadership. Similarly, the treaty relationships between settler and native were soon infused with the same racist claims. Without a stronger belief in equality grounded in the divine image, covenants and treaties became merely an instrument of domination severable at the will of the stronger party.

Both the domination through treaty relationships and the despotism of slavery found legitimation in biological claims. Simultaneously, the notions of election and vocation historically associated with covenantal ideas were reconstituted within a racial ideology. The democratic experiment launched on American soil began to be extolled as the product of "Anglo-Saxon genius"—something unknown to the Republic's founders. The idea of a people in promissory relationship with God and with each other was reconstructed as a theory of racial identity and superiority. It is this link between covenant, election, and race that leads to the closed societies Donald Akenson has explored elsewhere. Whether their covenantal heritage, along with that of the United States, can be reconstructed along the lines of an open and democratic republic is a question central to this inquiry.

Just as with the native peoples of North America, the churches were at first hesitant to engage in proselytization and conversion of the enslaved Africans. Some church leaders felt that slaves should be freed and repatriated to Africa. While this policy of return yielded such signal accomplishments as the founding of Liberia in the early nineteenth century, the repatriation dream, apart from its marked recrudescence in Marcus Garvey's movement of this century, never seized the imaginations of the majority of Americans, white or black.

The theological obstacle to an alternative policy of conversion and assimilation lay in the meaning of Christian baptism itself, since baptism still bore the mark of social membership from its European history. The key to conversion of slaves lay in stripping baptism of its wider meaning for citizenship. It became a ritual associated with the state of one's soul and psychology. This reinterpretation of baptism actually reversed the earlier reconfiguration of baptism's meaning in European history.[8] There, baptism had become associated with rites of royal consecration. One was anointed with oil just as the kings of David's house. Eventually all baptized people could be seen as heirs of Christ's kingship, eligible to participate in the governance of Christ over their lives. This centuries-long development was crucial to the eventual religious legitimation of democratic government in the seventeenth and eighteenth centuries. English settlers brought it as part of their deep memory, even preserving the kingship of Christ in their soul as they rejected kingship in the political realm. Now the psychologization of baptism that had undergirded democratization was being stripped of its political significance while retaining its psychological, individualistic meaning. This time psychologization of baptism meant renunciation of its meaning for citizenship. Only a fringe group of radicals, abolitionists, and Quakers held on to the connection.

But what about baptism as entry into the church? This indeed had to hold, first in the form of balcony membership for the baptized slaves, whose names can even be found as charter members of mixed race churches but who were in fact second class members—children never to be confirmed in full solely because of a status increasingly grounded in racial arguments. First in the northern states, with Richard Allen's founding of the African Methodist Episcopal Church in 1794, and then after the Civil War, with the founding of separate Baptist denominations, came the full development of a racially segregated ecclesial structure that survives to this day.[9] Within the walls of racism its rich culture has gradually nurtured a unique form of

Christianity that goes far beyond the questions of ecclesiastical distinctions from the other churches.

The voluntary character of religion and church association in the United States has permitted the exfoliation of a profusion of African-American religious forms. Sometimes the European immigrants have tried to control the religious life of the first natives or slave descendants, as with the prohibition of the Indian Ghost Dance in the late nineteenth century or the prohibition of secret gatherings of slaves with their own preachers and conjurers. Other times they have greeted new forms, such as the Nation of Islam among twentieth-century Americans, with watchful suspicion. In any case, religious forms that began in relationships of excruciating domination have come to form part of the pluralism so deeply valued by American culture. It is this pluralism rather than the broken treaties with native Americans and the abusive household of slavery that shaped the governmental forms of the new American republic.

Finally, we cannot overlook how deeply slavery and racism divided religious denominations at the time of the Civil War—divisions, as with the Southern Baptists and American (Northern) Baptists, which have persisted to this day. The more voluntaristic the church, the more it could be divided over slavery and the regional conflict in which it was embedded.[10] Presbyterians, Methodists, and Baptists experienced this division most acutely, but no denomination was immune to it. Within the forms created by slavery, both racial and organizational, distinctive pieties, modes of worship, and organizational culture developed that have had distinctive impact on their environing political culture. The bond between the fundamentalist Southern Baptist Convention of recent years and the emerging conservative Republicanism of the South is only one recent example of this intense interaction.[11]

Pluralism and the Necessity for Federal-Republican Government

From John Locke's standpoint the Americans of the New World were ready for republican governance because they had slipped the fetters of feudal patriarchy. They were not bound in the ascribed statuses of lordship and personal fealty. They were no longer perpetual children in the household of the king but free adults in relationships of promise and consent. While this estate permitted a republican order, it was the actual pluralism of the colonial situation that required the peculiar form of republicanism and federation that arose on American soil.

The linkage of monarchy with despotism that we find in the pamphlets of Thomas Paine and the Declaration of Independence could still find heady response hearkening back to the English civil wars of the seventeenth century. By the end of the eighteenth century, however, even English monarchy was undergoing a slow transition from being a form of rule to being a representative of social cohesion. While Parliament might control taxation and legislation, the monarch would gradually become a kind of "cultural president" legitimating parliamentary acts and representing in some sense the English as a people. It was precisely this link between kingship and the putative kinship of the people that could not survive in the plurality of nationalities present in the colonies from the earliest years, though English descendants have repeatedly tried to create such a conviction through pretense to aristocracy in the South and baronial architecture in the North.

The need to protect the plurality of peoples in America served simultaneously to support restrictions on tyrannical government as well as on the re-creation of kingship, a point that George Washington grasped with fortunate sapience. While he was later seen as father of his country, he subverted any effort to make him a king. Americans would have to be held together entirely by compact, covenant, and constitution. While tribal bonds and the later biological fictions of race might run strongly in the footlights, the promise making of the covenantal tradition rehearsed in a public unconstrained by parental control would form the set and scenery for American governance.

The plurality of "factions," as James Madison called the interest groups of his day, could not and ought not to be contained by appeal to some unifying force, whether king, congress, or religion. Any uniting power could also become tyrannical. Therefore, factionalism needed to be contained within a genuine plurality of countervailing powers, whether in society or in government itself.[12] Authority, rather than being unified like the head of a body, would have to be divided within itself in order to preserve the liberty of the parts—a claim quite inimical to the ancient political and ecclesial belief that governance was like the operations of a human body whose head was either the king or Christ. This division of the polity into separate parts that could be free agents was one side of the coin of covenant circulating in the colonies. The other side, which Madison tended not to stress, was that the only source of unity was the constitution holding these agents in tension with one another, whether it was the states and the national government, the legislative, executive, and judicial branches of government, or the various factions seeking to elect a representative or president. That is to say, a covenantal agreement is to a plurality of free agents what a "head" is to an organism requiring central control. Only by some kind of covenantal association could liberty be balanced with coordination for the public good. Such a conception had been nurtured for 150 years in the towns and assemblies of the British colonies.

Covenantal Association and Federal Governance

Assembly

The colonists came with charters and grants from the English Crown to settle in the New World. From the beginning, with the Mayflower Compact of 1620, they had to devise their own forms of immediate governance as public agreements emerging out of their assemblies, congresses, and conventions.[13] It was these public assemblies rather than any ancestral house that were the stage on which to erect the frame of government. It was public assembly that legitimated the solemn compacts of the people creating their governments. The God who had authorized biblical covenants and feudal oaths, even to the Mayflower Compact and colonial constitutions, began to recede into the consciences of the baptized citizens. The assembly of their witness and consent took over the role of the divine—*vox populi, vox dei.* By 1787 the new federal Constitution had to stand on the basis of its own assemblies of inspiration and consent.

This predilection for public assembly and argument began haltingly, but the principle of voluntary association was unstoppable. The claims of conscience led Roger Williams to oppose the religious establishment of Massachusetts and, in banishment, to establish a free and independent Baptist church in Rhode Island in 1635. The principles of voluntarism and congregational autonomy—that a religious congregation is an assembly of freely covenanted persons—eventually became the dominant form of religious organization in the United States.[14] These congregations would then be federated in various ways to create the "denomination," the peculiarly American form of religious organization distinct from a state-promoted church or a sect on the margins of society. The shape, meaning, and legitimacy of this denominational federalism forms the central question of the "Pacific Homes" case I shall examine shortly.

This congregationalism and denominationalism were entwined with their political twin—the party and the convention.[15] Indeed, the Baptists, at least, called their denominational form a convention rather than a synod, conference, or assembly. The U.S. Constitution, operating within the small-scale assumptions of the colonial period, made no provision for political parties and was even deeply suspicious of them. *The Federalist Papers,* in their apologia for the Constitution of 1787, saw them as one among the many factional elements of society that made a federal order necessary. As Hannah Arendt has pointed out, the Constitution was a mechanism for containing factions rather than for nurturing the assemblies of the people.[16] Even the First Amendment speaks of assemblies in terms of petitioning government—a kind of spontaneous uprising against grievance—rather than as the essential engine of democracy that they actually were. To the constitutionalists, the constructive practices of assembly for generating people's power were not as important as the constitutional constraints against the tyranny they might produce. Even the power of religion, which might possibly control people's passions, was more likely to contribute to factionalism than to the securing of the public good.[17] Better for this purpose to have a plurality of religions than only one to serve as the public conscience.

Covenants, Compacts, and Constitutions

The problem of assembly in both religious organization and civil order was not merely how to curb self-interested factions but how to link the positive energies of local publics with more expansive assemblies. The idea of constitution that had evolved from its covenantal ancestors had increasingly become seen as a mechanism for containing forces that could impel actors and factions into collisions—the famous billiard ball view of reality associated with Newton's physics.[18] What had been lost in this covenantal heritage were the deep emotional bonds between people and the land that nurtured them and the God that evoked their fundamental loyalties.

In order to escape the tendency of covenantal societies toward exclusion and constricting conformity, the liberty of assembly, with its freewheeling conversation, argument, and conflict, had to take center stage in the American drama. This tension of federal order with the republic's democratic expansion erupted in the struggle between New England Federalists, who defended church establishment and a franchise limited to the social elect, and Jeffersonian democrats, who vigorously supported separation of church and state and extension of the franchise to all adult white males (only a harbinger of the slow democratization that would take place over the next 150 years).[19]

Here we see once again a central theme of our inquiry into the federal-republican struggle: how to relate the dynamics of republican assembly and covenantal order. The assumption of this study is that this question is not only the fundamental political question of our era but also one that is deeply tied to basic issues of religious vision and organization. The question of right governance appears in both civil and ecclesial forms. By exploring this question in both spheres, we can come to a richer understanding of what is at stake in the way we respond to it. In the American scene it directs us to the civil questions of how to confirm and extend the publics of free participation and at the same time define appropriately the federal structure in which these publics can be responsible to one another. In the religious sphere it has been a question of how the person "revived" in a spirited convocation can be linked to all other assemblies of like-intentioned believers and, beyond that, how he or she can be linked to people even more distant in their faith visions.

The delicate balance of federal republicanism, both civilly and religiously, came to its definitive test in the Civil War of 1861–65. It was a war about economic power—the plantation versus the factory. It was a war about human domination and exploitation. But first of all it was a war about the meaning of federal order. Does the federation called into existence in 1787–89 have an authority independent of the original constituting states? Or do the constituting states maintain their original sovereignty to establish and maintain the federation? Put religiously, is God with the states or with the union they have created? This has been put as the conflict between "federation" (the union) and "confederation" (the seceding states), a meaningless distinction in early federal theories. More strictly speaking, however, it can also be seen as the difference between a contractualist view in which the interests of the parties have a higher salience, and a covenantalist view, in which God's authorization creates a much more permanent bond. Though the argument was settled by military force, the theoretical arguments over the proper meaning of federal order, of constitutional obligation, and of the relation of covenant to contract continue to the present, most recently in terms of the Republican Party's "Contract with America" and its effort to reorder federal structures.

From the perspective of biblical covenantal thought these American developments evince the loss of agreement about where "God" is a party to national covenant and where "the land" participates in these covenantal bonds. Both of these parties to covenant have been attenuated for the sake of the liberty of assembly and of market. The contractual reciprocities of these two spheres of putatively free and interested agents take precedence over the covenantal bonds with God, the people, and the land—bonds that have so often become tyrannical or exclusive. The present political and religious conflicts in the United States can be construed as efforts to ask the question whether assemblies and markets can exist without a fuller covenantal sense of their fundamental "constitution." Can they exist without the overarching institutionalized commitments that make them possible as well as accountable to other spheres of life, including the natural order? The provision of this overarching sense of covenantal responsibility was originally the province of the churches and religious organizations. However, they too have participated in and been deeply shaped by these wider cultural developments. They bear an ambiguous relationship to wider public life and to this central task.

Ecclesiastical Independence and the Voluntary Church

Disestablishment and Separation

Both the Puritan churches of Massachusetts and the Anglican churches of the southern colonies were established churches supported in part by taxation and enjoying many privileges of public support. While a high degree of toleration of various sects and movements arose within a few decades, state establishment of churches lasted well into the life of the new republic, in spite of the First Amendment's exclusion of religious establishment from the powers of the national congress. Ultimately Thomas Jefferson's argument for a "wall of separation" between religion and government has become the metaphor and the norm for American political culture and constitutional jurisprudence. Even this wall has fissures, with congressional chaplains, military chaplains with officer's rank, and numerous religious symbols in the works of government, including the dollar bill.

The First Amendment of the Constitution's Bill of Rights not only excludes laws "respecting establishment" but also any that would "prohibit the free exercise" of religion. American constitutional jurisprudence must constantly balance these two provisions, so that efforts to remove governmental hindrances to religious activity do not also in some way "establish" it, as when some religious groups claim they need public funding for their schools so they can freely practice a religion commanding such schools. Since the extension of the provisions of the First Amendment to the states in 1940, the Supreme Court has generated an increasing number of decisions involving the relations of religion to governments. Persons and organizations recur to the courts increasingly for resolution of a wide range of disputes, spawning a veritable industry of lawyers, academics, and other experts on "church-state" matters.[20]

The issue of religious separation takes us to the heart of the societal preconditions for a federal republic. The question of a federal-republican order is how to create and nurture public assemblies and how to constitute their internal and external relationships in a network of trustworthy expectations. Both aspects assume a relative differentiation of spheres of life in order to create enough freely chosen alternatives so that people can indeed engage in genuine action and promise making. The First Amendment fosters the differentiation of spheres so crucial to a federal republic and seeks to protect free assemblies from the interventions of coercive forces, whether governmental or social. What neither the First Amendment nor the Constitution does is offer any way to nurture these nongovernmental assemblies or order the way they might contribute to the wider implicit and explicit covenants of public life.[21] In fact, these religious and other voluntary assemblies have done so in a myriad of often unnoticed ways. One of the more celebrated recent forms of this interaction between religion and public order has been in the phenomenon known as American Civil Religion.

The Resonance of Civil Religion

John Locke spun out the lineaments of a contractual civil order within the assumptions of a Christian society. As this new experiment in republican governance developed, especially in a more anticlerical Europe, philosophers like Jean-Jacques Rousseau and later Alexis de Tocqueville emphasized the need for some sort of religious surrogate to undergird the rather frail and pale promises of the emerging constitutional orders. In the 1960s Robert Bellah gave contemporary American content to Rousseau's term "civil religion."[22] Drawing on the symbols and rituals of biblical religion, this American civil religion is nevertheless a distinct religious genus emerging out of the actual traumas and achievements of the new republic. This civil religion includes not only ceremonies like the president's inauguration but holidays, sacred burial grounds, slogans ("In God we trust"), symbols (the flag), and a pledge of allegiance. It has had both lofty aspirations to secure democracy around the world and the mean-spirited jingoism of American "manifest destiny" to dominate the hemisphere.

Bellah actually focused on what we might call the religion of the Constitution—those events, holidays, symbols, and ceremonies that ground the Constitution in more ultimate loyalties and in the history of the American people. This is what the Germans call "Constitution-patriotism." It functions to create and maintain a people whose covenant is crystallized in that

Constitution and the documents that augment it, including Abraham Lincoln's famous "remarks" at Gettysburg and his second inauguration address.[23]

What has become even clearer since Bellah's initiation of this modern discussion is the specificity and even narrowness of the content of this civil religion. Since then other publics have emerged—Native Americans, African Americans, women, Hispanics—who struggle with how or whether they might be included in the pantheon of this constitutional religion. Where are they in this national covenant? How does it legitimate and orient their own assemblies? Moreover, how is the land and the natural order caught up in this net of constitutional promises? Questions like these inform my second case study, on Indian sacred land claims and the status of their governments in the larger American republic.

The Ambiguity of Religion

Just as descendants of the original Americans contest the way their own public life is construed within the republic, so also religious movements and organizations chafe against the established order of normative religion and public order that surrounds the Constitution and its "sacred canopy" of civil religion.[24] Testing these limits is itself part of the story of the American covenant, whether with Roger Williams's expulsion from Massachusetts, the persecution of the Church of Jesus Christ of Latter Day Saints from New York to Missouri to Utah, or the ongoing struggle to define the government of the original inhabitants. In all of these struggles the mainline churches have played roles as dissidents as well as pillars of the existing order.

JINGOISM AND DISSENT.   With respect to the culture of the churches, regardless of their ethnic composition, one can find at one end of the spectrum a complete embrace of the civil religion, either in its cosmopolitan or its jingoist forms. The American flag stands in the sanctuary, the Boy Scouts are celebrated along with the saints, and the difference between the Pledge of Allegiance to the Flag and an affirmation of faith is lost on many.

On the other hand, one can find a fierce sense of opposition over against the established governmental order, not only in millennialist groups that have sprung up in the waning years of the twentieth century but in more modulated forms among Mennonites and other "peace churches" as well as socialist Christians baptized in the fires of opposition to the war in Vietnam.

In part what we see here is the expression of the plurality of positions already evident in the biblical writings, not to mention the histories of various Christian and Jewish traditions. The voluntarist character of American religion allows every one of these seeds to flower without interference from the state. Any effort to embrace these traditions as a systematic whole will inevitably produce deep ambivalence and conflict within any religious group. A second source of deep ambivalence is produced by the very engagement of these traditional groups with American government and its constitutional culture.

AUTONOMY AND ACCOMMODATION.   This second kind of ambivalence emerges from the way the internal traditions of faith and organization in these religious groups both absorb and reject key elements of American governmental order. This ecclesiological ambivalence applies not merely to the so-called fringe movements and churches but, as we shall see, affects even such mainline churches as the Methodists. It is this ambivalence I will focus on in my examination of the Pacific Homes case.

The first form of this ambivalence concerns the role of law and Constitution in defining church order itself. On the one hand, ecclesiastical self-governance (and one must add also the laws of Judaism and Islam) seeks to be considered as part of "free exercise." Not only beliefs and private practices but the very autonomy of the religious organization legitimates itself by appeal to God. At the very least, argue the churches, the First Amendment ought to protect this claim. Although this free exercise clause seems to parallel closely the historic admonition to "obey God rather than men" (Acts 5:29), the churches have almost always yielded to the US Supreme Court the legitimate authority to adjudicate conflicts between church and government, rather than go to jail as did St. Paul on several occasions. In exchange for this favor, as we shall see, the court always places hedges about free exercise, since it is only one among many rights to be adjudicated in the society. Thus, what is in contention is not so much the existence of the wall of separation but whether civil or ecclesiastical courts get to define where the wall stands and what people can do on the ecclesial side of it. It is a question of jurisdiction, which is in turn a question of how the various institutional actors in the society will be obligated toward one another. It is a question of deep cultural covenant and federal public order.

The second form of this ambivalence emerges in the relation between symbols of feudal monarchy and those of democracy, a cultural warfare that was ostensibly settled with the Declaration of Independence, the acceptance of the Constitution, and Washington's rejection of kingship. However, monarchy had been the bridge symbolism between traditional Christianity and political order for over 1,500 years. It dominates key elements of the Bible as well as the historic liturgies of the churches. What was to be done with it? How could Christians be monarchists at worship and democratic citizens of a republic the rest of the week?

The initial response to this dilemma, followed by many American Christians in the early days of the republic, was Deism, in which God was shorn of political attributes and construed as a God of nature and nature's laws and as the Maker of the great mechanism of the universe. While certain strands of this effort persevered into our own time, most notably in Unitarianism, the Romantic reaction to the excesses of the French Revolution and the revivalist upsurge of personal and charismatic religion stimulated by Methodists and Baptists reinstituted traditional symbols of God's rule, this time not as political symbols but as symbols of psychological and familial order. The individualism stimulated by a pluralist and voluntarist society required, especially in the absence of parental governance, an internal king to rule the passions and shape people's understanding of their best interests. Without external covenants to constrain the market and the assembly, an internal one would have to be installed. This was the role of revival, moral uplift, and settled worship. It was also the role of family in the social order promoted by the civilizing churches.[25]

With this uneasy truce the churches were able to preserve their monarchical symbols of God, Christ, and Christian life within a republican and democratic culture. They did this, of course, at the cost of severing the conversation between political theory and theology, not to mention ecclesiology, especially at the juncture between their covenantal and conciliar traditions and the development of American federalism or political assembly. The role of Christian symbols and theory, not to mention practice, was motivational and educational rather than structural.[26]

Despite this embrace of feudal and patriarchal culture in worship and spirituality, the churches have practiced in their ecclesial order patterns of governance much closer to those of the federal republic than to the English feudalism embedded in their worship. The Anglicans were especially affected by the Revolution. Renaming themselves "Protestant Episcopals," they ended up granting virtual congregational autonomy to their parishes. With much difficulty, the Roman Catholic hierarchy was able to beat back a strong lay trustee movement in the nineteenth century only to have it reemerge in different forms after the Second Vatican Council.[27]

As a result, across the wide spectrum of denominations runs a deep ambivalence about the relation of their church practices to the faith they rehearse symbolically. Just as the wider social order does not know how to relate parental ordering of people's welfare to their political rights as citizens, so the churches also have difficulty integrating the two historic principles of patriarchy and baptismal democracy in their own life.

Summary

This quick review of key themes in American history has focused on the existence of several peoples struggling for identity and participation within the same land governed by the U.S. Constitution. Both the dynamics of public assembly and covenantal order have been deeply shaped by the cultural currents of racism and of relations to the original inhabitants of the land, and by the forms and patterns of religious life. Moreover, the embrace of covenantal association and the rejection of patriarchal domination have deeply shaped the emergence of the federal republic within the conflicts over slavery, race, and subjugation of the aboriginal peoples in many ambiguous ways.

These themes may seem very abstract and diffuse, but in fact they have very particular bite in the lives of people. This bite is frequently conveyed through the actions of the courts of the land as they seek to adjudicate between the contradictory impulses of the constitutional order and of American life. It is only by exploring this specificity that we can then return to a genuinely comparative reflection on the dynamics of federal republicanism in various cultural contexts.

First, I shall turn to a case in the seeming mainstream of American life, involving what some people call the quintessential American church—Methodism.[28] Here we shall see from the center, as it were, some deep tensions over the meaning of federalism, public action, and religion. Our second case takes us in some sense "over the boundary"—to American Indian sacred land claims. Here we see from another angle a deep contest over the character of federalism, treaty, and covenant—with one's God, with the land, and with the meaning of being a "people."[29] We also gain some perspective on what it means to say that ecclesiology is central to the modern republican notion of liberty within a federal polity.

Methodism and the Quandaries of Republican Federation: The Pacific Homes Case

Since 1912 church organizations in southern California that later became part of the United Methodist Church had sponsored a number of nursing and retirement homes as part of their charitable mission.[30] These homes, including seven residential centers and seven convalescent hospitals, had by 1975 come to serve about 1,700 people under the corporate name of Pacific Homes, a nonprofit corporation created in 1929. The board of directors of Pacific Homes was elected annually by the Pacific and Southwest Annual Conference of the United Methodist Church.

Beginning in the late 1960s Pacific Homes began to encounter severe financial difficulties because the costs of care steadily exceeded the funds generated by the "life care" payment system, according to which retirees prepaid their lifetime care with a lump sum fixed on entry into the Homes. Increase in longevity of the population and sharp inflation of costs made this arrangement increasingly difficult. The Annual Conference arranged and guaranteed several loans for the Homes and finally appointed a "crisis management team" to reorganize the Homes and convert to a pay-as-you-go system over an extended period of time.

By 1976 the conference agreed to subsidize the Homes in the amount of $5 million over a nine-year period to bring them through this reorganization. However, the state of California, where the Homes are incorporated, refused to approve this conversion plan. As a result, Pacific Homes had to declare bankruptcy in 1977. Although 91% of the residents voted to accept a bankruptcy plan proposed by the management team to enable Pacific Homes to regain viability, two class action suits brought on behalf of approximately 150 of the residents blocked this arrangement. These two suits sought to hold not only the Pacific Homes corporation but various United Methodist entities and "The United Methodist Church" itself responsible for claims totaling $366 million. Subsequent suits against not only Methodist-related entities but also individuals involved in the administration of Pacific Homes brought the total to over $600 million.

Even though there is no legally incorporated body called "The United Methodist Church," plaintiffs sought to sue it as an "unincorporated association," a procedure under California law to give legal personality to groups who act like an incorporated association if they have a common purpose and "function under a common name under circumstances where fairness requires the group be recognized as a legal entity. Fairness includes those situations where persons dealing with the association contend their legal rights have been violated."[31] By breaking down the distinction between formally incorporated and unincorporated groups, courts had enabled people to sue labor unions, political parties, clubs, lodges, and churches with greater ease. Indeed, under the California definition the mere allegation of legal injury seemed to be enough to establish this corporate persona for an association.

As noted in various documents related to the case, no religious denomination as such had ever been held to be a jural entity liable to suit apart from its various incorporated units. Not even the Roman Catholic Church, with its purported hierarchy of command from the Vatican to the local parish, had been so treated. Because of the landmark character of the case, the National Council of Churches filed a brief amicus curiae with the defendants, and the case received extensive national coverage.

The Trial Court: Free Exercise vs. Ecclesial Corporality

The California trial court held that the UMC was not a jural body that can be held liable for the acts of its purported agents. The court accepted the church's argument that there is no central representative for "the United Methodist Church," much less a chief executive officer who could be a principal directing the activities of UMC "agents" around the world. The court held that the UMC was a "spiritual confederation" held together by shared beliefs. The many entities holding this common name and sharing adherence to the United Methodist *Book of Discipline* did not compose either a single jural body or an unincorporated association amenable to suit. Most importantly, treating churches like the UMC as simply another corporate body would violate First Amendment protections for religion.

Arguing from the standpoint of religious free exercise, the trial court judge, Ross G. Tharp, wrote:

A contrary ruling would effectively destroy Methodism in this country, and would have a chilling effect on all churches and religious movements by inhibiting the free association of persons of similar religious beliefs. If all members of a particular faith were to be held personally liable for the transgressions of their fellow churchmen, church pews would soon be empty and the pulpits of America silent.[32]

In short, constitutional protection of religion took precedence over the ordinary claims of liability.

The Appeals Court: Market Fairness vs. Freedom of Religion

The Fourth District Court of Appeals in California reversed this ruling, holding that such First Amendment protection gave churches an "unfair" advantage in "commercial affairs" such as nursing homes.[33] This claim rested on the courts' previous development of a doctrine of "neutral principles" by which to treat the "secular" aspects of religious and non-religious corporations which and contracts alike. In applying these "neutral principles" to the UMC the court argued that the UMC did not differ significantly from other corporations that carryied on the same activities. To give the church special consideration might even violate the First Amendment's prohibition of the establishment of religion. Upon removing this veil of protection for the UMC, the court then went on to examine its internal organization to find that it was indeed a corporate hierarchy that could be sued as a "principal" responsible for the actions of its "agent," in this case Pacific Homes, Inc.

To make this case for hierarchical agency, the court argued that "the Council of Bishops is equivalent to the board of directors of UMC." Quoting from the UMC *Book of Discipline,* the court lifted up the statement: "[The] Council of Bishops is thus the corporate expression of episcopal leadership in the Church" overseeing "the spiritual and temporal affairs of the whole Church."[34] In line with this reasoning the plaintiffs had indeed served their court summons and complaint to a former president of the council, who then claimed that he could not speak as a representative of the United Methodist Church—something only the quadrennial General Conference can do. Since this General Conference, as a legislative body, does not exist between sessions, the court looked to the Council of Bishops as its interim executive representative, in short, as its "board of directors," despite the *Book of Discipline*'s distribution of powers to a variety of bodies and agencies.

Drawing on corporate analogies, the court said in addition:

> It [UMC] is hierarchical; the 43,000 local churches and 114 Annual Conferences are governed through the structure described by the Book of Discipline of the United Methodist Church (Discipline). In United Methodism "the local church is a part of the whole body of the general church and is subject to the higher authority of the organization and its laws and regulations."[35]

The appeals court's argument thus drew on corporate models of executive authority to construe both the legislative and episcopal functions of the church. Having done this it could simply assert that the various parts of the whole UMC were agents of each other and mutually liable. To do otherwise would be unfair to similar corporate actors. In the court's view, any preferential treatment to religion, especially to treat it differently in civil law because of its own religious self-understanding, would do more injury to the establishment clause than to the free exercise clause. Moreover, it would provide a shield under which unscrupulous and fraudulent operators could seek religious immunity from lawsuits. The Pacific Homes case did not present any religious activities to the court but only commercial activities conducted by a religious body. Such secular activities had to comply fully with ordinary civil law.

Church defendants appealed to the U.S. Supreme Court to render a final verdict on its suability, but the court refused to do so on technical grounds. Fearing an even more ruinous siege of litigation the Pacific and Southwest Conference settled with the plaintiffs out of court for $21 million, not to mention legal costs of over $4 million to the conference and national agencies of the church also involved in the suits. Various conferences and agencies of the UMC loaned the conference funds to make these settlement payments.

As a result, every entity within the UMC "connection" had to take steps to establish "firewalls" to limit the liability of the entities constituting the entire denomination for the actions of its constituent parts.[36] Such firewalls called into question the nature of "connection" among conferences, agencies, and local churches.

One of the most striking effects of the Pacific Homes cases was to lead the Church's General Conference in 1984 to change the *Book of Discipline* so that the Council of Bishops, rather than being the "corporate" expression of episcopal leadership in the church, as cited by the Barr court, would now be the "collegial" expression of that leadership.[37] The language of corporate unity was replaced by that of cooperation among independent superintendents overseeing the work of the ministers—something that may have been more congenial to John Wesley's intention but nevertheless marked a change of course among United Methodists with regard to their conception of episcopacy.

The California appeals court ruling presently stands as an anomaly, and the U.S. Supreme Court has never issued a ruling that would settle the underlying constitutional issues. While courts in at least nine states subsequently dismissed suits brought against the denomination as a whole, suits of this kind continue to plague religious organizations.[38] The Pacific Homes decisions lie beneath the legal sands like a land mine. Religious bodies seek to restructure themselves to deal with possible liability suits, even if these moves distort their own theological understanding, and spend increasing time and money to defend themselves from liability suits rather than advance their mission.

Church and State: Reshaping the Agenda

This complex and costly legal battle serves as a stethoscope that can enable us to hear deep internal dynamics in the relationships between religious and civil constitutional forms in American culture. As we have seen, the litigation itself revolved around the tension between the establishment and the free exercise of religion, the legal standing of churches and their associations, and the competence of the civil courts to construe questions of church law and ecclesiology. These issues lead us first to questions of the role of religious liberty in strengthening the differentiation and plurality necessary for a vital republic. Secondly, they lead us to questions of the integrity of a church's ecclesiology within a society characterized by federal-republican order and market corporatism. The societal tension between markets and publics finds its religious expression in the United Methodist quandary over its organizational nature. This struggle brings to focus many of the tensions between ecclesiology and constitutional order in American society. I now turn to these wider issues revolving around the struggles of this "quintessential American denomination" for an appropriate place in American public life.

The Shifting Context of Religious Liberty

UMC authorities had argued the church's case not only on the grounds of sheer organizational structure but also as a case of autonomy and free exercise for religious groups whose organizational self-understanding should be protected from reinterpretation by a civil court. Such an insulation of internal church decisions was well grounded in constitutional law. A long series of legal precedents had confirmed that civil courts cannot interfere in internal church disputes, even when it appears that church authorities have acted in violation of their own established procedures.[39] There simply is no "higher court" to adjudicate theological matters.

However, this legal tradition was carved out largely in the face of governmental intrusions on religion. Liability suits now force the court to use these traditions in a radically different direction—a new context of consumer protection and marketplace performance. A church's dealings with an external marketplace are quite different from internal relationships historically insulated from court interference. In external matters the appeals court, and in a related case the U.S. Supreme Court, held that its arm of adjudication can be long indeed.[40] This change demands not only legal reinterpretation but ecclesiological rethinking as well.

The Challenge to Ecclesiological Integrity

Ironically, because of this assumed veil of religious protection, the UMC pleadings did not go into the actual theological grounds for the church's ecclesiological self-understanding. In fact, behind these claims lay both ancient traditions and ecclesiological confusion. This involves the conception of church and of the relations among its parts.

The UMC reflects the confluence of two ecclesiological traditions. The first, typical of the medieval church and the Anglican church that originally cradled the Methodist movement, focuses on the church in terms of the language of "bodies" and corporation. The other, which reflects the primitive church and the free-spirited revivalism of the early Republic, is rooted in the language of assemblies, councils, conferences, convocations, associations, and federations.[41] First let us follow the thread of "body thinking" about organization in this story of litigation.

The Church as a Corporate Entity

In the words of the body tradition, the church is "the Body of Christ" in two ways—as a spiritual or mystical body, with its unity in the resurrected Christ, and as a temporal body in which it is institutionalized for ordinary life among other worldly institutions. Language attaching to its life as a mystical body—corporate unity, common purpose, one baptism and faith, etc.—reflects this transcendent dimension of the church's ultimate character. This language of unity reflects the unity of its source in Jesus Christ and its anticipated unity in the consummation of all things at the end of history.

The church as a temporal, or secular, body takes on various institutional forms depending on history, culture, and circumstances of law and economics. This is, in this tradition, the continuing incarnation of Christ. The seeming fragmented character of this corporality is not necessarily a corruption of the mystical body but the form of its work in the world. The church's factual brokenness continues the cruciform brokenness of Jesus Christ. How these two ecclesial bodies—temporal and spiritual, visible and invisible, broken and consummated—are related has ignited a great deal of theological controversy over the centuries.

Despite these distinctions, however, the church's "temporal" body is not severable from its "spiritual" body. Both constitute the one "Body of Christ." Its unity is defended theologically by appeal to the doctrine of the Incarnation of God in Christ—a unity of divine and human elements. Its organizational form is in some sense an expression of its spiritual body and is not irrelevant to its existence as the "body" of Christ. Thus, the "religion" of which the First Amendment speaks must cover both aspects of this integrated "body." Within this tradition, the Methodist "connection" could not be merely otherworldly. It had to have real presence in the world of human action. But, the church argued, the real presence of this connection did not necessarily have an ordinary legal form. There is a real arena of human activity—indeed, the most important kind of public activity—that exists apart from civil law. Such a claim has implications for our understanding of the free publics that constitute any federal-republican order.

Without this claim concerning both "bodies" of Christ the Christian churches could not have created the *institutional* difference between religious and political spheres that has become fundamental to the civil government of republics. Government, including the courts of civil law, operates within a limited sphere. In the republican tradition that limit is posed by free aggregations of citizens—the publics of their conversation. The religious impetus behind this distinction was presented by the claim that the church—the ekklesia—is a peculiar public guided directly by the Holy Spirit. These free publics, grounded in an authority preceding the civil constitution, were both real actors in society and transcendent bodies. Severing that tie between real public presence and transcendent authority by disconnecting the UMC's self-understanding from its organizational form would have removed a theoretical keystone for this entire republican tradition of limited government. The autonomy of the church's public grounds the autonomy of public life over against governments, providing both their ground of legitimation and the critical basis for their reform. The trial court, standing in the mainstream of constitutional interpretation, refused to challenge this principle.

Like many in the tradition of corporate ecclesiology, Methodists had tended to focus this free public, at least in major part, in the *episcopal* office. The bishop in some sense represents the "head" of the church universal, who is present through the Holy Spirit. Indeed, many of the arguments in this case agreed on the use of language of body and corporation to describe the organizational issues at stake. The *Discipline* drew on this language in describing the Council of Bishops as the *corporate* expression of leadership in the church. In the episcopal heritage behind United Methodism this language refers to the way Christ is really and truly present through the teaching and general pastoral oversight (the root of the word *episcopal*) of the bishops. It is the way the mind of Christ really has a body among us. But the control of this body through the episcopal representative is essentially a matter of persuasion seeking the assent of faith rather than a command seeking automatic obedience. The appeals court, however, seized on this corporal language within the framework of contemporary business enterprise to argue that the Council of Bishops, with its president, is the chief executive organ of the church. Corporate leadership, rather than being a means of inspiring an assembly of faith, was seen as the command structure for a bureaucratic organization.

The Body of Christ from Public to Market

The appeals court thus followed the logic of corporate thinking in another direction—toward the marketplace of hierarchical business corporations rather than the assemblies of church and state. The decision of the appeals court devolved upon two crucial moves, one that reduces a church's ecclesiology to a choice between "hierarchical" and "congregational" forms, and the other that abridges distinctions among institutional arenas. The first move lifts up the difference between the ecclesiologies of body and those of public assembly. The second move leads us to questions of social pluralism central to federalism and public life.

In order to hold the entire denomination liable in the suit, the plaintiffs had to argue that it was a "hierarchical" denomination with a central principal agent, to which all subordinate agents were responsible. Drawing on corporatist language in the UMC *Book of Discipline* (1976) and seeing in the term "connectional" a hierarchical principal, the appeals court agreed with the plaintiffs' claim.

The court's division of churches into either "hierarchical" or "congregational" forms derives from an 1872 ruling by the U.S. Supreme Court in the case of *Watson v. Jones.* [42] That case arose from a struggle between two factions that emerged among Presbyterians in Kentucky at the end of the Civil War. One faction supported the decision of the Presbyterian General Assembly calling for repentance both of the sin of slavery and of the crime of rebellion against the federal government as conditions for ministerial or missionary standing. The other faction opposed this ruling and sought control of a local congregation in which to promulgate their views. In microcosm, it was the collision of slavery, federal order, and church autonomy.

The court ruled in favor of the Presbyterian General Assembly on two grounds. One was the unquestioned right of religious bodies to govern themselves without civil interference. The other rested on the court's identification of three forms in which such disputes need to be adjudicated. The first, hearkening back to the English law that also lay behind the Basel Mission Case in India, asks whether the church's property results from a trust that specifies the intent of the original donor. Those who most closely seek to administer that trust then have rightful claim to the property. The problem with such an approach is that it draws the courts into theological examinations in order to assess the meaning of the original trust. Such a theological function for the court would eventually erode the distinction between civil and religious spheres. Republican governance, with its inherent plurality of all kinds of expression, ought not go down that road, argued the court at that time.

The United Methodist Church, however, in keeping with this old English tradition and adapting it to the American civil environment, had explicitly construed its entire property arrangement in terms of trusts. All property under the United Methodist name is held "in trust for The United Methodist Church" to "be used, kept, and maintained as a place of divine worship of the United Methodist ministry and members of The United Methodist Church." [43] Such a web of trusts is what many Methodists mean today by calling their church a "connectional" church. That such a "connectionalism" is itself a complex and ambiguous formulation is a matter I will return to shortly. Because American civil law since *Watson v. Jones* has largely chosen not to pursue the trust arrangement for settling church disputes, courts have not developed sensitivity to the intricate meanings of this trust connectionalism and its relation to other, quite different ecclesiastical forms. What indeed does it mean to hold property "in trust" for the United Methodist Church if such a person, real or fictional, has no address and cannot appear in court? Furthermore, how do you take some scalpel of "neutral principles" to separate out the theological and the "secular" meanings of the trust? Such questions lay at the heart of the Pacific Homes cases.

The second form cited in *Watson v. Jones* involved congregations that are "strictly independent of other ecclesiastical associations" and owe "no fealty or obligation to any higher authority." Such cases can be resolved "by the ordinary principles which govern voluntary associations"—majority vote of the members or other procedures previously defined by the association. Because of the seemingly clean character of this ecclesial type within American law, it actually functions as the normative case.[44] Just as entrepreneurial corporatism is the normative type of American business, so is congregationalism the normative form of religion. To go beyond pure congregationalism for the sake of the cosmic spiritual unity of the church as the Body of Christ is to risk unceasing lawsuits in a litigious world.

The third form is one in which the conflicted group "is but a subordinate member of some general church organization in which there are superior ecclesiastical tribunals with a general and ultimate power of control more or less complete in some supreme judicatory over the whole membership of that general organization." In this case, the decisions of the highest judicial organ must be respected by the court. The decision in *Watson v. Jones* was the keystone for all subsequent honoring of ecclesiastical autonomy. However, it bore within it the simplistic ecclesiological distinction that bedeviled the Pacific Homes cases.

The court in *Watson* did not in fact use the term "hierarchy." Moreover, it focused on the judicial appeals process within a religious organization rather than its line of executive command. In this sense, it was working within the world of federalism more than corporatism. However, by the time we reach the Pacific Homes cases we find that the term "hierarchy" has been used to define such third types, possibly because of the use of that term in the context of priestly governance in cases involving the Orthodox Church.[45] Moreover, the hierarchy dealt with in those cases concerned not merely judicial appeals within a church but control over employment and property—typical concerns of a bureaucratic corporation.

The key turning point in this line of judicial reasoning is this: When "hierarchy" becomes conflated with the corporate forms of organization typical of American business firms, and when nonprofit organizations are interpreted in terms of for-profit organizations, then depiction of a religious organization as "hierarchical" departs from the effort to defend church autonomy over against the courts and becomes an effort to treat churches the same as other organizations engaged in commercial affairs. All of this is done in the name of fairness and justice with regard to the claims of persons against church-related agencies. Here we have moved from disputes between factions within organizations to those between church authorities and their "customers" or "clients," conceived in terms of business life. This business or market model of religion has worked to overturn the historic immunity to suit enjoyed by religious and charitable organizations. No longer do they represent a public or transcendent purpose rooted in a people's common good. They are treated like one interested party among others, all competing for the allegiance of free individuals in the marketplace.

The erosion of institutional differentiation implied in the appeals court's reasoning involves not merely piercing the wall of separation between religion and government by removing free exercise protection. More broadly, it involves reducing the difference between religion and business, between an ordinary commercial enterprise and a church. From the standpoint of business law, enterprises are either "for profit" or "not for profit." There is no third category peculiar to religion, as is the case for instance in Germany, where specific "public law" governs church organization and finance. "Fairness," which here means the universal application of laws arising out of commercial operations, means that one must subject all religious operations that look like commercial affairs (such as almost any charitable enterprise involving money) to the same law. Here we see that the struggle for differentiation of religion from government has been replaced by the struggle to differentiate religion from business. This is a very different struggle for differentiation from that in India, where kinship and religion are so tightly intertwined, or in Germany, with its historic ties between church and state.

Within this context of claims by "customers" and "clients" against church agencies, the formulation of *Watson v. Jones* becomes a question of who possesses liability within a complex church organization rather than who gets to decide church disputes. If the church is "congregational," then liability stops with the congregation. However, if it is "hierarchical," then liability touches all "levels" of the organization, conceived in corporatist terms.

It is within this context that we turn from the question of religious protection from legal claims to questions of the church's internal organization. We move from issues of differentiation among institutional sectors to issues of ecclesiology proper; that is, how to define "church" in ways that are theologically authentic as well as intelligible and viable in civil society.

The Methodist Search for Identity between Publics and Markets

It is clear that the court was ignorant of the theological language it was intruding on. Indeed, courts and government have lived for decades behind a self-imposed veil of ignorance on these matters. This ignorance is bearable if religion is considered a private matter of individual belief. However, loss of religious knowledge can wreak havoc when the interests and integrity of large institutions are at stake.

From the church's side this veil of ignorance accompanying the wall of separation has meant that the churches have not had to articulate the theological meaning of their forms of organization. They have not had to think hard about ecclesiology because they have also largely accepted the belief that religion is a matter of individual belief and practice. Indeed, thoughtful Christians might fear that concern about the rightness and wrongness of ecclesial organization would lead us back to the bloody controversies of the

Reformation and the Thirty Years War, in which conflicts over ecclesiologies lay at the heart of disputes among the emerging nations.

This amnesia about ecclesiology overlies, in fact, a rich experimentation in ecclesial order offered by the rise of the voluntary religious organization. The spontaneous mass meetings, revivals, camp meetings, and conferences driving the engine of personal revival in the early American republic did not fit the corporate understandings of the body thinking in established Christianity. Rather, they brought to mind the ideas of assembly, congregation, and convention—ideas resonant with the root word *ekklesia* and the ideas of public in the republican theorists of the day.

While a small number of theologians were able to grasp this eruption of religious assembly in the early nineteenth century as a fundamental ecclesiological change (or renewal, if you will), most people understood these "awakenings" as matters of individual experience—a psychological revolution. Thus, it was difficult to grasp these events ecclesiologically and theologically. Individualism rather than a sense of the total system of organized relationships carried the day. The meaning of these new understandings of organizational relationships—a shift from the hierarchy of command to a covenant or compact of distinct but related publics—was overwhelmed by individualistic concepts of personal experience.

This meant that Methodism oscillated between an effort to capture the import of the free meetings, conferences, and revivals that energized it and recurrence to the corporatist ecclesial language of its Anglican mother. Wesley himself never was able to resolve this tension, which persists to this day. Indeed, it was Wesley who introduced the major complicating factor ecclesiologically, namely, his understanding of the oversight associated with the ancient *episkopos*.

FROM EPISCOPAL OVERSIGHT TO CORPORATE CONNECTION.   Wesley wanted to exercise oversight of the preachers who sought to revive members of the Anglican establishment according to his teachings and methods (hence the term "Methodists"). Since the term "bishop" referred to Anglican prelates locked into the ossified church of his day, along with their membership in the House of Lords, Wesley chose the term "superintendent" to refer to this exercise of oversight. Though seeming to respect the claims of the bishops to their New Testament roots, he was actually undercutting them. The functional bias of supervision stood in sharp contrast to the corporate notion of the bishop as a representative of the church as the Body of Christ. Methodism, with its superintendents, would eventually separate from the Anglican and Episcopal churches altogether.

It was this original arrangement of oversight that constituted the "connection" between Wesley and his preachers. It was not a connection of corporate embodiment but of mutual accountability among preachers. Thus, the original Methodist connection was a relation among ministers, not among congregations. Ministerial "charges," not congregations, were—and theoretically remain so today—the units of "church." From the standpoint of Wesley's tradition, this connection of ministers charged to serve various "classes," "bands," and "societies" of believers existed to vivify the body of Christ. It existed to enable the mind and spirit of Christ to find visible articulation in this world, primarily through the vivid experience and activity of believers. The "connection" served the regeneration of individuals and through that a spreading of holiness through the world.

Over the two centuries of Methodist development in the American republic this connectionalism had to be accommodated to the forms of association known to American business and law. Thus, connection became equated with trust deeds for holding property, and the "charges" of the ministers began to become congregations. The connected ministers congealed into conferences. However, the original language of Wesley still dominates the church's discourse even if it has to sing it in an increasingly minor key—the language of corporations, liability, and hierarchical agency.

Within itself, Methodism was never able to identify the basic unit of "church," largely because it arose under Wesley's leadership as a reform within the Anglican church. Because Wesley's main organizational focus was on the connection of his ministers and the formation of intentional societies of believers, he did not attend to "church," since that was already taken up by the existing parish system. Over time, the highly intentional and disciplined societies in the American landscape became settled congregations. The circuit-riding ministers also settled down with them but retained the same authority structure of superintendency as before. At that point Methodists were challenged to reopen the problem of defining themselves as "church." Could they reclaim a corporate identity without rejecting the free-spirited meetings at the center of their emotional identity? Could they be both institutional and associational?

As Methodism grew and matured, it adopted the organizational patterns around it, since it was difficult to maintain Wesley's original conception of connection within a world Wesley (a devoted monarchist) could neither imagine nor desire. Toward the end of the nineteenth century Methodists adopted the forms of bureaucracy out of which they developed a myriad of agencies to serve the various functions of missions, finance, social service, and ministerial education and support. Along with the rest of America's business world they sought efficiency and centralization, not to mention the corporate forms that made this possible in law.[46] This is the leading edge of hierarchy and corporate liability that the court and plaintiffs engaged.

What this shift to stable organization produced was a clear distinction between clergy professionals and lay supporters, in spite of the heavily democratic import of revivalistic individualism, in which every spiritually regenerated person was the equal of all others. This tension between professional experts arranged in supervisory orders over against a democratic mass of supporters has come to characterize much of American life generally. The bureaucratization of professional service in recent decades further crystallized the move from a church typified by ecstatic assemblies to a church characterized by professional services for religious consumers.

In the course of this development Methodists could not clearly articulate what is "connected" and how these parts are connected to each other. Since congregations, conferences, and councils were not the original units of connection, they could not fit the original spiritual and ministerial meaning of Wesley. Yet these were the connections the court and the plaintiffs were looking for. They therefore took the theological language of the Wesleyan tradition and attached it to places totally unforeseen and even unimaginable to Wesley—and indeed to his present heirs in the leadership of the United Methodist Church.

But even Wesley's heirs are confused about the term "connection." In the pleadings and affidavits presented to the Pacific Homes courts we find a variety of interpretations. The UMC, claimed one church brief, is a "spiritual 'connection'" whose units—"churches, conferences, boards, agencies or institutions"—operate "within a loose, non-authoritarian confederation pursuant to the *Book of Discipline*." [47] In an important affidavit to the court the distinguished Methodist scholar Murray Leiffer put it this way:

> The general United Methodist denomination is a voluntary religious movement and connectional network of millions of persons, known as 'members,' and literally thousands of units, denominated as local churches, conferences, boards. . . . [This] connectional religious denomination and movement [is] structured around two fundamental church units, namely, (a) the local Charge, with its local congregation or congregations, and (b) the Annual Conference.

However, these fundamental units may not act as agents for other units nor "bind or obligate them in any way." Leiffer concludes: The "UMC is not a single entity. . . . It is not a unified corporate body, but in actuality is an international religious faith and denomination which constitutionally declares itself to be a branch of the Church universal and the ministry of Christ." [48]

On the one hand, Leiffer wanted to stress the autonomy of the various units in order to resist court intrusion in liability cases, in which plaintiffs assume relationships of agency and mutuality. At one point Leiffer appeals to the American suspicion of the centralization of power to support this dispersal, rather than to any specific theology or ecclesiology—a lesson drawn directly from Madison's conception of federalism. On the other hand, he wanted to preserve the organic sense of the universal Body of Christ—the corporatist tradition. The court pressed him to a congregationalism of "autonomous units," but his theology and ecclesiology pushed him to affirm the unity of the whole Church.

In the process, almost unnoticed, the understanding of the Methodist connection moved, again under the impact of corporation law, from being a relation of superintendents with ministers to being a relationship among "churches," "conferences," "units," and "members." Rather than the deep mutuality and accountability characterizing Wesley's relationship with his ministers, the meaning of "connection" brought before the court emphasized the autonomy of "spiritually confederated" groups. In fact, neither the connection of individual ministers nor the regenerative experiences of individuals could sustain themselves as an adequate basis for an ecclesiology, either internally or in relationship to civil society. In a society of associations an ecclesiology needs a compelling sense of "church" that can engage the general institutional order but also maintain its own integrity and distinctiveness in a critical way.

The problem with approaching a concept of church from the standpoint of business models of incorporation is that this move has little room for the independent initiative and extraorganizational activity so central to Methodist heritage. While the corporate analogies draw on important strands of theological tradition, they miss the peculiar mix of effervescence and order that characterizes not only Methodism but evangelical American religion generally. This peculiar mix is woven all through the rich tapestry of publics that generated the original American constitutional order.

THE SEARCH FOR A FEDERAL CONNECTIONALISM. In distinction to this corporatist business thrust, Methodists have also emulated America's own federal system and drawn on it to explain their polity. Congregations, or at least the "charges" of the ministers soon began to look like local wards, conferences began to look like states, and general conferences like the national Congress. This development was actually well in line with their actual practices of meetings and periodic local, regional, and national, indeed international conferences. The essential activity of Methodism was these experiences of conference, which had no ongoing corporate form.[49] Yet the impact of these collective experiences was enormous. They were the engine of the movement.

Similarly, the public meetings, conventions, and conferences typical of the early republican movement have no ongoing corporate form. They are not "constituted" in the U.S. Constitution. They are the ecstatic moments of inspiration without which a republic cannot be sustained. Without these "effervescent" moments, which we saw earlier in the German case, the ordinary barriers of family, race, class, geography, and even language cannot be bridged to create a wider republic. Methodism is an effort to sustain such peculiar publics within a culture that generally speaks the language of commercial individualism and legal positivism—a reaction against the

European traditions of corporatism and established religion. However, spontaneous publics and the "connections" that sustain them are neither legally real nor responsible. Whether this crucial public reality of religious assembly can be sustained in such an environment is not only the challenge facing the Methodism of the Pacific Homes cases but republican orders in general.

The plaintiffs in the Pacific Homes cases sought to establish hierarchical relationships of agency, accountability, and liability in order to reach the "deep pockets" of a very large international religious organization. The UMC couched its arguments in terms of a "connection" that is very real and deep but not accessible in legal terms. The more it tried to protect this "connection" from legal suit, the more otherworldly it became, quite contrary to the norms of moral accountability historically associated with the connection of ministers and superintendents, not to mention the early Methodist societies. In this tension, if not contradiction, appeals surfaced continuously to the *Discipline* as in fact the body of commitments constituting the connection.

In fact, it is the *Discipline* that defines the mutual accountability of the various units—including ministers, bishops, conferences, and agencies—constituting United Methodism. Whatever goes on within this web of lawlike pronouncements *is* the Methodist connection. What made it difficult to say this is that Methodists would be led to say that it is the embodiment of their covenant with God and with each other. But "covenant" is not part of Methodism's original vocabulary largely because of its Anglican mother, even though its practices are thoroughly immersed in the republican effervescence and lawlike mutual accountability typical of the covenantal tradition and its federalist expressions.

The Methodist *Discipline* embodies the deep tensions between covenant and constitution also present in the American political order. On the one hand, by including several historic Christian creeds, the *Discipline* points beyond itself to a kind of cosmos of covenants presented in Christian tradition. On the other hand, it is in many respects a compilation of legislation produced in General Conference, reflecting increasingly the jurisprudence of the American legal system within the treatylike commitments of classic covenant. Yet if anything *is* the "connection," it seems to be the form adumbrated by this covenant-like document. It is the interim authority, rather than any bishop, president, or council, between the periodic conferences that guide the organization.

In these respects Methodism rehearses, perhaps more explicitly, tensions and deficiencies within the American polity itself. The more one presses an emphasis on the centrality of the spirited public assembly as the practical center of the church or of a society, the more one moves to some notion of covenant as the connecting bonds within and among those publics. The more one stresses the bodily functionality of a group as a stable organism, the more one moves to some notion of legal headship as the connecting and representative bond. Methodism exhibits both this covenantal "connection" and this corporatism—tendencies that we see in American society generally. Its inability to give clear voice to its basic self-understanding within this tension reflects American disputes over federal order and public freedom as well as offers us some possibly illuminating entrees into a critical engagement with them. Such an inquiry raises at least two basic issues.

First, we can recognize that a constitutional order tends to be reduced to increasingly fine grades of positive law that envelops everything in its legal code. Therefore, in order to remain responsive to continual historical change it must be situated within a larger translegal covenant. This transcendent covenant, which works to federate people together at a prelegal level, is best known through the vitalities of free publics—the conferences, conventions, and assemblies that gave the constitution birth. How to interrelate the formative, constituting dynamic of this wider covenant with the spirited vitalities of free assembly is the balancing act central to the establishment and maintenance of a federal-republican order. While religious groups can be bearers of the claims of kinship, race, and biology that undermine free covenantal assembly, they can also, by carving out free spaces within a legal order, catalyze the rich blend of covenant and public conversation at the heart of a complex federation of publics.

Second, if we see Methodist ecclesiology as in some sense "federal," we can see that it is not a hierarchy of representation "up" and commands coming "down." Even in its Presbyterian counterpart, with an even more obvious federal order, this is not the case. What we have here is a set of quasi-legal relationships that are always interrupted, as it were, by the overarching commitments of the people making up the total church. Bishops interrupt to teach. Evangelistic movements offend and even bypass congregations to affect conferences. Conferences establish agencies that make demands on conferences and local congregations. What this confusing interaction can do is to lift up the way that a vital federalism is not a pyramid of representation and command but a web of crosscutting accountabilities always pressing the participants to articulate the fundamental covenant informing their constituted federal order.

The Pacific Homes cases have led us to the importance of defining the institutional character of religion within a constitutional order. But what if the meaning of religion and church escapes simple constitutional definition? What if the dimension of land, so important to biblical covenant, comes to the fore and that of corporate distinctiveness recedes to the margins? What if the wider covenant so necessary to the viability and legitimacy of a political constitution is broken or absent? These are questions posed by the religious claims of the original Americans, present today in an ambiguous treaty relationship with the U.S. government and sharing the land of its peoples.

Sacred Lands and Native Peoples in Federal Contestation

America's Federal Dilemma

The practices and claims of American Indians, like those of the tribal and Dalit peoples of India, pose formidable questions for federalism and for the meaning of religion and its relationship to the constitutional order of federal republics. While the Aryan invasion of the ancient Dravidian world is lost in the mists of mythology and the speechless shards of archaeology, the often brutal engagement between European settler and American aboriginal is painfully and extensively documented.[50] Native peoples have struggled for sheer survival in the face of endemic European diseases, military assault, forced expropriation, and legislative and judicial connivance, as well as the seductions of commerce, Christianity, and civilization. At the heart of this struggle have lain conceptions of land, of peoplehood and governance, of sacredness and religion, and of federative order—concepts at the center of this book's inquiry.

However, in this case the elements are thrown into the air and come down in unfamiliar ways, ways that test our concepts of religion and federal republicanism and suggest new understandings of the way these relationships may develop in the future. In the words of a foremost expert on American Indian law, the Indian is like the miner's canary, who "marks the shifts from fresh air to poison gas in our political atmosphere; and our treatment of Indians, even more than out treatment of other minorities, reflects the rise and fall in our democratic faith. . . ."[51] The canary need not merely die to warn others. It can also guide us to fresher air and broader horizons.

The United States has been called a "compound republic,"[52] but this reference to its internal formal organization must now be compounded further with the awareness that the formal federal republic exists within a wider internal and yet also external array of federative relationships with the original inhabitants of the land. The traditional native councils, assemblies, and confederations bore striking resemblance to many of the concepts and practices prized by the emerging republicans in the colonies yet were eventually subordinated to the new American states. Both the lattice of federal relationships and the intermingling of these republics further "compound" the American order. What does the "compounding" of this federal order say about the meaning of federalism? of republican order? of the sacred covenants that must undergird public trust?

Not only do we confront these classical questions, but we also come up against concepts of land, property, and religion constituting the wider environment within which federal and republican arrangements must sustain themselves. The case before us tests in new ways the European and Semitic traditions that spawned the federalist and republican lineage. To concretize these questions I lift out of the sea of legal cases and conflicts a struggle by some American Indians to defend a mountainous area of California from development by an agency of the U. S. Government.

Foresters and Worshipers: The *Lyng* Case

In the late 1970s the U.S. Forest Service developed a plan to construct a paved road through mountainous country in northern California traditionally sacred to the Yurok, Karok, and Tolowa tribes.[53] The mountains in this high country were the traditional living source of these people's powers. Their sacral leaders had to make ritual pilgrimages into these highlands to replenish the power of the earth and of the people bound to it.[54] While the exact boundaries of these sacred highlands were hidden in the secrecy accompanying these esoteric rites, it was clear that the mountains as a whole ecosystem, to use contemporary parlance, constituted the sacred context for these religious mysteries.

An extensive study commissioned by the Forest Service to evaluate the feasibility of the road reported that this "high country" was crucial to the conduct of tribal rituals ensuring the continuity and well-being of these tribes. Indeed, construction of a road disturbing this area would be "potentially destructive of the very core of Northwest [Indian] religious beliefs and practices."[55] Nevertheless, the Forest Service decided to proceed with the road, seeing the Indians' claim as just one factor to balance with others. While designing the road to avoid what it saw to be the center of this sacred area, it proceeded with its plans. Members of the three tribes, under the umbrella name of the Northwest Indian Cemetery Protective Association, sued in civil court to stop the road.

The tribal plaintiffs, in order to make their case in the trial court, compared this sacred space to a church—the environment of religious activity familiar to Christians. More precisely, they took shelter under the rubric of cemetery protection, a long-standing claim in the face of land use change. However, unlike a church this mountainous land was neither constructed by human hands nor should it be altered by them, they argued. It belongs, in the words of one witness, "to the spirit and it exists in another world apart from us."[56]

As such, this high country falls under the category of "religion," whose free exercise is protected by the First Amendment to the Constitution. The trial court agreed and blocked the construction of the road. The Forest Service appealed the ruling, which was upheld by the court of appeals. The Department of Agriculture appealed this decision and the U.S. Supreme Court agreed to hear the case in 1988.

In its opinion the Supreme Court agreed that indeed the forest road might desecrate this "high country" and by so doing destroy not only the religious practices conducted there but the very existence of the tribes dependent on them for their cultural integrity. However, the court held, competition between religious claims and other claims on government policy cannot be resolved by the courts. They are political matters best left to legislatures and other institutions.[57]

Thus, in this case the court set aside its historic role as the adjudicator of conflicts between religious rights and governmental action. Instead, it focused on the narrow question of whether governmental action was "coercing" behavior contrary to the plaintiff's beliefs or whether it was discriminating against them on the basis of their religion. Such a test was far narrower than the historic principles used in other free exercise cases, which included requirements that the government have no other means to achieve its ends.[58] Since this was not the case, the court could press to the central question: whether the government could do what it wanted to with what, after all, was "its land."[59] Granting the Indians' claims, said the court, would impose a "religious servitude" on the land that would divest the government of its rights to do with the land whatever it willed. Neatly dissecting the actual practices of the claimants from the sacred reality of the "high country," the court claimed that tribal members could still go into the high country to meditate and conduct other ceremonies, but they would have to share that use with other use rights, such as logging and recreation. That the other uses would desecrate the site was, the court claimed, beyond its control.

Justice William Brennan assailed this logic in his minority opinion, pointing out that the First Amendment's protection of religious exercise is much broader and applies to "any form of governmental action that frustrates or inhibits religious practice."[60] Moreover, the majority's opinion places the government's property rights, even as a trustee, above the claims of religious free exercise and a people's cultural (and therefore actual) survival. The court, averred Brennan, erred in its narrow construal of Indian religion and its overly broad interpretation of government "ownership."

Ironically, though the Forest Service was now free to build its road, it has not been built to this day for other reasons. Shortly after the litigation, the state of California further restricted development in this region, not for any religious reasons or concern for Indian sovereignty but because it decided to name much of this land a "wilderness area," further restricting its commercial value.[61] What the tribal litigants could not do by appeal to religious freedom and the survival of their distinct culture, the state could do on behalf of the general citizenry's longing for recreation in pristine areas undisturbed by human construction and destruction—a secular counterpart to aboriginal sacrality.

Assessing the Issues

It Begins with the Land

The *Lyng* case was only one of several similar cases litigated in the same period seeking to safeguard traditional sacred lands from private and governmental spoilation. The San Francisco peaks in Arizona were threatened by development of a ski resort, Bear Butte in the Black Hills of South Dakota faced state park incursions, and the headwaters of the Little Tennessee River sacred to the Cherokees were to be flooded by a TVA dam.[62] All of these Indian suits were unsuccessful, at least one because of the *Lyng* precedent.

Sacred land claims were only part of a wider constellation of land claims by tribes resulting in the return of the Blue Lake in New Mexico to the Taos Pueblo Indians (1970)[63] and Mt. Adams to the Yakima Indians in Washington (1972), both lands having sacred import for these peoples.

However, in the overall picture the lands of the aboriginal peoples have been steadily restricted by treaty, relocation, private and governmental purchase, condemnation, and forced allotment of tribal lands to individual members. Disposition of the land mirrors divergent concepts not only of ownership but of the nature of peoplehood and religion. The *Lyng* case was the outcome of the essential conflict over land that has controlled the relationship of immigrant and native American. American federalism cannot be understood apart from this crucible of land conflicts. To understand these conflicts we have to understand the bases by which the European settlers claimed the land.

First, the settlers appealed to concepts of "discovery" as well as of contract to legitimate their control over the land. Discovery meant that the lands settled by the Europeans were "empty," not in the sense of "unoccupied" but in the sense of not being "developed" by agriculture, manufacture, extraction, or permanent settlement. The Indians, claimed such Puritan divines as John Cotton, had only the natural right of occupancy, but the settlers, by mixing their labor with the soil, had it by civil right. Moreover, this development is not a matter of unjust conquest, something the English left to Spanish claims. Said Cotton, "[O]thers take the land by his [God's] providence, but God's people take the land by promise."[64]

At the core of this Puritan conception was the belief that the land was given to the Christian settlers, not for any merely commercial or military purpose but for the religious one of conversion and establishing righteous order. The wider covenant of God's promise framed the efforts of successive generations to create relations of guardianship and education with the tribes, sometimes based in treaty, sometimes in statute and executive order. At times this entailed ardent defense of Indian national integrity, as with Samuel Worcester's trial testing Georgia's usurpation of the United States' exclusive constitutional right to make treaties and regulate commerce with the Cherokee Nation.[65] Sometimes this entailed assiduous efforts to revoke treaty recognition of sovereign tribes in order to assimilate them into the mainstream of a "Christian civilization," as with the Lake Mohonk reformers at the end of the nineteenth century.[66]

Whose Courts? Whose Law?

Samuel Worcester, a missionary among the Cherokees with their consent and by the authorization of the president of the United States, was convicted by a Georgia court for violating its 1828 law requiring outsiders to gain the governor's permission to be on Cherokee soil. In defense of Worcester, a citizen of Vermont, the Supreme Court argued strenuously for jurisdiction and for the integrity of the Cherokees as a dependent but still sovereign nation in treaty with the United States. Georgia's act violated not only Worcester's right to protection under federal laws but the very force of the U.S. Constitution itself, which preempted Georgia's right to make laws affecting the Cherokee or any other Indian nation. The court declared Georgia's law null and void.

When the Cherokee nation itself was the plaintiff, however, the matter of jurisdiction changed. Immediately preceding the Worcester case Chief Justice John Marshall, in the case of *Cherokee Nation v. State of Georgia,* held, as he did the next year in the Worcester case, that the United States had consistently viewed the Cherokees as a "state, as a distinct political society, separated from others, capable of managing its own affairs and governing itself. . . ." Thus, its relation to the newly formed federal government, as to its British predecessor, had always been one of treaty. But, Marshall went on, "the relation of the Indians to the United States is marked by peculiar and cardinal distinctions which exist no where else." Because they reside wholly within the jurisdiction of the United States and have it as their sole treaty and trading partner, they are actually "domestic dependent nations." They are "in a state of pupilage. Their relation to the United States resembles that of a ward to his guardian."[67] Thus, they could not claim the Supreme Court's jurisdiction to adjudicate their dispute with Georgia—nor, by implication, would an international tribunal have availed them either.

The upshot was that the tribes were put in a permanent judicial limbo. On the one hand, they were not simply a population of citizens whose first citizenship is to the state in which they reside. The federal Constitution reserves to Congress the sole right to "regulate commerce with . . . the Indian tribes," as with foreign nations and among the states constituting the federal union. They were in some sense self-governing but peculiar republics. On the other hand, they were not able to appeal to the federal courts in an action against a state because they were not one of the constituting states of the federal union. A true international treaty relationship between the United States and the tribes would require appeal to some international court, to a third nation arbiter, or, as was tragically often the case, to force of arms. Lacking the arms and lacking the court, the tribes became wards of the union, first under the executive branch and then, after the termination of treaty making with the tribes in 1871, under the Congress.

From Treaty Partner to Dependent Ward

Between 1871 and 1934 government policy, in line with the heirs of the Puritan conversionist legacy, sought to eliminate even the vestiges of nationhood for these domestic dependent peoples. Principal among these efforts was the Allotment (Dawes) Act of 1887, which carved up most Indian lands into 160-acre parcels for the tribal individuals. The vast majority of the lands left over was then given away for homesteading by whites, sold, or held permanently by the national government. These former aboriginal lands in government hands were at least fictively held "in trust" for the interests of the Indians, thus evidencing a tatter of covenantal obligation among the shreds of solemn treaties. But, as we saw in the *Lyng* decision, even this sense of trust evaporates in the face of any assertion of bald ownership rights in fee simple. It is "after all" the *government's* land, held Justice Sandra Day O'Connor. As a "guardian" the Congress' has "plenary power" over the tribes and their land that is as absolute as the powers of the ancient Roman *pater potestas,* the German *Landesherr,* or the Indian raja.[68] Trusteeship thus moved from being obligations under a covenant with a greater sovereign to being the exercise of the rights of a parent over a child.

In 1924 Congress, without consulting the Indian tribes, acted to include all Indians as U.S. citizens. While almost two-thirds of all Indians had already gained citizenship on their own application or as part of land or other agreements with the U.S. government, a sizable number had either resisted this move as the last sign of their loss of sovereignty or simply had not been caught in the great net of assimilationist policy. However, for many, if not most, Indians this meant an additional citizenship, with some, such as the Oneida and Iroquois, still carrying their own tribal passports.

In 1934 the Congress reversed its course and, under the Indian Reorganization Act, discontinued the "allotment" of Indian Lands begun with the Dawes Act and sought to recreate the tribes as constitutional governments in the image of the federal republic that had been their guardian and tutor in civilization. While they ostensibly could simply recrystallize their traditional governments, only a few were capable of or willing to do this, so the majority simply picked up their constitution from the Bureau of Indian Affairs in order to recover as much as they could of their treaty relationship. This time, however, it was not even a putative relation of independent peoples. In the frame of covenantal analysis it was not even a "suzereignty" treaty of grace from above, much less a compact of equals. It was an administrative device clothed in the memories of republican federalism.

In general, though these constitutions looked like republican arrangements, in fact, because these reemergent governments actually had to go on relating to external government agencies, principally the Bureau of Indian Affairs, emphasis fell on a strong executive for each tribe rather than on the conciliar consensus formation typical of traditional tribal government.[69] The centralization of power for purposes of governmental contact and economic development opened the door in more than one case to later abuses of power.

Just as the government gave with the act of 1934, so it soon began to take back in 1953 with a policy of terminating treatylike relationships with tribes, thus "freeing" Indians from tribal governance and dependency and enabling them to become citizens like any others. This long tradition of assimilation and uplift took much of its legitimation and power from the history of America's struggle first to emancipate the slaves within the federal union and then to institute their full civil rights and economic participation after World War II. The moral force as well as the script of this drama then flowed into the quite different river of settler-native relations.[70] All America's "minorities" were herded into the same boat to rise on the same tide.

The termination period, however, was short-lived because the widespread faith in the American dream behind the assimilationist program began to crumble in the 1960s under the impact of the war in Vietnam, the assassinations of Martin Luther King, Jr., and the two Kennedy brothers, and internal political turmoil. Both the cultural climate fostered by the emergence of new nations around the world and the pragmatic political decisions of national leaders such as Richard Nixon led to a resurgence of tribal claims as quasi-sovereign governments. But the assimilationist and guardianship eras had eroded much of the basis for rectifying the injustices of the past by returning to a treaty form of federal relationship. The Indian Claims Commission, for instance, during its brief tenure (1946–52), could only compensate Indians for lost lands, not return them.

Tribal Survival as Religious Rights

The resurgence of cultural identity among Indians coincided with the loss of ordinary civil means to reclaim their lands. They therefore turned to appeals to religious protection as a way of repristinating their existence as a people bound to the land. It is this confluence that produced the litigation carried out by the plaintiffs from the Yurok, Tolowa, and Karok tribes. Though the Supreme Court could not recognize them as sovereign political entities, it might be able to adjudicate their claims as citizens and members of a religion entitled to First Amendment protection. The Indians spurned by Marshall's court came back in Worcester's boots.

This approach depended not only on the provisions of US constitutional law and the evolution of U.S.-Indian relations but on the peculiar character of traditional society, namely, the traditional fusion between religion, culture, government, people, and land typical of aboriginal societies. In the cases from India these were called communal groups. Aboriginal life wears a seamless institutional garment foreign to the differentiation that we have seen to be essential to American conceptions of federal order and public life. If the garment could not clothe the tribe's civil persona, perhaps it could its religious persona. Thus, the survival of Native American peoples was transformed into a religious question in order to appear before the bar of constitutional law.

This strategy had been opened up legally first by the Indian Civil Rights Act (ICRA 1968) and the American Indian Religious Freedom Act (AIRFA 1978). While the brunt of the Civil Rights Act was to carry into Indian life the civil rights gains extended to African Americans and others burdened by racial discrimination, it took enough note of the peculiarities of Indian culture to exclude application of the First Amendment's prohibition of the "establishment of religion." Because of the seamless garment, efforts to assist Indian culture, education, and traditional medicine would have been prohibited because they would have also had to support their "religion." Individual Indians could still, however, sue in tribal courts for protection of their own freedom to choose to follow nontraditional religions, such as Christianity. While "establishment" was permitted, tolerance would have to prevail.

With AIRFA the Congress made it government policy to protect and preserve for American Indians their inherent right of freedom to believe, express, and exercise the traditional religions of the American Indian, Eskimo, Aleut, and Native Hawaiians, including but not limited to access to sites, use and possession of sacred objects, and the freedom to worship through ceremonies and traditional rites. That this declaration of policy did not create any basis for legal claims was made transparent in *Lyng*.

In spite of these legal incentives the religious freedom strategy foundered for several reasons. The Indian seamless garment could not contain the whole body of land claims seeking entry through the door of religious freedom. Essentially, the concept of religion in the First Amendment actually refers to that religion which can bear the public face of a "church." It must, as we discussed in the Pacific Homes case, have a corporate public face distinct from other institutions and cultural facts. The Indians did not have a church. They did not have an "ecclesiology" to fit constitutional law, though in their case it was not merely because, like the Methodists, their religious reality is "of another world." It was also because the land itself constituted their "church." And when it comes to land, the courts are thoroughly captive to a conception of property far from Native American theories.

Secondly, the differentiation of "church" from other aspects of culture carries with it a presupposition that church is differentiated from land and nature. From the Christian theological point of view, ecclesiology concerns an institution of "grace," not of "nature," of redemption as distinct from creation. Thus American law assumes that the religious life contained in church is nongeographic and portable, like the Hebrews' Ark of the Covenant, which wandered the promised land until it was housed in Jerusalem, and that not by divine necessity but by political ambition. Those whose "religion," that is, whose core of legitimation as a people, flows from the land rather than from a God who promises them the land, face an uphill battle fitting into the Constitution's definition of religion—especially when the land in question is the "property" of the government of another, "chosen" people.[71]

Once religion is distinguished from nature it is hard to honor the sacrality of natural geographic formations. The U.S. Constitution contains no language about the land typical of ancient covenant.[72] The natural world has neither standing in court nor representatives before the law.[73] Only under the settlers' notion of "wilderness" does the sacral once again regain a legal form that can cover some of the religious claims presented by the aboriginal peoples. Moreover, once religion is differentiated from nature and culture— "peoplehood" generally—it can be treated increasingly as one interest among others. The *Lyng* court explicitly did this with Native American religion, thus relegating religious claims to the contest of political compromise, much as the court did in placing the United Methodist Church within a free and fair market.

The canary that expired with *Lyng* foretold with complete accuracy the court's reasoning and decision in the later case of *Oregon Employment Division v. Smith* (1990), which ruled that the traditional ritual use of peyote by an American Indian was not protected under the First Amendment.[74] The court's dicta in this ruling, following much the same line of reasoning as *Lyng*, swept aside all the traditional tests for government infringement on religious freedom. So breathtaking was the departure from precedent that all major religious groups in the United States lobbied Congress for statutory protections equivalent to the former constitutional principles to safeguard for the "historic" religions what had earlier been denied the Indians.[75] What had already emerged in the court's cavalier overriding of religious claims based on the sacredness of land now was carried out against the differentiated religions of historic revelation.

Clearly more was at work here than the contrast between nature and history, creation religion and redemption religion, distinct ecclesiology and seamless garment. Both the religion of tribal integrity and the religion of ecclesial redemption fell beneath the court's sickle. Why?

There seem to be two answers, both of which lead us back to the questions of land and property with which we started. First, the court seems to have assumed that "religion," whether it is tribal or ecclesial, is a private matter that must leave the public playing field to one player—the government. Constitutional law is not a matter of orchestrating the "deep federalism" of differentiated institutions underlying the governmental differentiations of a federal order. It is a matter of clearing away the impediments to the government's actions. In attacking the deep covenant among key institutions constituting a public order—whether these are tribal, ecclesial, or social—the court risks jeopardizing the differentiation of government itself. Without a wider institutional plurality in the society the internal federalism espoused in *The Federalist* begins to collapse in on itself. By clearing the field for the governmental actors, the probability of the hegemony of the strongest becomes very strong indeed. One untrammelled state stands over against private individuals, whether religious or not.

Second, in tune with this privatistic view of religion (and the concurrent supremacy of the state), the court reduces all claims formerly associated with the cultural underpinnings of the society to distinct "interests"—the *Lyng* outlook. When the government pits "the public interest" over against them, it needs no "compelling" reason to override them. Its own advocacy is enough. This is the judicial resonance of the dictum: After all, it is the government's "own" land.

What is important to notice here is the concept of private interest and property that lies behind this line of reasoning. "Ownership" as complete domination of an object translates into a political theory of state domination of the properties under its control. The "public domain" becomes "government property" no different from that of any private owner. This conception of ownership as exclusive dominion differs markedly from ownership as a web of rights and responsibilities within a larger system of interdependency. It is the difference between a corporatism of single headship and a federalism of pluralistic contest and cooperation.

Again, the *Lyng* case is instructive.[76] The court interpreted the government's land rights in terms of "ownership" of the land. Behind this shift from language of "trusteeship" to that of ownership lies the model of ownership in "fee simple." That is, all the rights pertaining to land are fused into one—the right to occupy the land, to use it, to enjoy its benefits, to alter and develop it, and to transfer these rights to others. All the rights, as with the corporate ideal, are lodged in one "head." This is quite different from a view that distinguishes these rights from each other, so that they start building a web of complex relationships anchored in the land and among various parties related to it.[77] The fee simple ownership doctrine informing the *Lyng* court hides this elemental reality, which had informed not only the previous doctrine of governmental trusteeship but the covenants into which the national government had entered since its inception. That the word "covenant" is most often attached to land in legal matters should alert us to the way land was once construed as part of a larger network of obligations and rights anchored in occupants, users, future beneficiaries, and the Creator of all. Covenants in the law are in some sense "held" by the land itself. The collapse of this wider covenantal notion reduces trusteeship to paternal sovereignty rather than compactual obligation.

Marshall's arguments in *Worcester* still resonate here. Marshall argued that the rights of discovery were used by the European nations only to exclude each other from an area, "but could not affect the rights of those already in possession, either as aboriginal occupants or as occupants by virtue of a discovery made before the memory of man. It gave the exclusive right to purchase, but did not found that right on a denial of the right of the possessor to sell."[78] Neither did this right of market access give the government a right to govern the people. Likewise, the fact of a treaty between unequals in power did not extinguish the sovereignty of both parties within their own jurisdictions. All these distinctions, so clear at the outset, had eroded away before the notions of absolute dominion. The landlord had replaced the feudal lord. Its malign face was that of the corporate despot, its kindly face a great white father. The refusal or inability to think and act covenantally had left the field to the great individual who held all the bundle of rights to the land. To share them as the plaintiffs asked in *Lyng* would be to impugn this fundamental concept of property informing the law.

What this reduction of relations to fee simple ownership does is to remove the fundamental character of land as a commons. It is no longer a medium for human intercourse but a set of boundaries separating people from one another.[79] Security takes precedence over publicity. This move exposes how the conception of land is critical for the viability of a federal-republican order. The ability to see land as the medium of a complexity of obligations among groups, individuals, generations dead, living, and yet un-born, and the Creator of all reverberates in the ability to see governance as an equally dense and comprehensive set of obligations. The ability to see land, at least fundamentally, as a medium of shared action, memory, and hope—in short, as a public—is crucial to envisioning publics locked in civil argument over the life they share in a common geography. This is not a question over whether land is "sacred" or not, or whether religious authority is "historical" or "cosmological," but whether land is seen covenantally or commercially, as medium of our relationships or as object of control. This is the central significance of this case for a federal-republican order. The pluralism of federal-republican order requires for its partner not the fee simple individualism attributed to Jefferson but the covenantal conception of common land familiar to Indian ears and in muted tones to Puritan notions of the commons and the town.[80]

Challenging the Historic Religious Foundations of Federal Republicanism

Cosmic Land and Sacred History

Indian sacred land claims both attack and reconfirm crucial elements of the traditional religious framework for federal-republican polities. On the one hand, their appeal to a more cosmological sense of sacrality calls into ques-tion the traditional Jewish and Christian appeal to historical promising—to covenant—as the basis for a federal culture. But the conception of land wrapped in this cosmological appeal reconfirms the complex web of cove-nant through which peoples can share the land and seek to respect its own integrity as a direct partner in God's creation.[81] What the historical ap-proach to covenant surrenders to nationalistic conceptions of election and destiny, the cosmological approach recovers by reclaiming the land as a part-ner to a universal covenant of shared existence.

What we have here is not merely a clash between "historical" and "cos-mological" sacrality. It might be better to see it as clashing views about what makes land "powerful." For the aboriginal peoples land mediated a life-giving relationship with past and future generations, with water and food, shelter and hand tools. It was more like the way people generally view the ocean—as something to fish in rather than to control absolutely. It was this bond of common life that made it sacred. For the settlers, the market of money, exchange, and "improvement" was what could convert the land from being a mere thing to being a greater power among people. By settling, improving, developing and transforming, even moving, the land, people could gain more financial and material power. Owning land in fee simple was the path to real power in a commercial market. Trade in real estate was the path to many fortunes. The contest in *Lyng* was over whose version of "sacrality" would prevail—at least in the short run.

Corporate Control and Conciliar Consensus

As with the Pacific Homes case, *Lyng* drives us to the deep tension between the centralizing tendencies of corporate notions and the pluralizing tendencies of conciliar consensus-formation. While both elements are necessary to complex social life, how we value them and where we locate them in our common life make enormous difference. Both conceptions are capable of great mystification, and both have very pragmatic consequences.

The difference between the two concepts is striking. Over against the "compound" federalism of land, people, and tribal republics stands the clean pyramid of corporatism. Over against the consensus of the council we find the single mind of the corporate head. Over against the harmonies of the created order we find the equilibriums of the market. Both *Lyng* and the Pacific Homes cases have shown us the power of the corporatist model and the market in reshaping both our conceptions of federal order and our sense of religion and the sacred. What one means by mutual accountability, authority, and "church," and how one perceives the relationship to the sacred are shaped by whether one views them from a corporatist perspective within a market framework or a conciliar one within a covenantal, federal framework. In India, and to a certain extent in Germany, the main threat to a fuller democratic order came from the bonds of tribe, kin, and ancestry. In America the threat comes from a quite different corner—the corporation and the market that are the antithesis of family and tribal order.

Through the lenses of these cases we can formulate the American debate as a struggle over which of these two principles will govern the other. It is not merely a debate over Alexander Hamilton's national empire and Thomas Jefferson's democratic republic. It is a debate framed more widely between two different principles for relating and reconciling settler and native in America. Whether the covenantal and conciliar patterns with which the nation emerged can regain parity or prominence with its present corporate structures is the question of whether we have the dead portent of the canary or the resurgent eagle of a vital people.

Where we locate the two principles of corporatism and conciliarism also makes a difference. The councils and publics of Indian governance have been thwarted by their position within the corporate bureaucracies of the U.S. government, rather than among the constituent assemblies of the U.S. Congress. This "disfederation" has seen them slide from being partners in treaty (and in the Hopewell Treaty of 1785 invitees to the Confederal Congress) to being wards of a welfare state. Their jurisdiction has oscillated between being a jurisdiction over land to being a "personal jurisdiction" over members of the tribe in family matters, religion, and small civil suits. Shorn of integral relations between people and land (over 50% of the land on Indian reservations is owned by non-Indians), tribal government may be tending toward the classical Hindu and British "personal codes" that are seen as obstacles to rather than media for democratic governance.[82] This would be a major departure from the geographic federalism that has shaped the settler-native contestation.

Both of these very different directions take us back to a web of reciprocal obligations, multiple citizenships, and intertwined rights familiar to a covenantal mind. Whether we locate these publics in administrative or congressional contexts is an enormous difference. Whether we locate the jurisdictions of these publics in land or in tribal relationships also makes a dramatic difference, as the cases of India's Shah Bano and Soosai remind us.

Transcendent Publics

The ambiguous position of the aboriginal nations in American law makes them "peculiar publics." The ghost of sovereignty still whispers in the conversations of their councils. The councils have their roots in claims and customs far beyond the apparatus of the government's internal administration. They transcend the frame of constitutional law even as they are buried in it.

This ambiguity echoes in the seemingly far distant struggles of the churches, whose assemblies, communions, connections, and covenants are both less than the law requires and more than it can grasp. The First Amendment echoes the Tenth; namely, the wider power and authority of the people's assemblies always stand beyond the law to constrain and renew it. But this can happen only if the spirit of these transcendent publics also is the spirit of the lawyers.

From the standpoint of the idea of covenantal publicity, the Bill of Rights amending the U.S. constitution is better construed as the limits these wider publics place upon the law. They are the publics in which the covenant forming the Constitution is generated and maintained. The extinction of these publics or their reduction to a collection of individual rights undermines the generation and renewal of this wider covenant, leading finally to the collapse of constitutional legitimacy as well. Both of the cases I have examined here were struggles to maintain transcendent publics in the midst of a law that has forgotten its wider covenantal base in publics that transcend the ordinary forms of power and law.

Covenants of Election, Covenants of Connection

The covenant-generating character of these peculiar and transcendent publics leads us to the question of these covenants themselves. These cases bring into sharper relief the ambiguous relation of covenantal traditions to federalism. From its biblical origins covenantalism has meant the "hierarchical" relation of election and subordination as well as the "egalitarian" relation of mutual obligation within a web of promises among relative equals. This hierarchical covenantalism can easily reinforce ideas of racial or national superiority that are implicitly present in the notions of American manifest destiny embedded in the Puritan materials we reviewed earlier. Through its connections with the monarchical heritage in Israel and the ecclesiological heritage of the Body of Christ in Christianity, it can also be used to legitimate the hierarchies of kingship and corporatism as well. Finally, it can make of federalism a pyramid of power devolving from a unified center rather than the construction of obligations among constituent partners. India and the United States have traveled different roads to union, but both must struggle with the distortions that centralism brings to a federal republic.

Covenant as compact among equals yields a web of complex allegiances. Methodist efforts to articulate their "connection" in the face of corporatist and even standard federalist conceptions evidence the difficulty in modeling this covenantal pattern. Native American efforts to disentangle treaty making from ownership of land represents another. This multifariousness of covenants is already evidenced in standard federalist accounts of the multiple citizenship of persons in a federal republic. But the covenantal side of federalism opens up people's citizenship to the nongovernmental "publics" of God and of the land—the classic covenantal partners of the people. It is with these citizenships that standard federalism has great difficulty, often retreating into a rigid corporatism, as with our cases, or a private conception of God and land that is amenable to the operations of the market. Both Pacific Homes and the sacred Siskiyou high country became trapped in these eddies away from the mainstream of a more expansive federalism.

It will probably always be human nature to seize on the pride of covenantal election by a transcendent Lord,[83] but it becomes demonic when it is not constrained by the nets of compacts among equals. American history has been an often tragic battle between the two, whether in the Removal Act of 1830 or the succession of contradictory "reforms" of Indian life after the end of treaty making in 1871. The new sense of ecological urgency can form some elements of rapprochement between the two cultures, but it requires a more expansive notion of the covenantal bonds underlying a federal culture.

The Covenantal Matrix of Limited Sovereignties

In bringing together the peculiar and transcendent publics with the complex web of covenant we come to the heart of the issues of covenantal publicity raised by these cases—that the American republic is more "compound" than the constitutional framers realized. This compounding began with the division of a sovereignty that once attached to the monarch into various branches of government among the several constituent states. The holding of all power and authority in one "head" had been a, if not *the*, crucial link between the character of earthly power and the nature of God—that God is one, just as the king is one. Here we also see the mirror of the idea of "fee simple" ownership, in which every person exercised the same rights as ancient kings.

This monarchical conception of God had, at least in the Christian tradition shaping European culture, always been challenged by the Trinitarian doctrine but without decisively reshaping people's notion of sovereignty. Since the tenth century the western church had subordinated the Spirit to the dynasty of Father and Son, just as the spirited assemblies of the people had been occasionally tolerated rather than honored.

While it secured an internal division of sovereignty, the American federal republic, through the exigencies of war as well as the greed of conquest, has tended to become a new sovereignty over against the assemblies of the people in the land. By emphasizing the importance of these wider publics and covenants, we expand the "compounding" of the republic, making it a covenantal matrix of limited sovereignties. The peculiar status of the tribes and churches thus becomes a signpost toward a more complex notion of shared power than even the one gained in the original Constitution of the American federal republic.

Whether this covenantal matrix of limited sovereignties can also become a cultural paradigm for global governance is the profound question before us. The American cases presently evidence a struggle between federalist and corporatist principles in the sharing of sovereignty. The struggle to share power becomes a contest of countervailing power between large corporations and governments. The cases from India lift up a struggle between federal-republican principles and the bio-piety of kinship, caste, tribe, and their attendant religious codes. In Germany we have not only these two factors, though in different degrees, but also the insistent pull toward a wider European federalism demanding a further compounding of limited sovereignties. In all these cases the struggle for greater publicity and a more expansive federalism requires an analysis not merely of law and government but of the religious cultures undergirding them.

Five

Assessing the Engagement, Evaluating the Inquiry

This comparative study began with four intentions: 1) to identify the religious issues at stake in the engagement between religious organization and federal republicanism; 2) to identify the crucial interinstitutional relationships that mediate the influences back and forth between religion and federal-republican polity; 3) to identify the roles religion plays in the process of legitimating, critiquing, or delegitimating the federal-republican project; and 4) to explore critical ethical dimensions of this reciprocal engagement through the bridge concept of covenantal publicity. Moreover, this inquiry has been both analytical and normative. I have sought both to understand the actual interplay of religion with the federalist struggle for more embracing publics and also to gain some normative vantage point for evaluating these complex connections.

We have now immersed ourselves in the historical, constitutional, and religious particularities of this engagement in three quite diverse cultural settings. The inquiry has uncovered peculiar elements in each setting, such as caste in India or the religious public corporation in Germany, as well as many themes that appear in differing ways in all three contexts. In some respects the otherwise very dissimilar countries of India and America reveal common themes of the tension between communal and constitutional federalisms as well as of the difficulties in redressing past injustices based on race, religion, and culture. In other respects, such as in the relatively close ties between religion, education, and government, Germany and India have more in common. In all three countries we find that the federal-republican project confronts issues of how to create and preserve genuinely participatory publics, whether in the face of market forces or communal exclusion; of creating appropriate federal bonds that avoid either simple pyramids of command or fissiparous fragmentation; and of respecting the autonomy of religion for the sake of social differentiation while at the same time curbing its possible tendencies to absolutize political debate or limit fundamental rights of public participation by its members, especially women.

From the religious side we see internal struggles over the nature of publics and federal forms within traditionally parental forms of governance as well as tensions between efforts to maintain the autonomy of religion and efforts to find effective ways to engage a largely secular state. In their interaction we find common struggles to form an appropriate political culture rooted in religious claims but not confined to them. Finally, this common struggle over the formation of an appropriate federal-republican culture leads us to questions of intergenerational and intergroup reconciliation as well as questions of the relation of people to land. The material here is rich and readers can do their own comparative work beyond the framework I am employing. At this point I can only focus on some critical assessments of these themes within the parameters established by the lens of covenantal publicity.

Three key issues emerge from our study of these religious institutions, communities, and traditions: (1) the establishment and maintenance of integrity between the deep faith commitments in the tradition and the institutional structures that bear them (the question of ecclesiology); (2) the securing of an appropriate degree of autonomy of these religious structures from other institutions or communities in order to maintain this ecclesiological integrity; and (3) the roles these religions can or ought to play in fostering a federal-republican order with widespread democratic participation, especially in terms of cultivating symbols, rituals, and worship for mediating between religion and political culture. In each of these areas of inquiry the overarching concept of covenantal publicity has directed us to ask both about the kind of public life fostered by various ecclesiologies and about how they are ordered with respect to the classic partners of covenant—God, people, and land. At the heart of these theologically informed questions lies the issue of how religion shapes the processes of group reconciliation essential to the emergence of new public orders.

These issues are intertwined with each other and reshape the original questions. In order to take up these issues my critical reflection will first treat the question of ecclesiology and the institutional forms of religion at play. Second, I will explore the interinstitutional dynamics, especially of the relation of religion to government, family, and economy. Third, I will turn to possible roles of religion in the federal-republican project, especially in shaping political culture and defining the process of reconciliation. Finally, I will take up the critical question of the adequacy of covenantal publicity as a lens for examining the relation of religion to the struggle for democratic publics within a federal order.

The Critical Role of Ecclesiology

Fundamental to this project is the conviction that the structural forms of religion are not externals. They are not merely expressions of the faith or belief of individuals. They are in fact essential to the religious. Ecclesiology is the study of the systematic and institutionalized practices of people with reference to the sacred, the divine, the transcendent. It studies the means by which these practices are transmitted across generations or to other people. In seeking to understand the relation of religion to political development, we should start not with religious ideas but with the institutional structures legitimated by appeal to these religious convictions. In short, religion is not merely a collection of cultural values but also a variety of institutional forms. It is these ecclesiologies that shape people's institutional habits, mobilize their powers, lift up public representatives, and knit the elements of their lives together in ongoing ways. The ecclesiological form or forms of a religion already set up its political as well as other institutional implications.

Communal, Institutional, and Associational Ecclesiologies

In the course of this study I have identified three basic ecclesiological forms, each with a differing impact on the effort to establish and preserve federal-republican order: communal, institutional, and associational.[1] This simple typology focuses first of all on their principle of internal organization and then, by implication, on how they tend to interact with other parts of the society.

In the communal forms ritual life and belief are embedded in the interknit practices of family, economy, land management, governance, and education. In India this has meant historically that it is the rituals, beliefs, and ethics legitimating the fusion of family, village, caste, economy, and land. It is an amalgam of bio- and geo-piety. In America it appeared among Native Americans, for whom caste did not exist but for whom land, ancestry, economy, and governance were fused as a "religious" reality. In Germany yet another version exists in the concept of a Volkskirche, which has deep roots in the fusion of people, land, feudal lordship, governance, and faith. The historical development of this Volkskirche into an increasingly differentiated institution manifests characteristics of the second ecclesiological form.

In an institutional ecclesiology religion gains a structural differentiation from other spheres of life. A religious institution seeks its own autonomy in order to preserve the integrity of its values, practices, purposes, and roles in the midst of a more differentiated society. In doing so, however, and this is the critical point in this typology, it still preserves a close connection with the traditional institutions of the society, especially those concerned with passing on that relatively integrated tradition. In some sense, it stands above and before any individual emerging into social consciousness. It is in this sense an "establishment." Such institutional forms appear in the religious public corporations of Germany and the Anglican church in India until 1928. Traces of it can still be found in United Methodism, and aspirations toward it occur in American Indian efforts to form indigenous churches.

Associational ecclesiologies, what H. R. Niebuhr called denominations,[2] legitimate themselves not by passing on a tradition but by organizing the purposes of individuals who covenant to form or join such associations. Unlike the institution, for which covenant usually emphasizes the hierarchical covenant of transmitting and receiving a heritage, the association emphasizes the present commitments of believers who covenant as relative equals in building up the religious organization. This form is in principle the most differentiated from other institutions of the society, because it requires the intentional efforts of persons who can act apart from other commitments to family, business, politics, education, and land.

Each of these types can have a wide variety of internal religious cultures and theologies, but each also exhibits some dominant tendencies. Communal ecclesiologies are often bound strongly to fundamental biological ties of family, clan, and tribe. A God of the created order who is like a great mother or father often shapes their fundamental view of authority, whether it be in the form of the Landesherr in Germany or the Raja in India. Individualist and voluntarist impulses have their own communal form, as illustrated most explicitly in India, but which have comparable devotional forms in Germany and America. Institutional ecclesiologies usually require a formal leadership, most typically a priesthood, which preserves the purity of doctrine, belief, and practice for the sake of believers. This pattern was well rehearsed by Troeltsch in his discussion of the European "church-type," which focuses on the mediation of divine grace to the people. The associational form rests on a more direct relationship of believers to the divine and to a voluntaristic individualism of obedience to the commands or ideals of a God known immediately by each person. The American Christian sense of disciplined devotion to Jesus exemplifies this kind of theology and ethics underlying an associational ecclesiology.

Each type also engages concepts and practices of covenantal publicity from significantly different angles. For the communal form, when covenant or covenantlike orientations emerge, they emphasize first of all the covenant between the whole people, their God, and their land. The givenness of this covenantal bond before all acts of adult consciousness tends to emphasize the hierarchical nature of the covenant.

For the institutional form, when covenant orientations emerge, they tend to have a more limited focus on the body of the religious organization itself. Covenantal and federal bonds may exist between the institution and other institutions, as revealed in the German case, and at that point have a negotiated and egalitarian character, but within the institution, covenantal practices, when they occur at all, are fairly hierarchical in order to preserve the emphasis on the stability of the institution over time.

Finally, in associational ecclesiologies covenantal orientations, which are often very strong, take on a highly egalitarian character in organizational life, even if each individual may preserve a hierarchical covenant directly with God. It is important to recognize in all actual cases in these three countries these ecclesiological and theological tendencies often exist in a complex tension within the same tradition. What is crucial for this inquiry is which directions these ecclesiologies will take to resolve their internal tensions as well as their effort to find a satisfactory engagement with emerging political forms.

We can see that religions might evolve from one to the other, namely, from communal to institutional to associational. The association could contain many elements of its past forms, especially in its liturgy or teaching, as with American denominations, or the increasingly associational form of the German *Großkirchen* (the "Great Churches" presently constituted as public law corporations), or the movement from communalism to political faction and religious sect in India. However, religions can also experience "devolution." An associational church can become so entrenched in a culture that it actually becomes institutional or communal, as with the Southern Baptist churches of the United States or the Protestant tribal churches in Northeast India. The voluntaristic individualism of the association becomes a kind of communal individualism that lacks the stable autonomy of the institution over against the wider culture. Even more complexly, American Indians now use associational religious concepts of free exercise to try to reclaim essentially communal religious practices in the high country of the American West.

Ecclesiology and the Federal-Republican Struggle

Awareness of these alternative ecclesiological types enables us to analyze the tensions, dynamics, and ambiguities present in the engagement of religion with federal-republicanism. It should be clear in this study that federal-republican structures generally prefer associational ecclesiologies. Communal ecclesiologies tend to be antagonistic to the federalist culture of governance through explicit, lawlike agreements and constitutions. Moreover, they have little conception of a public rooted in conceptions of egalitarian discourse. They prefer the traditions and customs of elders and the certainties of biological relationships to the flimsy bonds of the written word and human promises. Their positive contribution, however, lies in reminding increasingly fragmented societies of necessary and appropriate connections between people, land, and God, as well as of the intricate relationship between public and private life.

While having some affinities to communal forms, institutional ecclesiologies, as in Germany, can and have done a great deal to advance federal-republican culture. The institutional position of the Evangelical Churches in the former East Germany, for example, was indispensable to its role in generating the little publics that finally exploded in the collapse of the old regime. The problem they face, however, comes from the rebound of democratic voluntarism on church organization.

Federal-republicanism tends to generate the value of equality among religious groups and voluntarism within public associations. Ironically, however, this pressure toward voluntarist ecclesiologies tends to erode the differentiation of social institutions in the face of a growing state, or as we saw in the United States, a corporate marketplace. This erosion threatens models of federalism that depend on differentiation and a multiplicity of publics.

The question for the United Methodist Church was whether it could preserve its peculiar form of internal federalism and assembly in the face of this court-imposed corporatism. The question for the German churches was whether they could change and expand to preserve the dynamic associationalism aroused in the revolution.

In the last few years we have seen increasing financial and institutional pressures in Germany to make the religious public corporations into voluntary associations. Whether they can make this transition and still play a central public role in German life is a crucial question. Simultaneously, the American denominations are challenged to reclaim their own heritage of public assembly and federal order in the face of the dominance of corporate forms of organization.

Not only do these three forms reflect the spectrum of covenant from a hierarchical form emphasizing reception to an egalitarian form emphasizing negotiation, they also engage the values of publicity in various ways. First of all, the concept of *participation* has different meanings in the three ecclesiologies. In a communal ecclesiology everyone participates by nature of their being a member of the community. Religious participation is part of their identity, something ascribed to them rather than achieved through acts of commitment, expression, or ethical distinction. The institution shares some of this notion but does require some specific acts to express membership, especially cultic or ritual acts. However, the land is not tied to religion. In this case, several religious institutions can share the same land, as with Germany today, even though the 1648 Treaty of Westphalia still tied religion to prince and land. The associational type asks for a participation that goes beyond land, ritual, and community. It asks for regular intentional acts to maintain and lead the organization as well as receive its services. It is the most activistic and in this sense participatory form of ecclesiology, but also tends to be the most narrow in the way it construes covenantal bonds with land, other generations, and the wider community.

From an associational standpoint, communal ecclesiologies are often seen as hindering the participation of women in the political process, but from inside a communal perspective, women participate in the authority and power of the community from within their defined role. An institutionalist or associationalist defines political participation as activity within a sphere separate from the home, while the communalist finds true participation to be membership within the organic constitution of the community rooted in its households. Thus, the issue of women's political rights is at the same time a question of the degree to which one's ultimate vision of right relationships entails institutional differentiation.

Simply the development of institutional differentiation does not entail women's participation. In the West in the nineteenth century, middle-class wives and mothers at least stayed within a shrinking household as power and authority flowed to political, educational, and economic institutions. Many institutional and associational churches to this day resist their entry into leadership roles by appeal to a communal ethos centered in the household within a society that revolves around associations, corporations, and governments.

Finally, participation lifts up the question of how to integrate hitherto subordinated and excluded groups into the expanding public as well as how to repair the injustices accumulated over generations, whether by Nazi and Communist regimes, by caste and untouchability, or by genocidal invasion and slavery. From a biblical standpoint we call this the problem of reconciliation—the religious basis for participation.[3]

The value of public *plurality* also varies with each ecclesiological type. In one sense the communal type is the least pluralistic, because of the pervasiveness of a common culture it presumes. However, in the Indian case we can see a wide variety of religiousness, especially in Hinduism, based on the peculiarities of land—this rock, that river, or this caste. The political factions that have arisen in the more communal ecclesiologies of Islam and Hinduism as well as, of course, in the more institutional and associational forms of Christianity attest to the intense plurality that is at least latent to these communal forms. In institutional forms, as in Germany, plurality is more structured, with formal distinctions among the institutional parts or partners. This is an important source of the federal practices of the German churches, at least the Evangelical ones I studied. With associational churches, as with United Methodism, we see much of this institutional clarity, but we also see the confusing movements of assembly, revival, and voluntary association that baffled the court and the church itself, much as the Evangelical institutions were deeply strained by the movements and associations within them.

The mode of *persuasion* also varies among them. Communal persuasion occurs as much as possible through the slow habituation of rearing and ritual repetition. The word of the elders carries enormous weight. On the one hand, this shaping of consensus is very nonviolent, a characteristic of persuasion itself. On the other hand, because it lacks argument, refusal to consent to the communal consensus can lead to instant violence or exclusion. Certainly one reason the German revolution was relatively peaceful is because the people were already locked in argument through the network of little and often hidden publics, whereas in Romania and Yugoslavia this culture of persuasion seems not to have developed, especially in the churches.

Institutional persuasion takes place in formal settings and processes of synods, councils, and established centers of collective authority. The synods of the German churches nurtured a careful and often meticulous parliamentary procedure that gave great attention to the many institutional ramifications of each decision. In institutional settings there exists a high commitment not only to survival of the institution but to one's ongoing life in it. Persuasion occurs within these ongoing commitments in their widespread complexity. While argument can suffocate under the burdens of proof and consequence, it can also gain great precision and clarity.

In the association persuasion springs more from the convictions and experiences of the participants. While the association can gain very high loyalty from members, the members know ultimately they can associate for different purposes elsewhere. Thus, persuasion attends not so much to institutional consequence and complexity as to the immediate cogency of appeals within the specified purposes of the association. It focuses on processes of mobilizing support rather than on legitimation and control within a stable membership. In one respect associations depend more deeply on persuasion for their survival and vitality, but they also have trouble cultivating the depth of argument that this survival and adaptability need. This may be one reason why the American churches with a strong associational tendency have not developed arguments of ecclesiology strong enough to deal with the inquiries of lawyers and courts, as we saw in the Pacific Homes case.

Commonality, the fourth characteristic of publicity, has a fairly obvious relationship to these ecclesiological forms. The communal type has a very high degree of commonality, even though this may truncate efforts at open persuasion and plurality. The institution still displays a high degree of commonality in its institutional past, present organization, and embracing engagement of the people—the characteristics Troeltsch called the church type. The associational form has a much more specified set of commonalities, such as the distinctives of the denomination, the character of its covenant, its practices, or its name, but lacks the broader and often intangible commonalities that can be relied on to hold people together in argument or social change.

In forging this commonality the three ecclesiological forms tend to pick up different aspects of covenantal relationships. Communal forms, as Akenson and Bühlmann point out, tend to accentuate the covenant of election between the people as a whole and the God who guides their providential path in the midst of other groups. Institutional forms tend to emphasize the covenants among official representatives of the institution and other institutions. Within the institution they emphasize the hierarchical covenants that carry over the traditions of past generations or of divine power into the next generation. Associational ecclesiologies emphasize the process of negotiation among participants that yields up covenants to sustain their fragile publics. Each form of ecclesiology bears a different conception of the covenantal bonds that undergird the public. Each has different implications for the type of federal order they would sustain.

The fact that these three forms engage the principles of covenant and publicity in various ways gives us some guidance in seeing more precisely at what point they legitimate, critique, or delegitimate the federal-republican project. For instance, associational forms, as with the small groups of the German revolution or the original assemblies of the Methodists, can respond immediately to new opportunities in the society and give them at least a fleeting form of public expression, argument, and vivid symbolic form. The round tables or the conciliar process of the German revolution are vivid examples. However, they are not as good at institutionalizing these new publics or forming new patterns of federation and wider covenant.

Similarly, communal forms can lift up deep symbolic awareness of the bonds of people, land, ancestry, and the other givens of our existence. They can powerfully influence people's symbolic life, as with the communal traditions of America's original peoples. These new commonalities, especially in our own time the commonality of the land, can powerfully shape the deeper culture of a possible covenant among all the peoples on the land. However, they have great trouble, as we saw in the *Lyng* case, giving this commonality an institutional form that can represent this religious reality to other institutions. In the American case, this is not simply because of the intricate oppression under which native communities have suffered but also because the logic of a communal vision on the land does not press for the kind of institutional differentiation of family, government, economy, and education that requires such acts of representation and institutional specificity. This comes to poignant expression in the conflict between the U.S. government and the tribes of the high country, who sought to speak for a land that needs no representation to a court for whom neither trees nor land have legal standing at all. And yet it is this land that both precedes and succeeds humanity's pretensions of ownership and dominion. The Native American advocates challenged the wider American citizenry to rethink their understanding of land, people, and the sacred reality that bonds them, just as the court challenged the tribal advocates to reexamine their claims to representation, either of the tribes or of the land itself.

Ecclesiological Autonomy and Federal Unity

All these ecclesiological forms struggle to maintain integrity with their central commitments, but they also struggle to maintain relationships with other key dimensions of social life. Though the communal form seeks to absorb all these elements into a single overarching religious unity (the Sharia is a classic example), it too must struggle with relations to family, economy, politics, and science. The case of Shah Bano represents an intense struggle among Muslims over the proper relation of law, religion, and marriage. Moreover, communal forms are much more open to the geo-piety of land than are the others, as is clearest in the American Indian case. For them, land use issues are central to religious integrity in a way quite foreign to most Christians, who belong to a universal church rather than a particular place.

Communal forms tend to anchor social relations in kinship and propinquity—the village community and its council. The distinction of public and private, so crucial to a republican venture, is missing, as is the difference between intimacy and publicity. The relation of parent and child, husband and wife, defines the whole range of social roles. Changes in marriage and family, therefore, are critical to the maintenance of the whole structure of communal religion, which is very clear in the Indian situation, but still powerfully important even when communal religion is a subordinate type.

Institutional forms, such as the ones I explored in Germany, press for a full publicity for the institution in a public composed of other institutions. To stretch an analogy, they replace the princes and bishops that monopolized the public sphere in late medieval times. This public character of the institutions seeks both to form the society in accord with a higher ethical vision and to provide for its general cohesion. This places them historically in relatively close relation to government and law. The tension between these cohesive and prophetic roles of the Evangelical churches lay at the heart of their ambivalent relation to the groups germinating revolution under their roofs in 1988–89.

With the associational churches, especially in America, the market emerges as the most important partner institution shaping ecclesiology. Rather than the distinction between "public" and "private" churches that we find in Germany, or between communal minorities and institutions that we find in India, we find the market distinction between "for-profit" and "non-profit" corporations, in which the for-profit conception of associational life is becoming increasingly dominant, as we saw in the Pacific Homes case. Simultaneously, the autonomy of individual believers and covenanters becomes the purported autonomy of the consumer and producer in the free exchange of the economic market. Here autonomy, choice, and plurality—in short, freedom—become central. With this market orientation, religious institutions also begin to emulate the corporatist forms of the primary actors in the economy. Just as the German churches align their salary scales with the government civil service, so the American churches align their organizational models with the successful business corporation. The Pacific Homes case showed how deeply this market corporatism shapes not only the churches but also the way the courts perceive them. The threat this poses to the integrity of their faith and ecclesiology is hardly recognized because of the churches' wholesale immersion in this culture of market corporatism, while the threat to the integrity of a federal republic surfaces repeatedly in efforts to reform campaign financing and lobbying—the invasion of the corporate market into political persuasion and participation.

Thus, the question of the autonomy of religion is not merely one of the "separation of church and state," though this is indeed critical. For communal ecclesiologies, it is the autonomy of the whole community from outside interference. For institutional religions it is a question of capacity to participate in the interinstitutional sphere, which demands special provisions in constitutional law. For associationalists, it is as much autonomy over against communalism, on the one hand, and the state, on the other, as it is autonomy in the face of the forces of market and finance.

Communal religion can press for a quasi federalism to preserve its autonomy but usually has to give up many elements of its organic ethics if it is to fit the mold of equal political participation required in a republic.[4] Institutional churches, as in the German case, can establish federative relationships among themselves, but their large-scale bureaucratic tendencies toward central financing and control can override impulses toward congregational, associational, or synodal autonomy, as with the reintroduction of the *Kirchensteuer* and civil pay scales in the former East German churches. Both internal federalism and the formation of spirited publics compete with the corporatist impulses of the institution. Finally, autonomy for the associational churches, while it fosters the spirit of democratic assembly, also falls prey to the autonomy of private consumers and cannot preserve enough institutional integrity to confront the other large institutions in the society.

In each case, these dilemmas of autonomy affect the federal-republican project. The communal ecclesiology can lift up issues of organic unity and ecology but can undermine the establishment of political federation on a territorial basis. Institutional ecclesiologies can press for interinstitutional federative relationships, help develop deeper political covenants, and harbor associational developments, but have trouble nurturing the dynamic of public assembly over the long haul.[5] Associational ecclesiologies nurture the spirit of free assembly, but their tendency to overemphasize the autonomy of individuals tends to subordinate public covenants and ecological relationships to the contracts and exchanges of the market.

Each of these ambiguities in the relationship between religion and the federal-republican struggle for adequate differentiation shapes the way the specific relationship of religion to the constitutional state emerges. Because of the power of communal religion in India, the federal republic has emphasized its "secularity" but also has developed the conflicting principles of "equal protection" to protect these otherwise threatened religious communities and "compensatory discrimination" to overcome their deleterious effects on people's capacity for democratic participation. Both the Shah Bano and the Soosai cases show how these three principles come into enormous conflict.

For the democratic experiment to advance, communal religions will have to develop sufficient internal association and institutionalization to promote intentional change within them, especially regarding principles of equality, persuasion, and covenant-like agreements. At the same time, the state will have to preserve its neutrality and equal protection if not its very secularity in the face of religious plurality. That is to say, the process of political negotiation through voluntary party formation must take precedence over the strategy of religio-communal segmentation in order to serve the requirements of public participation on a democratic basis.[6]

Church-state relations in Germany are still deeply shaped by what Wolfgang Huber calls the "terraced parity" between public and private incorporation of the churches.[7] The Catholic and Evangelical "public corporation" churches have a privileged status in education, financing, broadcast media, and many other aspects of public life. All of this exists so that they can play a fully public role in the affairs of the republic. While this can make possible a vital role in shaping the religious basis for the federal republic, the experience of excessive entanglement between church and state under the kaiser and the Nazis has made them very reluctant until recently to try to support the movement for an appropriate civil religion for the expanded federal republic. Moreover, while they can sponsor forums and assemblies, they have understandable difficulty moving from a rootage in the institutions of social service and governance to rootage in the associations and free initiative of a shifting public.

However, it is this dependence on voluntary initiative that has sustained the many "private corporation" churches in Germany. While they have little direct impact on the institutional public life of Germany, they provide an ecclesiological model for the public corporation churches and nurture a kind of associational religiosity that the "Great Churches" will increasingly have to nurture if they are to survive.

Finally, the relation of church and state in America is defined constitutionally by the tension between "establishment" and "free exercise." We have rehearsed some of the difficulties of the Supreme Court as it seeks to steer decisions between these two principles. It seems fairly clear that this way of defining the autonomy of religion within a federal republic assumes that religion is fundamentally an association of believers. This constitutional configuration exists for the sake of individual liberty first of all, religious liberty being one form.

What gets left out in the process is the important, even positive role religion might play in the formation of public character and culture, although in the case of the American Indian Civil Rights Act it recognizes this role within the communal religion of the American Indians. However, this kind of religion is to be constrained to reservations or to private associations. Moreover, as we saw in the Pacific Homes and *Lyng* cases, the principle of free exercise is increasingly taken out of its original context as an aspect of political freedom and turned into an aspect of market exchange, whether of land, services, or commodities. Thus, both the possible positive dimensions of religion for the cultural underpinnings of a federal republic ("establishment") and the function of religion as a protopublic of free assemblies ("free exercise") are neglected or dismissed. Meanwhile, the inevitable need to ground and legitimate a federal republic in more ultimate commitments must turn to an increasingly autonomous civil religion of nationalism rather than the loftier form originally discerned by Robert Bellah and others.

Both the overall interinstitutional place of religion and its specific relation to government deeply shape how religion, whether communal, institutional, or associational, interacts with essential themes of the federal-republican struggle. Just as there exist tensions as well as mutual reinforcement between

federalism and its constituent republics, so there are points of possible reinforcement between the various structures of religion and specific aspects of
the overall federal-republican framework.

Roles of Religion in the Federal-Republican Project

I now turn to some of these specific roles religion can play within this
framework, given the variety of structures and orientations I have examined.
Four key roles have emerged in this study: church assemblies as protopublics, religious liturgies as crucial media of legitimation or delegitimation,
specifically religious culture as the generator of modal personalities for public life, and the role of religion in the process of reconciliation, including
reconciliation with the land.

In each of the studies we have seen the power of small publics gathered
for prayer, worship, education, and governance. Whether at the round tables
under the church's roof in Germany, the sometimes vociferous synods and
congregational meetings of South India, or the councils of aboriginal Americans or the congregations of European immigrants, churches and similar
religious organizations can and do create little publics in which people can
achieve enough trust to speak their convictions and seek the truth through
conversation and argument. In each case these free assemblies press beyond
the established structures of religious or political life. This was certainly clear
in Germany, but it also occurs in Soosai's struggle for full citizenship in
India. Sometimes, as with America's Methodism, the institutional dimension
of the church forgets or fails to grasp the import of its originating assemblies. Sometimes, as with the supporters of the Muslim Personal Law Board,
the communal and patriarchal elements crush aspirations for civil equality.
Communal religion overcomes publicity as well as the covenantal negotiation necessary for political federalism.

In the American Indian case, conciliar and egalitarian elements are
strong, but in taking the land as their religious base Native Americans are
largely unable to defend this peculiar religious public in American constitutional law. To do so would call into question the absence of the land as a
partner in the deeper covenant underlying that Constitution. Honoring their
bond with the land, aboriginal peoples and their associated republics require
a reconception of the nature of the federation that composes the American
federal republic, both in relation to the land and to its original inhabitants.
While this might in fact be politically feasible, we have already seen the
power of economic corporations and market forces to constrain the unfolding of religious publics, whether Yurok or Methodist, in American society.

In short, religious publics, when they arise out of commitments transcending the present political order, are protopublics. Religion is pre-
political in the sense of cultivating the fundamental orientations and mores
that make a polity possible. But even more, they can be protopublics that
challenge the limits of such orders as well, whether in their conception of

citizenship, of land, or of authority and the nature of power. However, these assemblies often have an effervescent life that can evaporate into purely personal memory without the capacity to lay down deeper covenants and cultures that can sustain an ongoing public life.

The covenantal lens helps us to see both the critical importance of constitutions as well as their limits. Constitutionalism helps people move beyond the bonds of kinship and tribe to a more expansive polity. However, constitutionalism can only function if it rests on a broader and deeper set of mutual agreements that are expressed by the idea of covenant. First of all, it pushes us to identify the actual publics, as with the American and Indian cases, that constitute the federal order. Second, it presses us to identify the bonds of people with their shared land, in terms of the land both as a partner in covenant and as a sacred trust. Third, it leads us to think of the way the compacts of the peoples of the land are related to their sources of ultimate trust and hope. Their life together in federal order is a promise about the future. Without some basis for trust in this common future their compact cannot be sustained. In short, covenantal concepts help us frame the question of constitutional order in terms of broader and deeper relationships.

Another critical means for sustaining public life in federal order is through liturgy, worship, and symbolism. These activities lie at the heart of a civil religion that both mediates the particular perspectives and patterns of religious groups and provides a common basis for their public interaction. From a federal-republican perspective such civil religion needs to rehearse the memory of critical experiences of public assembly and covenantal trust—the round tables in Germany, Gandhi's nonviolent fasts and demonstrations, and America's congregational meetings and conventions. Both the inspiring acts of constitutionmaking and the shameful violation of sacred promises need to be lifted up as times of recommitment to common public purpose.

Civil religion, especially in its contact with the deep religious forms of major religious traditions, also is shaped for good or for ill by their symbolization of the Divine and of the person. From time to time I have touched upon the symbolic dimensions of the churches and religious groups studied here, primarily in terms of their symbolization of the Divine. Most of the worship forms cultivating such images of God stand in ambiguous contradiction to republican aspirations. Patriarchal images of God reinforced the institution of the *Landesherr* in German tradition but also can remind people today of a kind of holistic care promised in a reformed socialism or an ecological care of the earth—missing dimensions in much of the republican struggle.

In India the Christian churches have faced the question of how to resymbolize their worship life in terms appropriate to India's history, cultures, and republican aspirations without losing their integrity as a distinct faith community. One move would be to concentrate not on traditional "Hindu" myths, symbols, and rituals but on the connection between the symbols of ecclesial publicity and covenantal responsibility often buried within their own heritage and relate these to the federal-republican struggle for cultural roots to sustain and guide it. Whether the churches can achieve persuasive compromise over communal factionalism and foster covenantal trust over contractual legalism is a serious question but also a critical opportunity for them and for the Indian republic.

In Germany, the memory of the churches' germination of new public life under the Communist regime threatens to be buried in recrimination over Stasi files or the desperate effort to sustain inherited institutional structures within a shrinking economic base. The symbols and memories of round tables and conciliar assemblies become buried under mounting bills and miles of files. However, it is these symbols of spirited public assembly and covenantal responsibility for creation that liturgy can vividly remember and anchor in the deeper culture. Though many of the concrete proposals for reform were thwarted by the economics of reunion, the culture from which they spring can be seeded in the ongoing cult of anticipation in worship. The fleeting memory of the ecstatic liberation of public assemblies returns as eschatological hope only if it can be nurtured in the regular worship life of the churches.

Methodists and American Indians are nurtured in liturgies for realities that have no proper home in the Constitution—the free assemblies of the people and the covenant with the land. Methodists struggle with how to regain an integral relation between their corporate-driven ecclesiology and the revivals of their origins without simply cultivating an individualism of experience typical of consumer life. Tribal peoples struggle with how to celebrate their bonds with the sacred land while at the same time they participate in and depend on the wider markets and publics of American life that spurn and exploit it. In both cases liturgies cultivating values for public life need to lift up relations of deeper covenant and conciliar assembly to counter the enormous forces of market individualism.

Symbolizations of the divine always imply a symbolization of the self. The communal individualism of Hindu puja works to undermine the conception of the self as participant in an ordered assembly but can preserve some sense of the person's autonomy before the Divine. The problem, of course, is how to link this sense of self both to notions of equality between men and women and to the almost liturgical procedures of public argument, negotiation, compromise, and agreement. In India the question is how to move from this communal individualism to an associational individualism that can avoid the worst aspects of an entrepreneurial individualism that knows neither bonds to land nor to public associations and institutions. German culture faces another version of this in moving from a citizenship based on biological ancestry to one based on commitment to a Constitution.

In both cases people ask whether rituals of covenant making, constitutional commitment, and public-spirited volunteerism can both supersede these communal bonds and also corral the forces of radical individualism unleashed in an unconstrained free market. In the American situation, where such free market individualism is already well advanced, people have to not only fan the embers of an inherited associationalism but also practically reinvent the bond of people and land cultivated in communal traditions.

To illustrate such reconstruction of worship symbolism I turn to the central Christian rites of baptism and Eucharist, or Holy Communion. For the Christian churches this reconstruction of individualism can focus on how baptism, with its original legitimation of public participation, can be reintegrated with the communal themes of the earth's produce and of human *convivium* that are found in the table symbolism of Eucharist. Here we rediscover the powerful meaning of baptism for the abolition of slavery and gender discrimination at the same time that we rediscover the Eucharist as the form of a new covenantal assembly that links the land, the intimacy of communal eating, and the hopes for a new creation. That this might occur at a round table could convey even more powerfully the aspirations for a truly participatory public generated in our contemporary struggles. This moves the Christian Eucharist away from its traditional institutional setting as the work of a duly ordained priest within a hierarchy of sacrificial order to a meal of memory and anticipation more redolent of its origins in Jewish Passover. These renewed and reconstructed connections, with their ecumenical implications, can then contribute to a wider cultural base linking a general American civil religion to its particular religious roots. How, then, this kind of religious shift relates to a growing Buddhist and Muslim presence in America leads us to yet further questions of the development of a civil-religious base for a pluralistic society.

With these brief summary explorations we see how religion, especially as seen in terms of ecclesiology, presents issues of societal differentiation as well as cultural underpinning. It struggles for an appropriate social autonomy as well as cultural permeation within a pluralistic milieu. Moreover, these religious forms shape and are shaped by federal-republican institutions in complex ways, depending to a high degree on the other dominant institutions in the society, whether they be communal, corporate, or governmental. Finally, each religious tradition faces deep choices about the evolution of its rituals and symbols in the context of the contemporary struggle for public life in federal association.

Religion, Reconciliation, and the Republican Struggle

At the heart of many of these struggles, as we saw, is the effort to reconcile historic antagonists in a way that promotes fuller participation in public life and an expanded sense of covenantal responsibility, both among the peoples of a republic and between them and their land, as well as other peoples' straining to a fuller federal order. In Germany it is the struggle for reconciliation within the shadows and devastations of Nazi and Communist totalitarianisms. In India it is the struggle to rectify the deprivations of caste and tribal discrimination as well as the deep enmities among religio-communal groups. In America it is the struggle for reparation between enslaving and enslaved populations and between immigrant settler and aboriginal inhabitant. The term "reconciliation" includes not only the acts of forgiveness that establish new standing among the historic parties but also reparation sufficient to enable people to participate in the common life of a republic.[8] Ultimately, it means, from the standpoint of covenantal publicity, the capacity to share a common future.

The concept of covenantal publicity seeks to hold together several dimensions of this dynamic of reconciliation. First, the idea of covenant points to the way in which new relationships, not rooted in the inevitability of repeating communally inherited habits of hatred and cycles of revenge, are forged through intentional acts of entrustment.[9] Such acts have to emerge in some sense in a miraculous manner in order to break the ordinary expectations forged in the oppressive relationships of the past. Sometimes they are the miraculous acts of individuals, such as Mahatma Gandhi in his search to bridge the mistrust of communal hatreds. Sometimes it is a historic miracle, such as the experience of nonviolence in Leipzig or the fall of the Berlin Wall. Without this miraculous appearance of a new starting point, there is nothing that the aspirations for reconciliation can fasten on in order to form a new order of relationships. From a covenantal standpoint, this is the "hierarchical moment" that extends to us a new principle of relationship.

This new moment, what the Germans aptly called a Wende, opens up the possibility of a new future. Again, covenant making, in its biblical origins, was a way to begin a new life together with the land. Without this new possibility, there is no reason to come together in an intentional, constructive way to secure that new future. Without this new possibility of a shared future on the basis of a new covenant, reconciliation is impossible. In Germany it has been the hope for a new German federal order of widespread publicity anchoring a new federal order for Europe that would overcome the nationalist adventurism that plunged the world into chaos in this century. For India, it has been the hope for a truly multicultural republic with democratic self-governance. For America it is the hope for a new plurality out of which to gain a new relationship with the land.[10]

Another way of putting this significance of a shared future for the work of reconciliation is to remind ourselves of the historic link between covenant and vocation. We already explored this somewhat in the German case and can lift it up again here. Reconciliation can occur as people share a sense of common vocation, that is, how they will participate in the vision of a common future. This sense of calling stands over against a fixation on the past, with its infinite complexity of sin and victimage, each act crying out for publicity and reparation. However, these acts, of an often incomprehensible brutality, must be approached from the standpoint of the miraculous opening up of a possible new order founded not on the consequences of the past and its compensations but on the new covenant forged in the midst of new hopes.

It is important to see how such a notion of public vocation is quite different from the kind of nationalism that is often legitimated by appeal to the ideas of national election frequently associated with covenant. It is only by seeing the connection between covenant, reconciliation, and vocation that a people might establish and pursue a collective purpose that is not focused on their own aggrandizement but on the fostering of just relations with other peoples as well as among historic enemies within. This is a rather hidden dimension of the German awareness that a new German federalism has to be a federalism within a federal Europe. In India it becomes a federative vocation of reconciling a vast variety of peoples in the mutual benefits arising from a common care for the land. In America it is a national vocation to find reconciliation among descendants of settlers, slaves, and aboriginal peoples in a renewed relation to the land.

With this awareness of how covenant, vocation, and reconciliation inform each other, we can turn to the way in which the consequences of the past must be addressed in order to live out this new covenant and its vocational requirements. How can we begin to entrust ourselves to each other once we have entrusted ourselves to a new future? Here the dynamics of publicity come more fully into play. The first involves the question of which contemporary groups or persons are responsible, whether from the standpoint of oppressive destruction or of victimage. The second involves the kind of public process for correcting the wrongs of the past in the light of the new republic emerging in the covenant for a new future.

In the German case we saw the importance of moving from the examination of files and other evidence—the pursuit of legal and documentary truth—to the many publics of personal confrontation, whether they be tribunals, forums, or round table discussions. Because of the complex interplay between oppressor and victim, these little publics provided a way both to clarify and assess the past and also to forge the bases for new public discourse, a new public culture of democratic openness. Without them the struggle to compensate victims would disintegrate into an endless legalism of recrimination and suspicion. With them, the struggle for forgiveness, understanding, and enough truthfulness to nurture new trust would be impossible.

This round table phenomenon—a product of the miracle of the Wende—thus persists as a crucial principle binding together a future order with the process of reconciliation it requires. Its importance goes beyond the legal questions of reparation, with their need for specifics about agents, properties, and times, to those of public entrustment and the formation of a new political culture. From the standpoint of covenantal publicity, it is this kind of dynamic that needs to be captured in religious ritual that can continually reinform the deeper covenants of the general public culture. That is, these assemblies to seek truth and trust are inseparable from the formation of covenants for a new order. Without them the legal expressions of this new order in constitution and law lack an adequate cultural basis for long-term survival.

Covenantal publicity, in weaving together these dimensions of the process of reconciliation, offer some normative tools for approaching the questions of compensatory discrimination in India and those of affirmative action and land reparations in America. They do not solve the many particular legal and economic problems that emerge in these struggles, but they do ask that we frame the question in a way that focuses on what is needful for the founding of a new order of covenantal responsibility and public participation.

The Concept of Covenantal Publicity: An Evaluation

The rich narratives explored in three different cultures can easily lend themselves to reflections and analyses far beyond the few I can attempt here. The concept of covenantal publicity offers only one important window into the intricate dialectic between religious and political institutions within the modern struggle for public life in a federal constitutional order. At this point I conclude with some evaluation of the adequacy of this concept for understanding this dialectic.

Covenantal publicity has functioned as both an analytical mirror for seeing what is going on and a normative lens to help us envision possible future directions. As an analytical instrument it has helped us to expand the range of factors at work in defining the institutional structure as well as the cultural ground of federal-republican orders. It directs us to the importance of the "deep covenants" of common consensus necessary for a public order as well as the way these covenants must engage people's deepest commitments to land and to the God who sustains them over time. It also directs us to the ways that forms of religious organization, that is, of ecclesiology, shape how a public sphere arises in the interstices of family, economy, and governance.

The idea of covenant leads us to expand our conception of what is necessary for a federal order while that of ecclesiology deepens our understanding of the way relationships in the public sphere must be sustained by the deep habits nurtured in religious publics. Moreover, the concept of covenantal publicity alerts us to the way that discussions of federalism and covenant require examination of issues of publicity and ecclesiology, just as discussions of democracy and of publics must lead us back to issues of federalism. Each side of this conceptual pair demands the other. In short, "covenantal publicity" can expand our horizon of inquiry for exploring some fundamental issues in contemporary federal-republicanism.

The obvious normative import of this concept has been to emphasize the need for some sort of mediating term like this to enable religious traditions to play a positive role in the contemporary struggle for public life and federal constitutionalism. Here we encounter more ambiguity. Certainly we can see how this might be the case. Covenantal and federalist ideas and practices have a long interaction in the West, as has conciliar ecclesiology and the development of modern publics. Moreover, where publicity and covenant have been absent in religious life, it is more difficult to find a cultural base for federal-republican order.

It is also clear, however, that such a heritage, or even analogs to it, exists in an often contradictory amalgam with elements of monarchy, patriarchy, communalism, privatism, and pieties of biology and land that can be quite inimical to such a political culture. Religious traditions can themselves form not only protopublics but also antipublics of diverse tendencies and possibilities. Their liturgies may be quite antirepublican, but their ecclesiological form may assist societal differentiation or pluralism necessary for federal-republican order. Conversely, their ecclesiology may be quite conciliar in many ways but unable to transcend ties of biology or geography to participate in a wider federalism. Moreover, religious resources to help advance group reconciliation may be present in a tradition but be unable to form the public structures necessary for people to actualize that reconciliation. Such ambiguities as well as many others have emerged repeatedly in this study, making it impossible in any simple way to assess how "religion" or even particular religious institutions positively engage the federal-republican struggle.

Some of this ambiguity is due to the way elements of covenantal publicity are related to other elements in a religious tradition. Is the idea of covenant largely hierarchical or egalitarian? Is it connected primarily to individuals or does it also undergird the formation of associations? Is it primarily a matter of identity and group "election" or is it a relational principle transcending communal heritage and exclusivity? Is the making of covenant a capacity of each believer or is this a representative function by religious, communal, or political leaders? All of these considerations have played a role in these cases, shaping the way religious traditions and structures have engaged federal-republican efforts.

Other aspects of this ambiguity involve the social location of the religion. It has made a big difference whether a relatively differentiated religion has found its nearest institutional partner in family, market, or government. Moreover, the kind and degree of its piety toward biological inheritance and to land has further shaped the way religion is mediated to the public sphere proper. At every turn, therefore, specifically religious as well as sociological factors have shaped the way religion, even bearing elements of covenantal publicity, has interacted with efforts toward federal order and expanded publics of political participation.

Thus, while covenantal publicity helps illuminate ways religion positively engages the federal-republican struggle, it also shows us the many tortured paths by which this engagement proceeds. The presence of these elements alone does not ensure such a positive religious contribution, even if they can make an important one. What is even more difficult to assess is how religious traditions can enhance elements like this by transformations in their own traditions. At this historical juncture, probably the most important question in this regard is whether and how the various Islamic traditions can find ways to bring latent elements of covenantal publicity to the fore from within. The answer to this question takes us far beyond this book but is, I believe, the kind of question we should be asking.

An Afterword

Over the desk where much of this book has been written is a large photograph taken of the Berlin Wall on November 9, 1989, with joyous Berliners climbing over it and standing on its top. People mill around in startled wonderment, trying to grasp this historical miracle. Across the room over my wife's worktable hangs a colorful calendar painted by some children at a school run by Jane Sahi near Bangalore, India. It depicts an ancient story from Rajasthan about the women of the Bishnoi community, who tied themselves self-sacrificially to trees that a callous prince was using to build his palace. Over 250 of these women died before the prince withdrew and spared the trees. The story has become an important mythic element of the ecological movement in India today. Out the window I can see a portion of the Smoky Mountains, the ancestral home of the Cherokee, with its sacred spaces and lush slopes and hollows. Down the hall hangs a poster from the first reunion, at Red Clay, Georgia, in 1984, of the two bands of Cherokees separated by the expulsion order of 1838. Their faltering efforts at reunion echo the even larger problem of reconciliation still facing American aboriginals, European and Asian immigrants, and the descendants of enslaved Africans.

These images have carried on a quiet subliminal conversation with each other and with me as I have struggled to understand the religious, cultural, and political dimensions of the experiences recounted in this book. The conceptual work of this book may be a helpful contribution, but it is the power of their actual witness that can lead us to new and deeper covenants within a wider public of common care for the earth we share with friends and strangers.

Notes

Introduction

1. Henry Sumner Maine, *Ancient Law: Its Connection with the Early History of Society and its Relation to Modern Ideas* (10th ed. [1884]; Boston: Beacon Press, 1963), 163–65, 300–335.

2. I have elaborated the theoretical framework utilizing these two key concepts in *God's Federal Republic: Reconstructing Our Governing Symbol* (New York: Paulist Press, 1988).

Chapter 1. Envisioning the Engagement

1. See my *God's Federal Republic: Reconstructing Our Governing Symbol* (New York: Paulist Press, 1988), 54–62, 129–44, for a fuller historical presentation of these characteristics. The work of Hannah Arendt, John Dewey, and Jürgen Habermas lies behind much of this formulation.

2. The literature on covenant is very extensive. Some key works influencing my thought and presentation are Dennis J. McCarthy, *Old Testament Covenant: A Survey of Current Opinions* (Richmond: John Knox, 1972); Ernest J. Nicholson, *God and His People: Covenant and Theology in the Old Testament* (Oxford: Clarendon Press, 1986); Perry Miller, *The New England Mind: The Seventeenth Century* (Boston: Beacon Press, 1961); Douglas Sturm, *Community and Alienation* (Notre Dame: Notre Dame University Press, 1988); *Documents of Political Foundation Written by Colonial Americans: From Covenant to Constitution*, ed. Donald S. Lutz (Philadelphia: Institute for the Study of Human Issues, 1986); and Max L. Stackhouse, *Creeds, Societies and Human*

Rights (Grand Rapids: William B. Eerdmans, 1984). See my *God's Federal Republic*, 103–28, for a more extensive discussion of these points.

3. George Mendenhall, "Law and Covenant in Israel and the Ancient Near East," *The Biblical Archaeologist* 18, nos. 2 and 3 (May and September 1954): 26–46, 49–76.

4. For major treatment of the concept of federalism see Daniel J. Elazar's expansive four-volume treatment, *Covenant and Polity in Biblical Israel* (New Brunswick, NJ: Transaction Books, 1994), *Covenant and Commonwealth* (New Brunswick, NJ: Transaction Books, 1996), *Covenant and Constitution* (New Brunswick, NJ: Transaction Books, 1996), and *Covenant and Civil Society* (New Brunswick, NJ: Transaction Books, 1997). See also Daniel J. Elazar and John Kincaid, *Covenant, Polity and Constitution* (Lanham: University Press of America, 1983); and Daniel J. Elazar, *Exploring Federalism* (University: University of Alabama Press, 1986).

5. See Daniel J. Elazar, "Federal Models of Civil Authority," *Journal of Church and State* 33, no. 2 (Spring 1991): 231–54; and Durga Das Basu, *Comparative Federalism* (New Delhi: Prentice-Hall of India, 1987).

6. See Donald Harman Akenson, *God's Peoples: Covenant and Land in South Africa, Israel and Ulster* (Ithaca: Cornell University Press, 1992) for a historical exploration of the way a covenantal "grid" has been used in this exclusivist way in Northern Ireland, South Africa, and modern Israel. Akenson focuses more on the social exclusion arising from covenant as election of a people rather than on the process of government through constitutional negotiation.

7. Questions of legitimation preoccupied Max Weber and Emile Durkheim as well as many of their successors—Talcott Parsons, Robert Bellah, and Peter Berger.

8. See the classic study by Norman Cohn, *The Pursuit of the Millennium: Revolutionary Millenarians and Mystical Anarchists of the Middle Ages*, rev. and exp. (New York: Oxford University Press, 1970), as well as the seminal theories of ideology and utopia by Karl Mannheim, *Ideology and Utopia: An Introduction to the Sociology of Knowledge*, trans. Louis Wirth and Edward Shils (New York: Harcourt, Brace, and World, 1936).

9. See the classic studies by Lewis Mumford, *Technics and Civilization* (New York: Harcourt, Brace, and World, 1963); and Max Weber, *The City*, trans. Don Martindale and Gertrud Neuwirth (New York: Free Press, 1958).

10. Anthony Black, *Council and Commune: The Conciliar Movement and the Fifteenth Century Heritage* (London: Burns & Oates, 1979).

11. Parker J. Palmer, *A Company of Strangers: Christians and the Renewal of America's Public Life* (New York: Crossroads Publishers, 1981).

12. Talcott Parsons, "Christianity and Modern Industrial Society," in *Sociological Theory and Modern Society* (New York: Free Press, 1967), 402–21; and Robert Bellah, "Religious Evolution," in *Reader in Comparative Religion: An Anthropological Approach*, 2d ed., ed. William A. Lessa and Evon Z. Vogt (New York: Harper and Row, 1965), 73–87.

13. The sociological concept of mediation goes back to Emile Durkheim. For recent discussions see Peter Berger and Richard Neuhaus, *To Empower People: The Role of Mediating Structures in Public Policy* (Washington: American Enterprise Institute, 1977); and Michael Novak, ed., *Democracy and Mediating Structures: A Theological Inquiry* (Washington: American Enterprise Institute, 1980).

Chapter 2. The Churches and Germany's "Peaceful Revolution" of 1989–90

1. The "Bund der Evangelischen Kirchen" (BEK) was a federation composed of the "Landeskirchen" (so-called state or regional churches) in the former German Democratic Republic (GDR). I will call them "Evangelical" rather than Lutheran, even though they are not necessarily evangelical in the American sense. This study focuses on the Evangelical Churches of the former GDR, most of which were members of the BEK.

For an absorbing history of this period see John Burgess, *The East German Church and the End of Communism* (New York: Oxford University Press, 1997). The theological examination by Gregory Baum, *The Church for Others: Protestant Theology in East Germany* (Grand Rapids: William B. Eerdmans, 1996), unfortunately came to me too late to inform this study.

2. For this history and perspective see Wolfgang Renzsch, "German Federalism in Historical Perspective," *Publius: The Journal of Federalism* 19, no. 4 (Fall 1989): 17–33.

3. For the argument for federalism in the face of democratic centralism see Carl Schmitt, "The Constitutional Theory of Federalism," *Telos* 91 (Spring 1992): 26–56, and the introductory essay by G. L. Ullmen in that volume.

4. As guides here I am using Wolfgang Huber, *Kirche und Öffentlichkeit* (Stuttgart: Klett, 1973), 49–98, 490–549, and Wolfgang Huber, *Kirche* (Munich: Kaiser, 1988), 150–72. See also Martin Honecker, *Cura Religionis Magistratus Christiani: Studien zum Kirchenrecht im Luthertum des 17. Jh.: Insbesonders bei Johann Gerhard* (Munich: Claudius, 1968), 31–40.

5. See Reinhart Koselleck, "Bund: Bündnis, Föderalismus, Bundesstaat," in *Geschichtliche Grundbegriffe: Historisches Lexikon Zur Politisch-Sozialen Sprache in Deutschland*, vol. 1 (1972), 600–09, 635–49; as well as J. F. Gerhard Goeters, "Föderaltheologie," in *Theologisches Realenzyklopädie*, vol. 11 (1983), 246–52; Gottlob Schrenk, *Gottesreich und Bund im älteren Protestantismus, Vornehmlich bei Johannes Cocceius* (Gütersloh: C. Bertelsmann, 1923); and Schweizerischer Evangelischer Kirchenbund Theologisches Kommission, *Bundestheologie und Bundestradition* (Bern: Schweizerischer Evangelischer Kirchenbund, 1987), 27–43. For the mix of monarchical and federal structures in Prussia see Rudolf Smend, "Protestantismus und Demokratie," in *Staatsrechtliche Abhandlungen und andere Aufsätze* (Berlin: Duncker und Humboldt, 1955 [1932]), 297–308.

6. See Schrenk, *Gottesreich und Bund*, 293–97.

7. See Huber, *Kirche*, 169–72, for a short description of the various concepts of Volkskirche.

8. Adelheid Bullinger, "Das Ende des Landesherrlichen Kirchenregiments und die Neugestaltung der Evangelischen Kirche," *Zeitschrift für evangelischen Kirchenrecht* 19, no. 1/2 (May 1974): 73–105, provides a helpful discussion of these dynamics within the Prussian-dominated churches that came to compose the BEK.

9. The "church tax" freed the pastors from unequal salaries and from dependence on local nobility. See Huber, *Kirche*, 154–60. For an example of the contemporary attack on the church tax see Horst Herrmann, *Die Kirche und unser Geld: Daten, Tatsachen, Hintergründe* (Hamburg: Rasch und Röhring, 1990).

10. See Huber, *Kirche*, 150–71, for further dimensions of this arrangement.

11. The use of "in" in the name bespeaks a critical distancing from a church that would be only an aspect of the state or nation. For a brief overview see Michael Ahme, *Der Reformversuch der EKD, 1970–76* (Stuttgart: Kohlhammer, 1990), 12–21. The main thread of this story concerns the dominant Protestant churches. The Ro-

man Catholic churches, a decided minority in the East, took somewhat different paths for historic as well as ecclesiological reasons.

12. Art. 140 of the Fundamental Law, confirming the Weimar Constitution's Articles 136–149, 140. For interpretations of this constitutional move see Rudolf Smend, "Staat und Kirche nach dem Bonner Grundgesetz," in *Staat und Kirchen in der Bundesrepublik: Staatskirchenrechtliche Aufsätze 1950–1967*, ed. Helmut Quaritsch and Hermann Weber (Bad Homburg: Verlag Max Gehlen, 1951), 34–43; Konrad Hesse, "Die Entwicklung des Staatskirchenrechts seit 1945," *Jahrbuch des Öffentlichen Rechts der Gegenwart, Neue Folge*, 1–80 (1961); Siegfried Grundmann, "Das Verhältnis von Staat und Kirche auf der Grundlage des Vertragskirchenrechts," in Quaritsch and Wever, eds., *Staat und Kirchen*, 248–64; Huber, *Kirche und Öffentlichkeit*, 491–95; and Konrad Hesse, *Grundzüge des Verfassungsrechts der Bundesrepublik Deutschland*, 17th ed. (Heidelberg: C. F. Müller, 1990), 150–53, 184–86.

13. Arts. 4, 5, 9, and 33 (Sec. 3) of the Fundamental Law.

14. For the history of this development see Hans-Gerhard Koch, *Staat und Kirche in der DDR: Zur Entwicklung ihrer Beziehungen 1945–1974: Darstellung, Quellen, Übersichten* (Stuttgart: Quell, 1975); Theo Mechtenberg, "Das Staat-Kirche-Verhältnis im 40. Jahr der DDR," in *Die DDR im Vierzigsten Jahr: Geschichte, Situation, Perspektiven: Zweiundzwangzigste Tagung zum Stand der DDR-Forschung in der Bundesrepublik Deutschland 16. Bis 19. Mai 1989*, ed. Ilse Spittmann and Gisela Helwig, Edition Deutschland Archiv (Cologne: Verlag Wissenschaft und Politik Berend von Nottbeck, 1989), 162–72.

15. See Karl Schmitt, "Kirche im Weltanschauungsstaat: Zur Situation in der DDR," in *Kirche und Demokratie*, ed. Dieter Oberndörfer and Karl Schmitt (Paderborn: F. Schöningh, 1983), 125–28.

16. Werner Krusche, "Rückblick auf 21 Jahre Weg- und Arbeitsgemeinschaft im Bund," *epd-Dokumentation* 14 (March 11, 1991): 1–38, provides a review of this history. See also Reinhard Henkys, "Von der EKD zum DDR-Kirchenbund," in *Bund der Evangelischen Kirchen in der DDR: Dokumente zu seiner Entstehung*, ed. H.-W. Hessler, Epd-Dokumentation, vol. 1 (Berlin: Witten, 1971), 11–27; Richard Henkys, "Ein Jahrzehnt nach Fürstenwalde: Feststellungen und Erwägungen zur 'Besonderen Gemeinschaft der Ganzen Evangelischen Christenheit in Deutschland,' " in *Kirche in der DDR, Heft III: Aspekte und Probleme des Selbstverständnisses: Dokumente und Kommentare*, ed. Uwe-Peter Heidingsfeld and Hans-Jürgen Röder, Arbeitshilfe für den Evangelischen Religionsunterricht an Gymnasien, Themenfolge 48 (1977), 23–36; Schmitt, "Kirche im Weltanschauungsstaat," 123–52; Heino Falcke, *Die Unvollendete Befreiung: Die Kirchen, die Umwälzung in der DDR und die Vereinigung Deutschlands*, Ökumenische Existenz Heute, vol. 9 (Munich: Kaiser, 1991), 11–30; Uwe-Peter Heidingsfeld, "Der Bund der Evangelischen Kirchen in der DDR: Aspekte der Entstehung und des Wirkens aus Westlicher Sicht," *epd-Dokumentation* 21 (May 11, 1992): 1–45.

17. For the Catholic side see Schmitt, *Kirche im Weltanschauungsstaat*, 123–52; Clemens M. März, "Aus Langem Winterschlaf Erwacht," in *Unser Glaube Mischt Sich ein: Evangelische Kirche in der DDR 1989: Berichte, Fragen, Verdeutlichungen*, ed. Jörg Hildebrandt and Gerhard Thomas (Berlin: Evangelische Verlagsanstalt, 1990), 111–20; Ulrich von Hehl, "Der deutsche Katholizismus nach 1945 in der zeitgeschichtlichen Forschung," in *Christentum und politische Verantwortung*, ed. Jochen-Christof Kaiser and Anselm Doering-Manteufel (Stuttgart: Kohlhammer, 1990), 146–75; Martin Höllen, "Katholizismus und Deutschlandfrage," in *Christentum und politische Verantwortung*, ed. Jochen-Christof Kaiser and Anselm Doering-Manteufel (Stuttgart: Kohlhammer, 1990), 122–45. For the Free Churches see Günter Lorenz, "Die 'Stille im

Lande' Reihten Sich ein: Wo die Freikirchen ihren Platz im Reformgeschehen hatten," in Hildebrandt and Thomas, eds., *Unser Glaube Mischt Sich ein,* 121–26; Karl Zehrer, "Die methodistische Kirchen in Kontinentaleurope 1912–1936/40: Ausübung der sozialen und politischen Verantwortung," in *Der kontinentaleuropäische Methodismus zwischen den beiden Weltkriegen,* ed. Michel Weyer (Stuttgart: Christliches Verlagshaus, 1990), 133–54.

18. For the theologically informed account of this development see Falcke, *Die unvollendete Befreiung,* 11–51. For the increasing efforts at infiltration of the churches by the GDR regime and its security apparatus see *Pfarrer, Christen und Katholiken: Das Ministerium für Staatssicherheit der ehemaligen DDR und die Kirchen,* 1st ed., ed. Gerhard Besier and Stephan Wolf (Neukirchen-Vluyn: Neukirchener, 1991), 1–34.

19. A meeting between Eric Honecker and Bishop Albrecht Schönherr in March 1978 crystallized this development. See Hans-Jürgen Röder, "Kirche im Sozialismus: Anmerkungen zum Selbstverständnis der evangelischen Kirchen in der DDR," in *Kirche in der DDR, Heft III: Aspekte und Probleme des Selbstverständnisses: Dokumente und Kommentare,* ed. Uwe-Peter Heidingsfeld and Hans-Jürgen Röder, *Arbeitshilfe für den Evangelischen Religionsunterricht an Gymnasien,* Themenfolge 48 (1977), 5–18; Uwe-Peter Heidingsfeld, " 'Kirche Im Sozialismus:' Das Gespräch vom 6. März 1978 zwischen Staat und Kirche in der DDR und seine Folgen," in *Zum Verhältnis von Staat und Kirche: Dokumente und Kommentare,* ed. *Arbeitshilfe für den Evangelischen Religionsunterricht an Gymnasien, Themenfolge 48* (1978), 85–100; *Kirche in der DDR, Heft 1: Zum Verhältnis von Staat und Kirche: Dokumente und Kommentare,* ed. Röder, *Arbeitshilfe für den Evangelischen Religionsunterricht an Gymnasien,* Themenfolge 48 (1980), 81–84; and Bund der Evangelischen Kirchen, *Kirche als Lerngemeinschaft: Dokumente aus der Arbeit des Bundes der Evangelischen Kirchen in der DDR* (Berlin: Evangelische Verlagsanstalt, 1981), 164–71, 211–20.

20. Technically the Communist Party in the GDR was constituted as the Sozialistische Einheitspartei Deutschland (SED). After the fall of 1989 it reconstituted itself as the Partei des Demokratischen Sozialismus (PDS).

21. See Heino Falcke, "Die Kirche und die Friedensgruppen—Wie Gehören Sie Zusammen?" in *Gemeinsam Unterwegs: Dokumente aus der Arbeit des Bundes der Evangelischen Kirchen in der DDR 1980–1987,* ed. Bund der Evangelischen Kirchen (Berlin: Evangelische Verlagsanstalt, 1989), 114–17.

22. Gerhard Rein, *Die protestantische Revolution 1987–1990: Ein deutsches Lesebuch* (Berlin: Wichern, 1990), 186.

23. Joachim Garstecki, "Die Stunde der Pharisäer," in *Die Opposition in der DDR: Entwürfe für einen anderen Sozialismus,* ed. Gerhard Rein (Berlin: Wichern, 1990), 315.

24. Ehrhart Neubert, "Gesellschaftliche Kommunikation im sozialen Wandel: Ausgewählte Aspekte einer Bewegung," in *Die DDR im vierzigsten Jahr,* ed. Spittmann and Hellwig, 51; Ehrhart Neubert, "Sozialethische und Charismatisch—Evangelikale Gruppen in der Kirche aus soziologischer Sicht," Arbeitspapier der Forschungsstätte der Evangelischen Studiengemeinschaft (Heidelberg, 1991). See also *Die Legitimität der Freiheit: Politische alternative Gruppen in der DDR unter dem Dach der Kirche,* ed. Detlef Pollack, Forschungen zur Praktischen Theologie, vol. 8 (Frankfurt: Peter Lang, 1990), and *Leipzig im Oktober: Kirche und alternative Gruppen im Umbruch der DDR: Analysen zur Wende,* ed. Wolf-Jürgen Grabner, Christiane Heinze, and Detlef Pollack (Berlin: Wichern, 1990) for further perspectives on these groups.

25. One estimate gives 345 groups with 5,000 members. See the interview with Pastor Hans-Jochen Tschiche in Rein, *Die protestantische Revolution,* 427.

26. The overwhelming majority of Stasi surveillance activities documented in Besier and Wolf's *Pfarrer, Christen und Katholiken* and in *Ich Liebe Euch Doch Alle: Befehle und Lageberichte der MfS*, ed. Armin Mittler and Stefan Wolle (Berlin: Basis-Druck Verlag, 1990), deal in some way with groups like these.

27. See Rein, *Die protestantische Revolution*, 91; and Günter Krusche, "Gemeinden in der DDR sind Unberuhigt: Was Soll die Kirche Sich zu den Gruppen stellen?" *Lutherischer Monatsheft* 27, no. 11 (November 1988): 494–97. I am indebted to Christof Ziemer (Dresden) and Günter Krusche (Berlin) for interpretations of these problems.

28. Rudi Pahnke, "Wohl und Übel Mitgesteuert," in Hildebrandt and Thomas, eds., *Unser Glaube Mischt Sich ein*, 42.

29. See BEK, *Gemeinsam Unterwegs*, 219–46, 247–63; and Heino Falcke, "Unsere Verantwortung für Umwelt und Zukunft des Menschen," in *Kirche als Lerngemeinschaft*, ed. BEK, 250–59.

30. BEK, *Gemeinsam Unterwegs*, 242, 248, 250.

31. Op. cit., 284.

32. The 1986 call for the Assembly also came out of Dresden on February 13. For perspectives on the process see the essays by Epting, Garstecki, and Kühn in *Unterwegs in Sachen Zukunft: Das Taschenbuch zum Konziliaren Prozeß*, ed. Lothar Coenen (Stuttgart: Calwer; Munich: Kösel, 1990), 12–24, 139–70. Falcke and Ziemer describe their experiences in *Mit Pflugscharen gegen Schwerter: Erfahrungen in der Evangelischen Kirchen in der DDR 1949–90: Protokolle*, ed. Manfred Richter and Elsbeth Zylla (Bremen: Edition Temmen, 1991), 226–44. For the documents see Ökumenische Versammlung für Frieden, Gerechtigkeit, Bewahrung der Schöpfung, *Dresden—Magdeburg—Dresden: Eine Dokumentation* (Berlin: Aktion Sühnezeichnen—Friedensdienste, 1990); *and Dresden—Basel—Seoul: Vergleich der Schlußdokumente* (Bonn: Kommission Justitia et Pax der Berliner Bischofskonferenz, 1990).

33. On Jarowinsky see Ziemer's account in Richter and Zylla, eds., *Mit Pflugscharen gegen Schwerter*, 238; Mechtenberg, *Das Staat-Kirche-Verhältnis*, 169; Rein, *Die protestantische Revolution*, 87–90. For Mielke see Besier and Wolf, eds., *Pfarrer, Christen und Katholiken*, 573, 563.

34. *Ökumenische Versammlung*, 17–18. See also Rein, *Die protestantische Revolution*, 220, 318.

35. *Ökumenische Versammlung*, 28. The German is able to use *Umkehr* (return, turn back) and *Bekehrung* (conversion) almost interchangeably to distinguish but also relate societal and spiritual change to one another.

36. Op. cit., 94.

37. Interview with Manfred Stolpe in Richter and Zylla, eds., *Mit Pflugscharen gegen Schwerter*, 142–46. See also Falcke, *Die unvollendete Befreiung*, 24–26.

38. For the march see Joachim Garstecki, *Zeitansage Umkehr: Dokumentation eines Aufbruchs* (Stuttgart: RADIUS-Verlag, 1990), 73–78; Rein, *Die protestantische Revolution*, 19–23; and Besier and Wolf, eds., *Pfarrer, Christen und Katholiken*, 50–51. For the library events see Rein, *Die protestantische Revolution*, 37, and Besier and Wolf, eds., *Pfarrer, Christen und Katholiken*, 52–54.

39. *Die Revolution der Kerzen: Christen in den Umwälzungen der DDR*, 2d ed., ed. Jörg Swoboda (Wuppertal-Kassel: Oncken, 1990), 12; Mittler and Wolle, eds., *Ich Liebe Euch Doch Alle*, 11–16; and Rein, *Die protestantische Revolution*, 58–71.

40. Rein, *Die protestantische Revolution*, 143.

41. The citation is from Luther himself. See Rein, *Die protestantische Revolution*, 93.

42. See, for example, the letter by Magdeburg Bishop Christoph Demke to church members on September 3, 1989, in Rein, *Die protestantische Revolution,* 193–99.

43. See Christof Ziemer, "Wachen und Beten für die Stadt: Christen-und Bürgergemeinde am Beispiel Dresden," in Hildebrandt and Thomas, eds., *Unser Glaube Mischt Sich ein,* 100–110; *Die Opposition in der DDR,* ed. Rein, 199–96; Rein, *Die protestantische Revolution,* 228–37; Swoboda, ed., *Die Revolution der Kerzen,* 207–11; and Eckhard Bahr, *Sieben Tage im Oktober: Aufbruch in Dresden* (Leipzig: Forum Verlag, 1990).

44. In an interview with me Ziemer recounted that the police chief in Dresden had even greeted him with a salute!

45. For this "Dresden Model" see Rein, ed., *Die Opposition in der DDR,* 188–96.

46. For the events in Leipzig see Friedrich Magirius, " 'Selig sind, die Frieden Stiften . .' Friedensgebet in St. Nikolai zu Leipzig," in Hildebrandt and Thomas, eds., *Unser Glaube Mischt Sich ein,* 92–99; Friedrich Magirius, "Leipzig, Nikolaikirche: Erfahrungen und Ernüchterungen in der 'Revolution der Kerzen,' " in *Wieviel Religion Braucht die deutsche Staat? Politisches Christentum zwischen Reaktion und Revolution,* ed. Walter Sparn (Gütersloh: Mohn, 1991), 39–48; Rein, *Die protestantische Revolution,* 147–50; Swoboda, ed., *Die Revolution der Kerzen,* 140–58; Hans-Jürgen Sievers, *Stundenbuch eines deutschen Revolution: Die Leipziger Kirchen im Oktober 1989* (Göttingen: Van den Hoeck u. Ruprecht, 1990); Rein, ed., *Die Opposition in der DDR,* 169–87; and Wolfgang Schneider, *Leipziger Demontagebuch,* 3d ed. (Leipzig: Gustav Kiepenheuer, 1991).

47. See the volume compiled by the Magdeburg Cathedral advisory board, *Anstiftung zur Gewaltlosigkeit: Herbst '89 in Magdeburg,* ed. Beratergruppe Dom des Gebetes um gesellschaftliche Erneuerung im Magdeburger Dom (Magdeburg: imPULS Verlag, 1991), 10–42.

48. Op. cit., 27.

49. See Rein, ed., *Die Opposition in der DDR,* for an introduction with documents. See also Rein, *Die protestantische Revolution,* 219–86. For a critical evaluation see Hans-Jochen Tschiche, "Wende ohne Wandlung: Zum Ende der DDR," in *Deutschland, Deutschland . . Politische Kulturen im gesamtdeutschen Staat—Traditionen, Ängsten, Erwartungen.,* ed. Tilman Evers, Hofgeismar Protokolle (Hofgeismar: Evangelische Akademie Hofgeismar, 1991), 135–47.

50. For their development, esp. in Berlin, see Wolfgang Ullmann, "Der gemeinsame Boden einer geschichtlichen Erfahrung," in Hildebrandt and Thomas, eds., *Unser Glaube Mischt Sich ein.,* 80–81; Rein, *Die protestantische Revolution,* 310–11; Sievers, *Stundenbuch eines deutschen Revolution,* 130–32.

51. Hannah Arendt, *On Revolution* (New York: Viking Press, 1965), 260.

52. Interview with Sibylle Leu of Neuenhagen, in Richter and Zylla, eds., *Mit Pflugscharen gegen Schwerter,* 200.

53. See Ullmann, "Der gemeinsame Boden einer geschichtlichen Erfahrung," 84, 87.

54. Rein, *Die protestantische Revolution,* 398–407.

55. Ullmann, "Der gemeinsame Boden einer geschichtlichen Erfahrung," 89–90.

56. The desire for unification was poignantly expressed in the popular saying: "Helmut [Kohl] take us by the hand, lead us into economic wonderland." Reported by Joachim Garstecki in "Marktbeherrscht oder Selbstbestimmt? Die Vereinigung der Deutschen als Demokratie-Gewinn," in *Nach der Wende: Wandlungen im Kirchen und Gesellschaft: Texte aus der Theologischen Studienabteilung beim Bund der Evangelischen Kirchen in der DDR,* ed. Rudolf Schulze (Berlin: Wichern, 1990), 71.

57. For the treaty of May 18 with commentary see *Staatsvertrag zur Währungs-Wirtschafts- und Sozialunion,* ed. Klaus Stern and Bruno Schmidt-Bleibtreu (Munich: C. H. Beck, 1990). Art. 23 of the Fundamental Law enables states outside the three Allied zones that formed the Federal Republic to join the FRG by vote of their legislatures. See Hesse, *Grundzüge des Verfassungsrechts,* 33–36, for explanation.

58. "Die Erklärung von Loccum," *epd-Dokumentation* 12 (March 12, 1990): 1. For the reunification resolutions with the tough questions see *epd-Dokumentation* 14 (March 17, 1991): 47–55, and *epd-Dokumentation* 49 (November 19, 1990): 1–5, 63–67.

59. Ulrich Duchrow, Heino Falcke, Joachim Garstecki, and Konrad Raiser, "Berliner Erklärung von Christen aus beiden deutschen Staaten," *epd-Dokumentation* 12 (March 12, 1990): 17–21.

60. See, for instance, the lament from church executive Martin Ziegler of the BEK in February 1991: "The idea that two partners could come together and together create something new in partnership has shown itself to be an illusion. We aren't experiencing such a conjoining but an annexation. We are simply being plugged in. We are getting unity without change." Cited in Falcke, *Die unvollendete Befreiung,* 82.

61. Gottfried Forck, "Interview mit Dieter Stächer," *epd-Dokumentation* 12 (March 12, 1990): 26. Falcke, *Die unvollendete Befreiung,* 18, reports that one-third of the church's income came from western churches.

62. *Staatsvertrag zur Währungs-Wirtschafts- und Sozialunion,* 63, and Art. 9, Para. 5, of the Unification Treaty. See also Richard Henkys, "Freiwilligkeitskirche Abgeschrieben? Kirchen in der DDR Wünschen Einzug der Kirchensteuer durch den Staat," *epd-Dokumentation* 14 (March 26, 1990): 16; Axel von Campenhausen, "Romantische Vorstellungen helfen nicht weiter," *epd-Dokumentation* 14 (March 26, 1990): 17–18; and *epd-Dokumentation* 43 (October 15, 1990), 56–58.

63. This return to civil servant status would soon make it more difficult to staff smaller parishes and would force their consolidation.

64. See, for example, the assessment by Richard Schröder, "Das vereinte Deutschland aus der Sicht eines Politikers: Der Kontext der Kirche," *epd-Dokumentation* 9 (February 18, 1991): 13.

65. For some views on this issue see Jürgen Lott, "Reform (West) und Einführung (Ost): Ein Plädoyer für einen nichtkonfessionellen Religionsunterricht," *Frankfurter Rundschau,* June 6, 1991, 15; and Dieter Reiher, "Religion in der Schule: Entwicklungen—Auseinandersetzungen—Regelungen in den Ostdeutschen Ländern von 1989 bis 1991," *epd-Dokumentation,* 6 (January 27, 1992): 1–18.

66. Huber, *Kirche und Öffentlichkeit,* 247–59.

67. Jens Müller-Kent, *Militärseelsorge im Spannungsfeld zwischen kirchlichem Auftrag und militärischer Einbindung* (Hamburg: Steinmann und Steinmann, 1990), 80–82, 99–105. See also the statements by Walter Ulbricht, former party secretary, in *Bund der Evangelischen Kirchen in der DDR,* ed. Hessler, 63.

68. See Falcke, *Die unvollendete Befreiung,* 103–07.

69. See proposals in the West from Bishop Martin Kruse (EKD) to the Synod in Lübeck, November 4, 1990, in *epd-Dokumentation* 48 (November 7, 1990): 7; discussion of major issues in *epd-Dokumentation* 24a (June 3, 1991); proposals from the Dietrich-Bonhoeffer Union in Karl Martin, ed., *Frieden statt Sicherheit: Von der Militärseelsorge zum Dienst der Kirche unter der Soldaten: Positionen und Beiträge* (Gütersloh: G. Mohn, 1989); and "Ein kirchliches Dienstverhältnis," *Deutsches Allgemeines Sonntagsblatt,* June 17, 1994. From the East see the resolution of the BEK in Berlin, February 24, 1991, in *epd-Dokumentation* 14 (March 11, 1991): 55.

70. This was, for instance, central to the concerns of the Synod of the Church Province of Saxony in the fall of 1991. The concern for an appropriate federal structure had permeated the deliberations of the BEK from its inception. See, for example, Bund der Evangelischen Kirchen, ed., *Kirche als Lerngemeinschaft,* 13–29.

71. *Christliche Existenz im demokratischen Aufbruch Europas: Probleme—Chance—Orientierungen,* ed. Jürgen Moltmann (Munich: Kaiser, 1991), 38. See also Jürgen Moltmann, "Im Bund gegen den Leviathan: Mit der Theologie gegen die Politikverdrossenheit," *Evangelische Kommentare* 27, no. 1 (January 1994): 24–28, for a fuller treatment of covenant and federalism in light of these events.

72. Hartmut Löwe, "Was ändert Sich in der evangelischen Kirche in Deutschland durch die neue Gemeinschaft mit den alten Gliedkirchen-Ost?" *epd-Dokumentation* 14a (March 18, 1991): 4–5. For critical discussion see Uwe-Peter Heidingsfeld, "Anmerkungen zu dem Vereinigungsprozeß von EKD und Kirchenbund," *epd-Dokumentation* 18a (April 15, 1991): 1–25.

73. For a complete analysis see Martin Heckel, "Die Wiedervereinigung der deutschen evangelischen Kirchen," *Zeitschrift der Savigny-Stiftung für Rechtsgeschichte* 109 (1992): 401–516.

74. For the theoretical side of this effort see Helmut Zeddies, "Zur Wirkungsgeschichte von Zwei-Reiche-Lehre und Lehre von der Königsherrschaft Christi in den evangelischen Kirchen in der DDR," in BEK, ed., *Gemeinsam Unterwegs,* 289–332. For documents and commentary see BEK, ed., *Gemeinsam Unterwegs,* 23–57.

75. Ziemer, in Richter and Zylla, eds., *Mit Pflugscharen gegen Schwerter,* 242.

76. See, for example, Rainer Kessler, "Das Selbstbestimmungsrecht der Kirchen," in *Die Kirchen und die Politik: Beiträge zu einem ungeklärten Verhältnis,* ed. Heidrun Abromeit and Göttrik Wewer (Opladen: Westdeutscher Verlag, 1989), 136–60; Clemens Vollnhals, "Kirchliche Zeitgeschichte nach 1945: Schwerpunkte, Tendenzen, Defizite," in *Christentum und politische Verantwortung,* ed. Jochen-Christof Kaiser and Anselm Doering-Manteufel (Stuttgart: Kohlhammer, 1990), 176–91. For an analysis of the issue of church identity and role see John Burgess, "Church-State Relations in East Germany: The Church as 'Religious' and 'Political' Force," *Journal of Church and State* 32 (Winter 1990): 17–35.

77. Huber, *Kirche und Öffentlichkeit,* posed the questions anew. For the continuing debate see Ulrich Scheuner, "Das System der Beziehungen von Staat und Kirchen im Grundgesetz: Zur Entwicklung des Staatskirchenrechts," in *Handbuch des Staatskirchenrechts der Bundesrepublik Deutschland.* 2 vols., vol. 1, ed. Ernst Friesenhahn, Ulrich Scheuner, and Joseph Listl (Berlin: Duncker und Humboldt, 1974), 69–86; Ulrich K. Preuss, "Die verfassungsrechtliche Verankerung der Kirchen in der Bundesrepublik und ihre politische Bedeutung," in Abromeit and Wewer, eds., *Die Kirchen und die Politik,* 125–35; Heidrun Abromeit, "Sind die Kirchen Interessenverbände?" in Abromeit and Wewer, eds., *Die Kirchen und die Politik,* 244–60; and Wolfgang Bock, *Das für alle geltende Gesetz und die kirchliche Selbstbestimmung* (Tübingen: J.C.B. Mohr [Paul Siebeck], 1995). See also Falcke, *Die unvollendete Befreiung,* 12.

78. Unification Treaty of May 18, 1990, Preamble.

79. For the Board's proposals see *Eine Verfassung für Deutschland: Manifest, Text, Plädoyers,* eds. Bernd Guggenberger, Ulrich K. Preuss, and Wolfgang Ullmann (Munich: Carl Hanser, 1991), esp. 8–13, 23–27, 38–40. For the round table original see Arbeitsgruppe 'Neue Verfassung der DDR' des Runden Tisches, *Entwurf: Verfassung der Deutschen Demokratischen Republik* (Berlin: BasisDruck Verlagsgesellschaft, 1990). See also the statement by former Supreme Court Justice Helmut Simon, "Brauchen wir eine Verfassungsreform?" *epd-Dokumentation* 27 (June 24, 1991): 59–65.

80. The ratification through action of the Bundestag and Bundesrat, not the states, did not come about until 1994. While environmental protection and equal rights for men and women were included, other elements of social security and plebiscites were not. For the reaction of a popular theological journal see Peter Hölzle, "In Guter Verfassung? Die Reform des Grundgesetzes lässt viele Wünsche offen," *Evangelische Kommentare* 27, no. 3 (March 1994): 125.

81. For proposals for popular petition, referendum, and recall see *Direkte Demokratie in Deutschland: Handreichungen zur Verfassungsdiskussion in Bund und Ländern,* ed. Otmar Jung, Tilman Evers, and Diemut Schnetz, Brennpunkt Dokumentation, vol. 12 (Bonn: Stiftung MITARBEIT, 1991). That direct democracy at the national level would collide with strengthened federalism did not seem to enter the discussion. For diverging views on democratization and federalism between the politically active theologians Richard Schröder and Wolfgang Ullmann see John P. Burgess, "Theologians and the Renewal of Democratic Political Institutions in Eastern Germany," *Journal of Church and State* 37, no. 1 (Winter 1995): 87–102.

82. On this often controversial topic, especially with regard to the churches' role, see Helmut Quaritsch, *Recht auf Asyl: Studien zu einem missdeuteten Grundrecht* (Berlin: Duncker u. Humboldt, 1985); *Flüchtlinge und Asylsuchende in unserem Land,* ed. Evangelische Kirche Deutschland, EKD-Texte, vol. 16 (Hannover: EKD, 1986); Manfred Köhnlein, *Aus aller Herren-Länder: Asylbewerber unter Uns* (Stuttgart: Quell-Verlag, 1988); Günter Renner, "40 Jahre Asylgrundrecht: Zeit für eine grundlegende Reform," *Neue Juristiche Wochenschrift,* no. 20 (1989): 1246–54; Hans-Richard Reuter, "Kirchenasyl und staatliches Asylrecht: Ein rechtsethischer Beitrag" (Heidelberg: Forschungstätte der Evangelischen Studiengemeinschaft, 1991); and *Kirchenasyl: Ein Leitfaden für die Praxis,* ed. Wigbert Tocha and Matthias Drobinski (Oberursel: Publik-Forum, 1990), esp. 28–40.

83. Unification Treaty of August 3, 1990, Art. 31, Para. 4. For church statements see the Declaration on Abortion from the EKD and BEK of June 20, 1991.

84. For a review of the key issues see Arthur B. Gunlicks, "German Federalism after Unification: The Legal/Constitutional Response," *Publius: The Journal of Federalism* 24, no. 2 (Spring 1994): 81–98.

85. Mittler and Wolle, eds., *Ich Liebe Euch Doch Alle,* and Besier and Wolf, eds., *Pfarrer, Christen und Katholiken.* For discussion of the law regulating disclosure of the files see *Die Kontinuität des Wegsehens und Mitmachens: Stasi-Akten oder die schwierige Bewältigung der DDR-Vergangenheit,* ed. Heinrich-Boll-Stiftung (Cologne: Heinrich-Boll-Stiftung, 1991).

86. For an example of their extensive scope see the last five-year plan of the Stasi, which included extensive penetration of the churches, in *Frankfurter Rundschau,* February 1, 1992, 10.

87. Helmut Matthies, "Schuld offen bekennen," *idea Spektrum* 51/52 (December 19, 1991): 4.

88. *Der Spiegel* 18 (1992): 36–43; Sermon by Pastor Bernd Albani, Gethsemane Kirche, Berlin, February 23, 1992.

89. For only two samples see "Kirche und Stasi: Materialien zu der aktuellen Diskussion um das Besier-Buch und die Angriffe auf Manfred Stolpe," *epd-Dokumentation* 8 (February 3, 1992); "Kirche und Stasi: Weitere Materialien zu der aktuellen Diskussion," *epd-Dokumentation* 11 (February 24, 1992). The question continues both theologically and sociologically in Ehrhart Neubert, *Vergebung oder Weißwascherei: Zur Aufarbeitung des Stasiproblems in den Kirchen* (Freiburg: Herder, 1993).

90. See, for instance, Robert Leicht, "Wende zum Tod," *Die Zeit,* March 13, 1992, 1; Wolfgang Templin, "Das schlechte Vorbild der Anpassung," *Die Zeit,* March 13, 1992, 15; and Carl-Christian Kaiser, "Gut verdrängt ist halb gewonnen," *Die Zeit,* February 28, 1992, 77.

91. For the Stolpe case see *Der Spiegel,* 4 (1992): 18–27, and 8 (1992): 24–28; *Frankfurter Rundschau,* February 1, 1992, 10; *Berliner Zeitung,* February 22–23, 1992, 3; *Die Zeit,* April 24, 1992, 3; and Manfred Stolpe, *Der schwierige Aufbruch,* 2d ed. (Berlin: Siedler, 1992).

92. See, for example, the controversy around Berlin Brandenburg General Superintendent Günter Krusche's disclosure of his relations with the Stasi over the years in *Berliner Zeitung,* February 22–23, 1992, 1–2.

93. For similar problems in the political sphere see Jutta Braband, "Warum habe ich so lange geschwiegen?" *Die Zeit,* February 28, 1992, 47.

94. The Church Province of Saxony, one of the most assiduous synods in pursuing this matter, voted not to take this full-scale juridical approach in a special synod meeting May 21–23, 1992. See also Richard Schröder, "Nischen im Zwielicht," *Frankfurter Allgemeine,* December 6, 1991, 33; Bascha Mika, "Das Judassyndrom," *die tageszeitung,* January 6, 1992, 11.

95. "Bericht vor der 11. Synode des Kirchenprovinz Sachsen," Halle, October 31–November 3, 1991, 6. See also Arndt Haubold, "Der Wann der Saubermänner," *epd-Dokumentation* 11 (February 24, 1992): 2.

96. *Berliner Zeitung,* February 21, 1992, 5 and February 24, 1992, 1; *Frankfurter Rundschau,* February 24, 1992, 3.

97. For the EKD declaration "Kirche—Staat—Staatssicherheitsdienst" see Rat der EKD, "Kirche—Staat—Staatssicherheitsdienst," *epd-Dokumentation* 8 (January 27, 1992): 7–8. Further dokumentation is in Bund der Theologische Studienabteilung, Evangelischen Kirchen, *Recht und Versöhnung: Texte aus den Kirchen zum Stand der Aufarbeitung der Vergangenheit—Staatssicherheitsproblematik,* Information und Texte, vol. 5 (Berlin, 1991); and Theologische Studienabteilung Bund der Evangelischen Kirchen, *Recht und Versöhnung: Texte aus den Kirchen zum Stand der Aufarbeitung der Vergangenheit—Staatssicherheitsproblematik,* Information und Texte, no. 6 (Berlin: Bund der Evangelischen Kirchen, 1992). For the interchurch effort see the EKD agreement in "Information über den Stand der Überlegungen zum Umgang mit durch Zusammenarbeit mit dem Ministerium für Staatssicherheit belastete kirchliche Mitarbeiter," *epd-Dokumentation* 48 (November 11, 1991), 27–31.

98. *Frankfurter Allgemeine,* March 13, 1992, 1.

99. *Deutsches Allgemeines Sonntagsblatt,* February 14, 1992, 20. See also Matthies, "Schuld offen bekennen," 1–7, and Ehrhart Neubert, "Recht, Verantwortung und Versöhnung: Zum Stasiproblem der Kirchen," in *Recht und Versöhnung, Folge II,* ed. Theologische Studienabteilung BEK, 36–40.

100. Interview with Günter Krusche, February 23, 1992.

101. For a fuller history see John S. Conway, "The 'Stasi' and the Churches: Between Coercion and Compromise in East German Protestantism 1949–89," *Journal of Church and State* 36, no. 4 (Autumn 1994): 725–46.

102. Joachim Garstecki, "Eine riskante Berührung," unpub. ms. (1992); Günter Krusche, "Kirche im Sozialismus Kirche im Zwielicht?" *epd-Dokumentation* 11 (February 24, 1992), 17; Heino Falcke, "Verdrängen, vergelten oder versöhnen: Über den Umgang mit der Wahrheit: Vortrag in der Evangelischen Akademie Berlin," unpub. ms. (February 22, 1992); Bishop Christoph Demke, "Bericht vor der 11. Synode des

Kirchenprovinz Sachsen," Halle, October 31–November 3, 1991, 10; Clemens Vollnhals, "Der böse Vorwurf der SED-Kumpanei," *Süddeutsche Zeitung,* April 7, 1992, 12; and Edgar Sebastian Hasse, "Die stille Klage über den Westen," *Deutsches Allgemeines Sonntagsblatt,* May 29, 1992, 19. For a thoughtful review of the way the churches might redeem a new approach to society out of their often ambivalent participation in the 'peaceful revolution' see Wolf Krötke, "Die Kirche und die 'friedliche Revolution' in der DDR," *Zeitschrift für Theologie und Kirche* 87, no. 4 (1990), 521–544.

103. For a defense of the church's complex way see Richard Schröder, *Deutschland schwierig Vaterland: Für eine neue politische Kultur* (Freiburg: Herder, 1993), 135–44.

104. See Ulrich Duchrow, *Christenheit und Weltverantwortung: Traditionsgeschichte und systematische Struktur der Zweireichelehre* (Stuttgart: Klett, 1970); Ulrich Duchrow, *Zwei Reiche und Regimente: Ideologie oder evangelische Orientierung?* (Gütersloh: Mohn, 1977); *Two Kingdoms and One World,* ed. Karl Hertz (Minneapolis: Augsburg, 1976); Huber, *Kirche und Öffentlichkeit,* 435–89; Wolfgang Huber, *Folgen christlicher Freiheit: Ethik und Theorie der Kirche im Horizont der Barmer theologischen Erklärung,* 2d ed. (Neukirchen-Vluyn: Neukirchener Verlag, 1985), 33–70; and Zeddies, "Zur Wirkungsgeschichte von Zwei-Reiche-Lehre," 289–332, for a review of these interpretations and the movement toward a more eschatological, world-transforming interpretation of the Two Realms.

105. See, for instance, Huber, *Kirche und Öffentlichkeit,* 441–53. Huber is now Bishop of the Evangelical Church in Berlin-Brandenburg.

106. For examples see Swoboda, ed., *Die Revolution der Kerzen,* 135; Annemarie Schönherr, "Umkehr und Neuanfang," in *Christliche Existenz in demokratischen Aufbruch Europas,* ed. Moltmann, 42–43; *Räumt die Steine Hinweg: DDR Herbst 89. Geistliche Reden im politischen Aufbruch* 3rd ed., ed. Andreas Ebert, Johanna Haberer, and Friedrich Kraft (Munich: Claudius, 1990), 50; Horst Hofmann, "Bericht auf der Synode der Evangelischen Kirche in Hessen und Nassau," unpublished report to the synod, June 22, 1991, 14; and Falcke, in Rein, *Die protestantische Revolution,* 320.

107. See Hans-Joachim Maaz, *Der Gefühlsstau: Ein Psychogramm der DDR* (Berlin: Argon Verlag, 1990); Hans-Joachim Maaz, *Das gestürtzte Volk oder die verunglückte Einheit* (Berlin: Argon Verlag, 1991). Maaz, a therapist in the former GDR, explores the deep ambiguity of this process, since both church and state were historic institutions of "tutelage" (*Vormundschaft*) and parental control. See Rolf Henrich, *Der vormundschaftliche Staat* (Leipzig: Gustav Kiepenheuer, 1990), for the full theory of tutelage.

108. I am indebted to Heino and Almuth Falcke for this insight. See also Douglas W. Hatfield, "Reform in the Prussian Evangelical Church and the Concept of the Landesherr," *Journal of Church and State* 24, no. 4 (Autumn 1982): 553–72, for an earlier ecclesiological outcome. See Alexander Mitscherlich, *Auf dem Wege zur vaterlosen Gesellschaft,* Sozialpsychologie I, ed. Helge Haase, Gesammelte Schriften, vol. 3 (Frankfurt: Suhrkamp, 1983 [1963]), 173–204, 337–43, for some psychosocial aspects.

109. For a movement toward a reinterpretation of this image see Jürgen Moltmann, *Der Gekreuzigte Gott: Das Kreuz Christi als Grund und Kritik christlicher Theologie* (Munich: Kaiser, 1972).

110. For efforts toward this reinterpretation see Falcke, *Die unvollendete Befreiung,* 94; Moltmann, ed., *Christliche Existenz im demokratischen Aufburch Europas*; and Konrad Raiser, *Ökumene im Übergang: Pardigmenwechsel in der ökumenischen Bewegung* (Munich: Kaiser, 1989), 143–58, 172–82.

111. See Ludger Kühnhardt, "Multi-German Identity," *Daedalus* 123, no. 1 (Winter 1994): 193–210.

112. See Anne-Marie Le Gloannec, "On German Identity," *Daedalus* 123, no. 1 (Winter 1994): 129–48; and Mary Fulbrook, "Aspects of Society and Identity in the New Germany," *Daedalus* 123, no. 1 (Winter 1994): 211–34, for discussions of the problem of identity.

113. This effort begins with the "Stuttgart Confession of Guilt" (October 19, 1945) and the "Darmstadt Words" (August 8, 1947). See Martin Greschat, *Die Schuld der Kirche: Dokumente und Reflexionen zur Stuttgarter Schulderklärung von 18/19 Oktober 1945* (Munich: Kaiser, 1982); Martin Greschat, *Im Zeichen der Schuld: 40 Jahre Stuttgarter Schuldbekenntnis: Eine Dokumentation* (Neukirchen-Vluyn: Neukirchener, 1985); Gerhard Besier, " 'Durch Uns ist unendliches Leid über viele Völker und andere gebracht worden:' Schulderkenntnis und Schuldbekenntnis in der Geschichte unseres Jahrhunderts," *Glaube und Lernen* 1, no. 2 (October 1986): 120–30; Gerhard Sauter, "Schulderkenntnis in der Bitte um Vergebung," *Glaube und Lernen* 1, no. 2 (October 1986): 109–19; and Konrad Raiser, "Schuld und Versöhnung: Erinnerung an eine bleibende Aufgabe der deutschen Kirchen," *Kirchliche Zeitgeschichte* 4, no. 2 (1991): 512–22, for the ongoing process.

114. See, for example, Ingo Müller, *Furchtbare Juristen: Die unbewähltigte Vergangenheit unserer Justiz* (Munich: Droemersche Verlagsanstalt, 1989). For the indispensable psychology of this confessing and grieving see Maaz, *Das gestürtzte Volk*, 173–77; Margarete Mitscherlich, *Erinnerungsarbeit: Zur Psychoanalyse der Unfähigkeit zu Trauern* (Frankfurt: M. Fischer, 1987); and Alexander Mitscherlich and Margarete Mitscherlich, *Die Unfähigkeit zu Trauern: Grundlagen kollektiven Verhaltens* (Munich: R. Piper & Co. Verlag, 1967).

115. See the articles by Schröder, Clausen, and Vogel in *Ein Volk am Pranger? Die Deutschen auf der Suche nach einer neuen politischen Kultur,* ed. Albrecht Schönherr (Berlin: Aufbau Taschenbuch Verlag, 1992).

116. See Joachim Gauck, "Gegen den Schlußstrich: Gespräch mit dem Stasi-Akten-Verwalter Joachim Gauck," *Evangelische Kommentare* 6 (1994): 6–9, for the argument for ongoing examination of the files.

117. Hannah Arendt, *Eichmann in Jerusalem: A Report on the Banality of Evil,* rev. and enl. (New York: Penguin, 1977).

118. For the difficulties involved in this providential view within the context of German history see Gerhard Sauter, "A Certain Speechlessness: Theological Reflections on the Political Changes in Europe," *Soundings* 77, nos. 1–2 (Spring/Summer 1994): 163–77.

Chapter 3. Religious Organization and Constitutional Justice in India

1. Klaus K. Klostermaier, *A Survey of Hinduism* (New York: State University of New York, 1994), 31.

2. And, we need to add, Christian nationalism as well. See George Thomas, *Christian Indians and Indian Nationalism, 1885–1950: An Interpretation in Historical and Theological Perspectives* (Frankfurt: Peter Lang, 1979), esp. p. 25–27, 66–69 passim.

3. For a modern interpretation see Pandharinath H. Prabhu, *Hindu Social Organization: A Study in Socio-Psychological and Ideological Foundations* (Bombay: Popular Prakashan, 1990), 73–100, 284–335. For Prabhu the varnas are better seen as classes of people, with actual occupational segmentations divided into *jatis* by birth.

4. For discussions see J. Duncan M. Derrett, "Social and Political Thought and Institutions," in *A Cultural History of India,* ed. A. L. Basham (Oxford: Clarendon

Press, 1975), 128–30, and the esp. says in *Way of Life: King, Householder, Renouncer: esp. says in Honour of Louis Dumont,* ed. T. N. Madan (New Delhi: Vikas, 1982).

5. Derrett, "Social and Political Thought," 132.

6. I am indebted to Prof. M. Thomas Thangaraj, of Emory University, for the concepts of "geo-piety" and "bio-piety," which we developed in our paper, "Religious Human Rights in India," presented at the Conference on Religious Human Rights sponsored by the Law and Religion Program, Emory University, in Atlanta, October 1994.

7. Ronald Inden, "Hierarchies of Kings in Medieval India," in Madan, ed., *Way of Life,* 99–126.

8. K. J. Shah, "Of Artha and the *Arthasastra,*" in Madan, ed., *Way of Life,* 55–74. See also Abraham Vazhayil Thomas, *Christians in Secular India* (Rutherford: Fairleigh Dickinson Press, 1974), 23.

9. J. D. M. Derrett, *Religion, Law and the State in India* (London: Faber and Faber, 1968), 118.

10. Romila Thapar, *Exile and Kingdom: Some Thoughts on the Ramayana* (Bangalore: Mythic Society, 1978), 21. Derrett mentions that ancient Buddhists spoke of a "people's compact" as undergirding a political order ("Social and Political Thought," 137).

11. A. V. Thomas, *Christians in Secular India,* 25.

12. For the early development of the *samgha* (also spelled *sangha*) in India before Buddhism's expulsion see Trevor Ling, *The Buddha* (New York: Charles Scribner's Sons, 1973); Roland Fick, *The Social Organization in Northeast India in the Buddha's Time* (Calcutta, 1920); Sukumar Dutt, *Buddhist Monks and Monasteries of India: Their History and Their Contribution to Indian Culture,* 2d ed. (London: Allen & Unwin, 1962). The fuller unfolding of the relationship between samgha and civil order took place in Sri Lanka, Burma, and Thailand. See Stanley J. Tambiah, *World Conqueror and World Renouncer* (New York: Cambridge University Press, 1976); E. Michael Mendelson, *Sangha and State in Burma: A Study of Monastic Sectarianism and Leadership,* ed. John Ferguson (Ithaca: Cornell University Press, 1975). I am indebted to Prof. David C. Scott, United Theological College, Bangalore, for help on this point.

13. A. V. Thomas, *Christians in Secular India,* 25.

14. Durga Das Basu, *Introduction to the Constitution of India* (New Delhi: Prentice-Hall of India, 1991), 4.

15. For this general depiction, which by necessity overlooks many historical changes, I am indebted to James A. Bergquist and Kambar Manickam, *The Crisis of Dependency in Third World Ministries: A Critique of Inherited Missionary Forms in India* (Madras: Christian Literature Society, 1974), 100–113.

16. For relevant literature on these origins see *History of Christianity in India: Source Materials,* ed. M. K. Kuriakose, Indian Theological Library, vol. 9 (Madras: Christian Literature Society, 1982), 1–8.

17. Resolution 13, East India Company Charter of 1813, cited in Kuriakose, ed., *History of Christianity in India,* 88.

18. George Thomas, *Christian Indians and Indian Nationalism,* 69–81.

19. Fear of Hindu hegemony also fueled missionary loyalty to the Crown. See George Thomas, *Christian Indians and Indian Nationalism,* 101.

20. Because of the close ties between the Anglican Church and the colonial government, numerous property disputes linger even to this day as churches and governments try to figure out title claims in the absence of adequate surveys.

21. See esp. A. V. Thomas, *Christians in Secular India*, 105–24.

22. The use of Qu'ranic concepts of covenant in a similar way seems to be much less developed. The Qu'ran continues the idea of God's covenant with Abraham and his successors and refers to this basic divine covenant at many places (Surah 2.40, 3.81, 7.172, 33.7, etc.). Muhammed himself esp. tablished many compacts to form a quasi-federative polity in his early years. See *The Cambridge History of Islam. Vol I. The Central Islamic Lands*, M. Holt, et al., eds. (Cambridge: Cambridge University Press, 1970), 41–56. Moreover, the period of the Caliphs in the early centuries of Islam saw numerous suzereignty treaties with subjected Christian and Jewish communities. See A. S. Tritton, *The Caliphs and Their Non-Muslim Subjects: A Critical Study of the Covenant of 'Umar* (London: Frank Cass, 1970). In addition, some Indian Islamic leaders saw the new Constitution as a form of covenant rooted in these old Islamic covenants. See Ziya-Ul Farugi, "Indian Muslims and the Ideology of the Secular State," *South Asian Politics and Religion*, ed. Donald E. Smith (Princeton: Princeton University Press, 1966), 138–49. Needless to say, this relation of covenant and federalism in Islam is worthy of much more study.

23. J. N. Farquhar, *Modern Religious Movements in India* (New York: Macmillan, 1924) and David Kopf, *British Orientalism and the Bengal Renaissance: The Dynamics of Indian Modernization, 1773–1835* (Berkeley: University of California Press, 1969).

24. Kopf, *British Orientalism*, 315.

25. Kopf, *British Orientalism*, 252–65. The Christian theologian David C. Scott has assembled some of Sen's writings in Keshub Chunder Sen, *Keshub Chunder Sen: A Selection*, ed. David C. Scott (Bangalore: Christian Literature Society, 1979).

26. Farquhar, *Modern Religious Movements*, 35. The Samaj was reorganized in 1843 under Tagore's leadership. See Kopf, *British Orientalism*, 12.

27. Kopf, *British Orientalism*, 135–43.

28. Kopf, *British Orientalism*, 154. V. D. Sarvarkar expressed great contempt for "treaty nations" and exalted the "common affinities" of culture, race, religion, and language that had molded India into an "organic nation." See A. Appadorai, *Documents on Political Thought in India* (New Delhi: Oxford University Press, 1973), 506.

29. Basu, *Introduction to the Constitution of India*, 5.

30. Farquhar, *Modern Religious Movements*, 308–14.

31. Basu, *Introduction to the Constitution of India*, 6.

32. Indian Round Table Conference, *Indian Round Table Conference, 12 November 1930 to 19 January 1931. Proceedings* (Calcutta: Government of India, 1931), 189.

33. Judith M. Brown, *Modern India: The Origins of an Asian Democracy* (New York: Oxford University Press, 1985), 264–84.

34. *Indian Round Table Conference*, 438–41.

35. Cited in Granville Austin, *The Indian Constitution: A Cornerstone of the Nation* (London: Oxford University Press, 1966), 192.

36. Austin, *The Indian Constitution*, 188.

37. See Austin, *The Indian Constitution*, 243–51. The northwestern states of Jammu and Kashmir, however, are a special case due to earlier agreements by the British. Their contested status continues to be a volatile issue.

38. See Donald Smith's prescient book, *India: A Secular State* (Princeton: Princeton University Press, 1963).

39. Austin, *The Indian Constitution*, 30. Ambedkar called the villages "a sink of localism, a den of ignorance, narrow-mindedness and communalism." See Upendra Baxi, *The Crisis of the Indian Legal System* (New Delhi: Vikas, 1982), 295. Baxi, an advocate of village councils (*Panchayats*), also points out how communal and caste

spirit as well as governmental resistance have made it difficult to institute a kind of indigenous federalism based in these Panchayats.

40. Nathuram Godse, the actual assassin, was a fanatical follower of V. D. Sarvarkar's Hindu nationalist movement, the Mahasabha. See Larry Collins and Dominique LaPierre, *Freedom at Midnight* (New York: Avon Books, 1975), 414–525, for a gripping account.

41. Marc Galanter, *Competing Equalities: Law and the Backward Classes in India* (Delhi: Oxford University Press, 1984), 29–37.

42. The speech was printed as *Annihilation of Caste ("An Undelivered Speech"),* ed. Mulk Raj Anand (New Delhi: Arnold, 1990 [1936]).

43. Ambedkar's public conversion to Buddhism came some 20 years after his electrifying declaration, "I will not die a Hindu." See T. S. Wilkinson and M. M. Thomas, eds., *Ambedkar and the Neo-Buddhist Movement* (Madras: Christian Literature Society, 1972) and John C. B. Webster, *A History of the Dalit Christians of India* (San Francisco: Mellen Research University Press, 1992), 100, 204.

44. Jawaharlal Nehru, *Jawaharlal Nehru: An Autobiography* (New Delhi: Oxford University Press, 1980), 374.

45. Galanter, *Competing Equalities.* See also his *Law and Society in Modern India* (Delhi: Oxford University Press, 1989), chapters 8, 9, 11.

46. Galanter, *Competing Equalities,* 25, 34.

47. See B. A. V. Sharma, "Secular State and Civil Service," in V. K. Sinha, ed., *Secularism in India* (Bombay: Lalvani, 1968), 44–70.

48. 1985 (Supp) Supreme Court Cases 590.

49. Shriram Maheshwari, *The Mandal Commission and Mandalisation: A Critique* (New Delhi: Concept, 1991), 40.

50. See Max Stackhouse, *Creeds, Society and Human Rights: A Study in Three Cultures* (Grand Rapids: W. B. Eerdmans, 1986), 199–258, for discussion of covenantal culture and human rights and the peculiar challenges they face in the Indian context.

51. The Indian sociologist T. K. Oommen traces this communalist antisecularism back to the lack of institutional differentiation between Hindu religion and society in "Religious Pluralism in India: A Sociological Appraisal," *Christian Perspectives on Contemporary Indian Issues,* ed. Ram Singh (Madras: Institute for Development Education, 1983), 123–33. For a wide-ranging discussion of communalism and political order in India see *Towards Understanding Communalism,* ed. Pramod Kumar (Chandigarh: Centre for Research in Rural and Industrial Development, 1992).

52. See Julian Saldanha, "Hindu Sensibilities Towards Conversion," *NCCI Review* 102, no. 1 (January 1983): 17–39.

53. I am indebted to Prof. Frederick S. Downs of United Theological College, Bangalore, (correspondence of March 5, 1994) for this critical point.

54. Julian Saldanha, *Conversion and Indian Civil Law* (Bangalore: Theological Publications in India, 1981), 3.

55. For some introduction to the Dalit movement and its theology see M. E. Prabhakar, "Developing the Common Ideology for Dalits of Christian and Other Faiths," *Religion and Society* 37, no. 3 (September 1990): 24–39; A. M. Abraham Ayrookuzhiel, "Dalit Liberation: Some Reflections on their Ideological Predicament," *Religion and Society* 35, no. 2 (June 1988): 47–52; M. E. Prabhakar, ed., *Towards a Dalit Theology* (Delhi: SPCK, 1988), and K. L. Wilson, *Twice Alienated: Culture of Dalit Christians* (Hyderabad: Booklinks, 1982).

56. I hope it is clear that neither all Hindus nor all Muslims are communalists. Muslim or Hindu influentials such as Asghar Ali Engineer or Justice V. K. Krishna

Iyer are clearly supporters of democratic constitutionalism, though they are often speaking for a less strident majority.

57. Paul Devanandan (with M. M. Thomas), *Problems of Indian Democracy* (Bangalore: CISRS, 1962), 90; and Paul Devanandan and M. M. Thomas, *India's Quest for Democracy* (Bangalore: Committee for Literature on Social Concerns, 1955). This is also a major theme in A. V. Thomas, *Christians in Secular India.*

58. The directive itself almost became a fundamental right, losing this status by a 5 to 4 vote in the Fundamental Rights Sub-Committee of the Constitutional Assembly. In dissent three of these four (B. R. Ambedkar abstaining) noted: "One of the factors that has kept Indians back from advancing to nationhood has been the existence of personal laws based on religion which keep the nation divided into water-tight compartments in many aspects of life. We are of the view that a uniform civil code should be guaranteed to the Indian people within a period of five or ten years . . . ." Cited from *Indian Express*, January 7, 1986, in Asghar Ali Engineer, ed., *The Shah Bano Controversy* (Hyderabad: Orient Longmans, 1987), 97.

59. Derrett, *Religion, Law and the State in India* and J. D. M. Derrett, *The Death of a Marriage Law: Epitaph for the Rishis* (New Delhi: Vikas, 1978).

60. E. D. Devadason, "Christian Personal Law," *People's Reporter*, December 16–31, 1990, 4.

61. The Indian Divorce Act of 1869, the Christian Marriage Act of 1872, and the Indian Succession Act of 1925.

62. Arun Shourie, *Indian Controversies: esp. says on Religion in Politics* (New Delhi: ASA, 1993), 197.

63. Khan was in fact her cousin. He also took another cousin as his second wife. For this narrative I am largely relying on Engineer, ed., *The Shah Bano Controversy*, 66–70; Shourie, *Indian Controversies*, 193–289; and the court record. For a recent review of the issues in the case see Bruce Lawrence, "Woman as Subject/ Woman as Symbol: Islamic Fundamentalism and the Status of Women," *Journal of Religious Ethics*, 22, no. 1 (Spring 1994): 163–185.

64. 1985 Supreme Court Cases 556.

65. In 1979 the Allahabad High Court and in 1980 the Supreme Court had already ruled that provisions of the criminal code could be invoked to provide for maintenance if other provisions under the Muslim Personal Code did not suffice. See Shourie, *Indian Controversies*, 265.

66. English translation of Shah Bano's letter in Engineer, ed., *The Shah Bano Controversy*, 211–12.

67. See the summary report in Shourie, *Indian Controversies*, 193.

68. In fact, the bill had been introduced in March 1985 by G. M. Banatwala of the Muslim League before the Supreme Court's ruling in April. See Engineer, ed., *The Shah Bano Controversy*, 43–45, and Shourie, *Indian Controversies*, 254–55.

69. For the bill see Engineer, ed., *The Shah Bano Controversy*, 85–88, and for critiques by various parties see 89–110. See also Lawrence, "Woman as Subject/ Woman as Symbol," 166–72.

70. *Stanislaus v. State of Madhya Pradesh*, 1977. See Saldanha, *Conversion and Indian Civil Law*, 168 ff. Similar laws were passed in the states of Orissa (1967) and Arunachal Pradesh (1978). Earlier efforts (the "Niyogi Commission" in 1954) to extend similar anticonversion measures to all of India never succeeded due to Nehru's insistence on a secular state as well as to strong Christian resistance. Subsequently, these laws have been virtually unenforced. See Ronald W. Neufeldt, "To Convert or Not to Convert: Legal and Political Dimensions of Conversion in Independent India,"

in *Religion and Law in Independent India,* ed. Robert D. Baird (New Delhi: Manohar Publishers, 1993), 313–32.

71. See, for instance, the attack on Christian opposition to anticonversion legislation in Basu, *Introduction to the Constitution of India,* 112–15.

72. Engineer, ed., *The Shah Bano Controversy,* 126.

73. The complex problems of Indian federalism cannot be explored adequately here. See Durga Das Basu, *Comparative Federalism* (New Delhi: Prentice-Hall of India, 1987); Amal Ray, "Politics, Economic Development and Second-Generation Strains in India's Federal System," *Publius* 18 (1988): 147–67; and Sharada Rath, *Federalism Today: Approaches, Issues and Trends* (New Delhi: Sterling, 1984).

74. See Helen Ralston, *Christian Ashrams: A New Religious Movement in Contemporary India* (Lewiston, NY: Edwin Mellen, 1987).

75. Marcus Ward, *Pilgrim Church: An Account of the First Five Years of the Church of South India* (London: Epworth, 1953) and *The Church of South India After 30 Years: Report of the Special Committee . . . .* (Madras: Christian Literature Society, 1978).

76. Excerpt from *The Basel Mission Liturgy* (1880), foreword, cited in Brief to the Supreme Court by Appellants (Civil Appeal No. 84(N), 1975). For further background see *Wholeness in Christ: The Legacy of the Basel Mission in India,* ed. Godwin Shiri (Mangalore: Karnataka Theological Research Institute, 1985).

77. Code of Civil Procedure (1908), Order 39, Rule 1.

78. Notes 13 and 14 in Order 39, Rule 1.

79. There were other related claims, such as the use of the Apocrypha in worship, which could be organized under these broader issues.

80. *District Council of United Basel Mission Church and Others v. Salvador Nicholas Matthias and Others* [(1988) 2 Supreme Court Cases 31]. In this report I am also relying on briefs prepared by the CSI in its appeal in 1975 as well as conversations with Counsel to the CSI, H. N. Srinivas Anand, and Jesu Prasad, advocate in the case.

81. Any perusal of the *North India Churchman* or the *Bulletin of the National Council of Churches of India* or other church publications immediately exposes this immense problem.

82. Kakar takes a psychoanalytic approach in *Intimate Relations: Exploring Indian Sexuality* (New Delhi: Penguin, 1989) and *The Inner World: A Psycho-analytic Study of Childhood and Society in India,* 2d ed. (Delhi: Oxford University Press, 1981). Nandy combines this with a radical social criticism in *On the Edge of Psychology: esp. says in Politics and Culture* (Delhi: Oxford University Press, 1990). See also Richard Lannoy, *The Speaking Tree: A Study of Indian Culture and Society,* part 2 (London: Oxford University Press, 1971).

83. Except, of course, when the British introduced legislation such as the Caste Disabilities Removal Act (1850) and the Hindu Inheritance (Removal of Disabilities) Act (1928) enabling people to convert from one "religion" to another without forfeiture of inheritance. This illustrates how family law has been the point of introduction of civil freedoms of voluntary association.

84. See David Hardiman, "The Indian 'Faction': A Political Theory Examined," *Subaltern Studies I: Writings on South Asian History and Society,* Ranajit Guha, ed. (Delhi: Oxford University Press, 1982), 198–231.

85. See the efforts in 1993 to outlaw the appeal to religion in political life introduced by Prime Minister Narasimha Rao.

86. The use of the body as a metaphor for social organization has also been widespread in the West, where the idea of the "body of Christ" and the "body poli-

tic" has been pervasive. In Christianity this reinforced the institutional distinction between the church and other social orders, esp. pecially the family and government. In India, through the idea of the *maha-purusha*, which contains the four major castes, the body metaphor in religion reinforced the organic character of the whole society. Interestingly enough, the Buddhist tradition has the idea of the "three bodies" of Buddha—the Buddha himself, his teachings, and the samgha—which tends to articulate the difference between religious life and the rest of the society. See my "Body Thinking in Ecclesiology and Cybernetics," (Diss., Harvard University, 1970) and "Cybernetics and the Symbolic Body Model," *Zygon* 7, no. 2 (June 1972): 98–109.

87. Both the male Christian missionary and his pastoral successors in the newly independent church had deep affinities with this authoritarian tradition. Since the missionaries were accountable to their sending agency rather than the indigenous congregations they spawned, they served to reinforce traditional notions of headship. See the critical analyses in Bergquist and Manickam, *The Crisis of Dependency*, 26–42, and Graham Houghton, *The Impoverishment of Dependency: The History of the Protestant Church in Madras, 1870–1920* (Madras: Christian Literature Society, 1983).

88. In 1978 conflict over an episcopal election led to the firebombing of the car of one Karnataka candidate, Bishop Anandarao Samuel, in which his wife was killed.

89. See W. H. Morris-Jones's discussion "India's Political Idioms," in Thomas R. Metcalf, ed., *Modern India: An Interpretive Anthology* (New Delhi: Sterling, 1990), 402–23.

Chapter 4. Sacred Lands and Religious Assemblies in America

1. I am using the term "America" rather than "United States" to emphasize the open texture of what constitutes the United States in light of the peculiar position of the governments of the original inhabitants. The confusion over what to call the "First Americans" is compounded by the proximity of our study of India. I shall use terms like "aboriginal peoples," and "Native Americans" as well as "American Indians" or recognized tribal names.

2. John Locke, *Two Treatises of Government* . . . , ed. Peter Laslett (Cambridge: Cambridge University Press, 1960), 319.

3. Carl J. Friedrich, *The Impact of American Constitutionalism Abroad* (Boston: Boston University Press, 1967).

4. Daniel J. Elazar, *Covenant and Polity in Biblical Israel* (New Brunswick, NJ: Transaction Books, 1994), 45–51.

5. Donald Harman Akenson, *God's Peoples: Covenant and Land in South Africa, Israel and Ulster* (Ithaca: Cornell University Press, 1992).

6. Sharon O'Brien, *American Indian Tribal Governments* (Norman: University of Oklahoma Press, 1989), 14–33.

7. Robert Bellah, *The Broken Covenant: American Civil Religion in Time of Trial* (New York: Seabury Press, 1975).

8. For this development see my *God's Federal Republic: Reconstructing Our Governing Symbol* (New York: Paulist Press, 1988), 45–46, 75–76, 112.

9. Will B. Gravely, "African Methodisms and the Rise of Black Denominationalism," in *Perspectives on American Methodism: Interpretive Essays*, ed. Russell E. Richey, Kenneth E. Rowe, and Jean M. Schmidt (Nashville: Abingdon Press, 1993), 108–26; and Gayraud S. Wilmore, *Black Religion and Black Radicalism*, 2d ed. (Maryknoll: Orbis Books, 1983).

10. H. Richard Niebuhr, *The Social Sources of Denominationalism* (Cleveland: World Publishing, 1964), and James M. Gustafson, "The Voluntary Church: A Moral Appraisal," in *Voluntary Association*, ed. D. B. Robertson (Atlanta: John Knox Press, 1966), 299–322.

11. Nancy Tatom Ammerman, *Baptist Battles* (New Brunswick: Rutgers University Press, 1990), and Bill J. Leonard, *God's Last and Only Hope: The Fragmentation of the Southern Baptist Convention* (Grand Rapids: William B. Eerdmans, 1990).

12. *The Federalist* [1788]. See also Morton White, *Philosophy, The Federalist, and the Constitution* (New York: Oxford University Press, 1987), 55–81, 136–45, 159–71.

13. *Documents of Political Foundation Written by Colonial Americans: From Covenant to Constitution*, ed. Donald S. Lutz (Philadelphia: Institute for the Study of Human Issues, 1986), and Donald Lutz, "Religious Dimensions in the Development of American Constitutionalism," *Emory Law Journal* 39, no. 1, 1990: 21–40.

14. See James L. Adams, "The Voluntary Principle in the Formation of American Religion," in *Voluntary Assocations*, ed. J. Ronald Engel (Chicago: Exposition Press, 1986), 171–200; and O. Kendall White, "Constitutional Norms and the Formal Organization of American Churches," *Sociological Analysis* 33, no. 2, 1972: 95–109.

15. Richard Carwardine, "Methodist Ministers and the Second Party System," in *Perspectives on American Methodism*, ed. Richey et al., 159–77.

16. Hannah Arendt, *On Revolution* (New York: Viking Press, 1965), 241–44.

17. Papers No. 10 and 51 in *The Federalist*. See also White, *Philosophy, The Federalist, and the Constitution*, 63, 133–34. On this point Madison was considerably less sanguine than De Tocqueville after him, who saw in religion a key source for the morality and voluntary association indispensable for democratic life. See Alexis De Tocqueville, *Democracy in America*, 2 vols., trans. Henry Reeve (New York: Schocken Books, 1961), vol. 1, 355–73; vol. 2, 30, 128–33. At this point we see how Madison's federalism worked more to curb democratic excess than to enable democratic participation.

18. See White, *Philosophy, The Federalist, and the Constitution*, 146–48, 204–06, who explores the relation of the Federalist thinkers to David Hume's natural philosophy.

19. Carwardine, "Methodist Ministers and the Second Party System," 168.

20. For a recent introduction to the meaning of establishment and free exercise see Ronald B. Flowers, *That Godless Court? Supreme Court Decisions on Church-State Relationships* (Louisville: Westminster/John Knox, 1994). For a typology of the actual configurations of church-state relations in the United States see Carl H. Esbeck, "Five Views of Church-State Relations in Contemporary American Thought," *Brigham Young University Law Review* (1986), 371–404.

21. See Michael Walzer, "Liberalism and the Art of Separation," *Political Theory* 12, no. 3 (August 1984): 315–40. See Robert A. Horn, *Groups and the Constitution* (Stanford: Stanford University Press, 1956), for an earlier discussion of the lack of associational theory in the First Amendment.

22. Robert N. Bellah, "Civil Religion in America," in *American Civil Religion*, ed. Russell Richey and Donald Jones (New York: Harper & Row, 1974), 21–44, with a number of critical responses.

23. See Garry Wills, *Lincoln at Gettysburg: The Words That Remade America* (New York: Simon and Schuster, 1992), and William J. Wolf, *Lincoln's Religion* (New York: Pilgrim Press, 1970), for Lincoln's critical role in resituating the Constitution and Declaration of Independence in American civil religion.

24. The phrase is from Peter L. Berger, *The Sacred Canopy: Elements of a Sociological Theory of Religion* (Garden City: Doubleday, 1967)—a classic introduction to the legitimating function of religion in society.

25. See Janet F. Fishburn, *The Fatherhood of God and the Victorian Family: The Social Gospel in America* (Philadelphia: Fortress Press, 1982); Gregory A. Schneider, "Social Religion, the Christian Home, and Republican Spirituality in Antebellum Methodism," in *Perspectives on American Methodism,* ed. Richey et al., 192–208; and Carolyn DeSwarte Gifford, " 'For God and Home and Native Land': The W.C.T.U.'s Image of Woman in the Late Nineteenth Century," in *Perspectives on American Methodism,* ed. Richey et al., 309–21, for some perspectives.

26. Even when one looks at the thought of the preeminent political theologian of America's twentieth century, Reinhold Niebuhr, one searches in vain for an enunciation of these connections, since he was drawing still on the Augustinian heritage of sin, love, and moral ambiguity in laying out the contours of his theory of democracy and Christian political realism. Martin Luther King, Jr., while drawing more deeply on the American civil and religious heritage, also makes little use of this central concept. Jesse Jackson, however, has made extensive use of it, as with the symbol of the rainbow.

27. For the lay trustee movement see Patrick Carey, *People, Priests and Prelates: Ecclesiastical Democracy and the Tensions of Trusteeism* (Notre Dame: University of Notre Dame Press, 1987). For the democratizing and confederating of American Anglicanism after the Revolution see Frederick V. Mills, *Bishops by Ballot: An Eighteenth-Century Ecclesiastical Revolution* (New York: Oxford University Press, 1978).

28. Still the second largest Protestant group in the United States, the evangelical practices and theology that Methodism shares with many Baptist, Holiness, and Pentecostal groups on both sides of the racial divide make it a virtual prototype of peculiarly American Christianity. The focus of the following case study, the United Methodist Church, with approximately eight million members, is only the largest part of the Methodist family. For a discussion of Methodism's significance see Nathan O. Hatch, "The Puzzle of American Methodism," *Church History* 63, no. 2 (1994): 175–89.

29. It is clear from this analysis of American religion and constitutional history that we would do well to take up a case from African-American church history that would expose the legal dimensions of ecclesiology in the black churches. This is beyond the capacities of this book and awaits further development of this kind of inquiry.

30. Information for this section draws on Edward McGlynn Gaffney, Jr., Philip C. Sorenson, and Howard R. Griffin, *Ascending Liability in Religious and Other Nonprofit Organizations* (Macon: Mercer University Press, 1984); Jean Caffey Lyles, "Methodist Litigations and Public Relations," *The Christian Century,* December 19, 1979, 1256–57; Report of the General Council on Finance and Administration, *Journal of the 1980 General Conference of the UMC,* 1777–1784; official court documents, and materials graciously provided by the General Council on Finance and Administration, United Methodist Church, Evanston, Illinois.

31. *Barr v. United Methodist Church,* 90 Cal. A3d 266, 153 Cal. Re 328 (1979) [cited henceforth as *Barr.*]. For discussion of liability of unincorporated associations see Gaffney et al., *Ascending Liability,* 20–40.

32. "Minute Order" of the Superior Court of California, County of San Diego, No. 40–4611 (1978).

33. *Barr* at 328, 333.

34. *Barr* at 329. But this ruling forced a change in this very wording, discussed below.

35. *Barr* at 328. (Internal quotation from *Carnes v. Smith* (1976), 236 Ga. 30.)

36. See "The Methodist Approach," by Kent M. Weeks, in Gaffney et al., *Ascending Liability,* 133–37, for some examples. Some Lutheran organizational adjustments are described by Philip Draheim in the same volume, 137–42.

37. Compare the United Methodist *Book of Discipline* (1980), para. 524.2, and *Book of Discipline* (1984), para. 526.2. In addition, the 1984 *Book of Discipline* added specific language denying that either "master-servant" or "principal-agent" relationships—both conveying legal meanings of liability—defined the relationship of general agencies and the General Conference.

38. See Gaffney et al., *Ascending Liability,* 103–32.

39. However, in two Georgia cases involving Presbyterian churches in 1969 and 1979 courts developed the concept of "neutral principles" by which to approach church property disputes without entangling courts in doctrinal matters. In fact, however, "neutrality" simply means formulations familiar to civil law. See Gaffney et al., *Ascending Liability,* 60–75; and Douglas Laycock, "The Right to Church Autonomy as Part of Free Exercise of Religion," in *Government Intervention in Religious Affairs,* ed. Dean Kelley (New York: Pilgrim Press, 1986), 28–39.

40. A separate appeal by the General Council on Finance and Administration of the UMC was rebuffed by the U.S. Supreme Court with Justice William Rehnquist's claim that "the First and Fourteenth Amendments [cannot] prevent a civil court from independently examining, and making the ultimate decision regarding, the structure and actual operation of a hierarchical church and its constituent units in an action such as this" (439 U.S. 1355 [1979]). Cited with comment in Gaffney et al., *Ascending Liability,* 75.

41. For an insightful presentation of the dynamic of conference within Methodism see Russell E. Richey, *Early American Methodism* (Bloomington: Indiana University Press, 1991), 65–81.

42. U.S. (13 Wall) 679 (1872).

43. *Book of Discipline,* 2501, 2503.

44. See White, "Constitutional Norms and the Formal Organization of American Churches," 95–109, for a detailed examination of this point.

45. *Kedroff v. St. Nicholas Cathedral,* 344 U.S. 94 (1952) and *Serbian Orthodox Diocese v. Milivojevich,* 426 U.S. 696 (1976) involved matters of ecclesiastical appointment and related control of church property.

46. See William McGuire King, "Denominational Modernization and Religious Identity: The Case of the Methodist Episcopal Church," in *Perspectives on American Methodism,* ed. Richey et al., 343–55, for a description of this process in the late nineteenth century.

47. "Memorandum . . . to Dismiss . . ." by attorneys representing persons served as representing the United Methodist Church in *Trigg, et al., v. Pacific Methodist Investment Fund, et al.,* before the US District Court for the Southern District of California, No. 78-0198-S (1978), 5.

48. Affidavit of Murray H. Leiffer to California Superior Court, San Diego, in the case of *Barr v. United Methodist Church,* January 6, 1978, also used in other Pacific Homes cases. References are to 4, 20, 21.

49. Richey, *Early American Methodism,* 21–32, 65–81.

50. *Of Utmost Good Faith,* ed. Vine Deloria, Jr. (San Francisco: Straight Arrow Press, 1971), and *The American Indian and the United States: A Documentary History,* ed. Wilcomb E. Washburn (New York: Random House, 1973).

51. Felix S. Cohen, *Handbook of Federal Indian Law* (Albuquerque: University of New Mexico Press, 1982), v.

52. Vincent Ostrom, *The Political Theory of the Compound Republic* (Lincoln: University of Nebraska, 1987).

53. For this account I am relying on Robert S. Michaelsen, "Is the Miner's Canary Silent? Implications of the Supreme Court's Denial of American Indian Free Exercise of Religion Claims," *The Journal of Law and Religion* 6, no. 1 (1988): 97–114; and *Lyng v. Northwest Indian Cemetery Protective Association*, 485 US 439, S. C. 1319 (1988). That both American cases in this study arose in California is purely fortuitous.

54. Robert S. Michaelsen, "Dirt in the Courtroom: Indian Land Claims and American Property Rights," in *American Sacred Space*, ed. David Chidester and Edward T. Linenthal (Bloomington: Indiana University Press, 1995), 43–96.

55. D. Theodoratus, "Report for U. S. Department of Agriculture, Forest Service, On Cultural Resources of the Chimney Rock Section, Gasquet-Orleans Road, Six Rivers National Forest," April 9, 1979, 420. Cited in Michaelsen, "Is the Miner's Canary Silent?", 99.

56. Quoted from the trial transcript in Michaelsen, "Is the Miner's Canary Silent?" 99.

57. 108 S. Ct. at 1327. Justice O'Connor wrote the majority opinion in the 5–3 decision.

58. The litigants' case had already avoided the pitfall of the Sequoyah case by showing that the sacral place and activity in question were "central and indispensable" to their "religion." The Cherokees had lost their case by allowing the court to distinguish between "religious" and "cultural and historical" aspects of their life and by not showing that the headwaters in question were "central and indispensable" to that religion.

59. *Lyng* at 1327.

60. Ibid. 1330.

61. The California Wilderness Act of 1984 allowed, however, a corridor to be left open for the possible construction of the G-O Road. The rest of the area was designated the Siskiyou Wilderness.

62. *Wilson v. Block*, 708 F. 2d 735 (1983); *Frank Fools Crow v. Gullet*, 706 F. 2d 856 (1983); *Sequoyah v. T.V.A.*, 620 F. 2d 1159 (1980). Others included *Badoni v. Higginson*, 638 F. 2d 172 (1980), regarding tourist incursions around Rainbow Bridge in Arizona, and *U.S. v. Means*, 627 F. Su247 (D.S.D. 1985), rev'd, 858 F. 2d 404 (1988), involving access to the Black Hills National Forest for religious rites.

63. For the Blue Lake story see R. C. Gordon-McCutchan, "The Battle for Blue Lake: A Struggle for Indian Religious Rights," *Journal of Church and State* 33, no. 4 (Autumn 1991): 785–97.

64. John Cotton, "God's Promise to His Plantation" (1630), in *The Indian and the White Man*, ed. Wilcomb Washburn (Garden City: Doubleday-Anchor, 1964), 102–05. For John Winthrop's views see C. E. Eissinger, "The Puritan's Justification for Taking the Land," *Essex Institute Historical Collections* 84 (1948): 135–43, in *Law and the American Indian*, ed. Monroe Price (Indianapolis: Bobbs Merrill, 1973), 367. See also *Puritans, Indians and Manifest Destiny*, ed. Charles M. Segal and David C. Stineback (New York: G. Putnam's Sons, 1977) for the wider arguments among the Puritans and dissidents such as Roger Williams, who defended the integrity of Indian culture.

65. *Worcester v. State of Georgia* (1832).

66. For the Worcester case, with concurring and dissenting opinions to John Marshall's classic defense of Cherokee claims, see *The American Indian and the United States: A Documentary History,* ed. Washburn, 2603–48. The Christian assimilationist reformers are well presented by *Americanizing the American Indians: Writings by the "Friends of the Indian" 1880–1900,* ed. Francis Paul Prucha (Cambridge: Harvard University Press, 1973).

67. *Cherokee Nation v. State of Georgia* (1831).

68. As evidenced in court rulings in *Tee Hit-Ton v. United States,* 348 US 272 (1955), *Three Affiliated Tribes of Fort Berthold Reservation v. United States,* 390 F. 2d 686, 691 (1968), and *United States v. Sioux Nation,* 448 US 371 (1980). See Michaelsen, "Dirt in the Courtroom," 74–77.

69. For a strong statement of this point see Vine Deloria, Jr., *Behind the Trail of Broken Treaties: An Indian Declaration of Independence* (New York: Delacorte Press, 1974) and other writings. O'Brien, *American Indian Tribal Governments,* presents a more sanguine view.

70. For a critique of this confluence see Vine Deloria, Jr., *God Is Red* (New York: Grosset and Dunlap, 1973), 57–65.

71. Again, Deloria presents a vivid and wide-ranging discussion of the conflict between Christian "historic" faith and Native American "naturalism" in *God Is Red.* See also Vine Deloria, Jr., "Sacred Lands and Religious Freedom," *American Indian Religions* 1, no. 1 (Winter 1994): 73–84.

72. Nor, for better or worse, like the twentieth-century constitutions of South Africa and Israel. See Akenson, *God's Peoples,* for perspectives on a racial-ethnic incorporation of land in a national covenant.

73. See, however, Christopher Stone, *Earth and Other Ethics: The Case for Moral Pluralism* (San Francisco: Harper & Row, 1987), and Christopher Stone, *Should Trees Have Standing? Toward Legal Rights for Natural Objects* (Los Altos: William Kaufman, 1974) for arresting efforts to challenge this tradition.

74. 110 S. Ct. 1595. Ironically, the users of this traditional "sacrament" were members of the Native American *Church.* For an analysis of the case see "Abridging the Free Exercise Clause," *Journal of Church and State* 32, no. 4 (Autumn 1990): 741–52, and for arguments supporting a legislative remedy see James E. Wood, Jr., "The Religious Freedom Restoration Act," *Journal of Church and State* 33, no. 4 (Autumn 1991): 673–79.

75. The Religious Freedom Restoration Act, signed into law by President William J. Clinton in 1993, has still to face the test of constitutionality before the Supreme Court—another land mine in relations of religion and government.

76. See Michaelsen, "Dirt in the Courtroom," 43–96, for an extensive and penetrating analysis of these themes.

77. See William W. Everett, "Land Ethics: Toward a Covenantal Model," in *Selected Papers from the Twentieth Annual Meeting of the Society of Christian Ethics,* ed. Max L. Stackhouse (Waterloo, Ontario: Council on the Study of Religion, 1979), 45–73, for a fuller development of these points.

78. *Worcester v. Georgia* (1932) in *The American Indian and the United States: A Documentary History,* ed. Washburn, 2610.

79. For themes of boundary and medium in the law see Milner S. Ball, "Law Natural: Its Family of Metaphors and Its Theology," *Journal of Law and Religion* 3, no. 1, 1985: 141–65.

80. For further discussion of the relation of land to polity see Daniel J. Elazar, "Land Space and Civil Society in America," *Western Historical Quarterly* 5, no. 3 (July

1974): 261–84; and Daniel J. Elazar, "Land and Liberty in American Civil Society," *Publius: The Journal of Federalism* 18, no. 4 (Fall 1988): 1–31.

81. Whether we should view this integrity in terms of rights or dignity or some other political-legal way is not yet settled. See Wolfgang Huber, "Rights of Nature or Dignity of Nature?" *Annual of the Society of Christian Ethics*, 1991, 43–59.

82. O'Brien, *American Indian Tribal Governments*, 77–79, 216. For a possible step in the "personal codes" direction see the Indian Child Welfare Act (1978), discussed by O'Brien at 89–90.

83. See Walbert Bühlmann, *God's Chosen Peoples*, trans. Robert R. Barr (Maryknoll: Orbis Books, 1982) for a survey of these conceptions outside the European context.

Chapter 5. Assessing the Engagement, Evaluating the Inquiry

1. While I am working in the historic tradition of Ernst Troeltsch, I have transmuted his classic categories of Church, Sect, and Mysticism under the impact of these studies. These categories both expand his typology, making it more political, and also narrow it by concentrating on structural dynamics. See Ernst Troeltsch, *The Social Teachings of the Christian Churches*, trans. Olive Wyon (New York: Harper & Row, 1960). For alternative typologies that pick up some of these additional themes see H. Richard Niebuhr, *Christ and Culture* (New York: Harper & Row, 1956 [1951]); Avery Dulles, *Models of the Church*, expanded ed. (New York: Doubleday, 1978); Peter Rudge, *Ministry and Management* (London: Tavistock Institute, 1968); and Ross Scherer, "A New Typology for Organizations: Market, Bureaucracy, Clan and Mission, with Application to American Denominations," *Journal for the Scientific Study of Religion* 27, no. 4 (December 1988): 475–98.

2. H. Richard Niebuhr, *The Social Sources of Denominationalism* (New York: Henry Holt & Company, 1929). For a further development of Niebuhr's concerns see James M. Gustafson, *Treasure in Earthen Vessels: The Church as a Human Community* (New York: Harper & Brothers, 1961).

3. The South African Commission on Truth and Reconciliation (1995), chaired by Bishop Desmond Tutu, represents the most recent expression of this civil-religious need in the effort to esp. tablish a new federal republic with democratic participation. For a theological and ethical reflection on this development see Dirkie J. Smit, "The Truth and Reconciliation Commission: Tentative Religious and Theological Perspectives," *Journal of Theology for Southern Africa*, no. 90 (March 1995): 3–16.

4. See Will Kymlicka, *Multicultural Citizenship: A Liberal Theory of Minority Rights* (New York: Oxford University Press, 1995), esp. chapter 8, for arguments on this point from a classic liberal perspective.

5. For the German churches, the biannual *Kirchentag* and *Katholikentag* provide some of this function of free assembly on a dramatic scale, though their wider impact on the churches is difficult to assess.

6. Paul Brass critiques the segmented character of a federalism of religio-communal groups ("consociationalism") on this basis in Paul R. Brass, *Ethnicity and Nationalism: Theory and Comparison* (New Delhi: Sage Publications, 1991), 333–48.

7. Huber developed this idea in a seminar we conducted at Emory University in 1989.

8. For a sensitive examination of the political dynamics of forgiveness and repentance, including the practices of reparation, see Donald W. Shriver, Jr., *An Ethic for Enemies: Forgiveness in Politics* (New York: Oxford University Press, 1995).

9. For covenant as an act of entrustment see Joseph L. Allen, *Love and Conflict: A Covenantal Model of Christian Ethics* (Nashville: Abingdon Press, 1984), 32.

10. For the American ethicist Theodore Weber, reconciliation is thus intrinsic to the tasks of government itself: "Reconciliation, politically understood, is the process of eliciting, coordinating, and strengthening the elements of community in both domestic and international society." ("Security, International Responsibility, and Reconciliation," *Quarterly Review* 6, no. 2 [Summer 1986], 24.)

Index